I0812680

POSTCARD HISTORY SERIES

Manchester

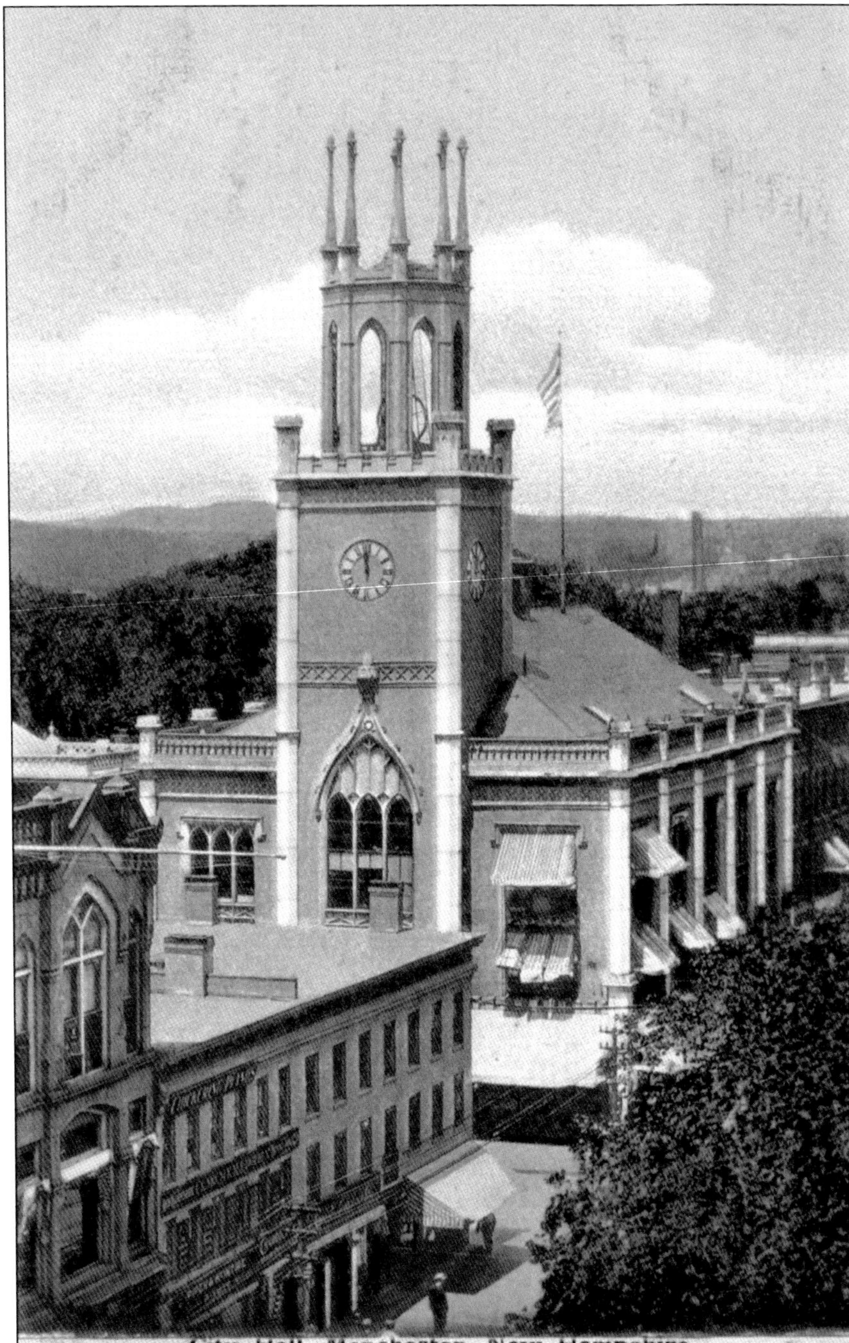

Fortunately for Manchester residents of today, Ulric Bourgeois had no qualms about lugging his heavy view camera and tripod up to the roof of his employer, John B. Varick Company, to capture for posterity a unique bird's-eye view of City Hall about 1905. Since the construction in 1992 of the NYNEX Building, renamed City Hall Plaza, the old Gothic structure remains dwarfed in the shadow of its modern neighbor.

POSTCARD HISTORY SERIES

Manchester

Robert B. Perreault

ARCADIA PUBLISHING

ISBN 978-0-7385-3783-2

Published by Arcadia Publishing
Charleston, South Carolina

Printed in the United States of America

Library of Congress Catalog Card Number: 2004117603

For all general information contact Arcadia Publishing at:
Telephone 843-853-2070
Fax 843-853-0044
E-mail sales@arcadiapublishing.com
For customer service and orders:
Toll-Free 1-888-313-2665

Visit us on the Internet at www.arcadiapublishing.com

Pour Charles, voici l'histoire en images d'un aspect de l'héritage que nous partageons. Avec amour, Papa.

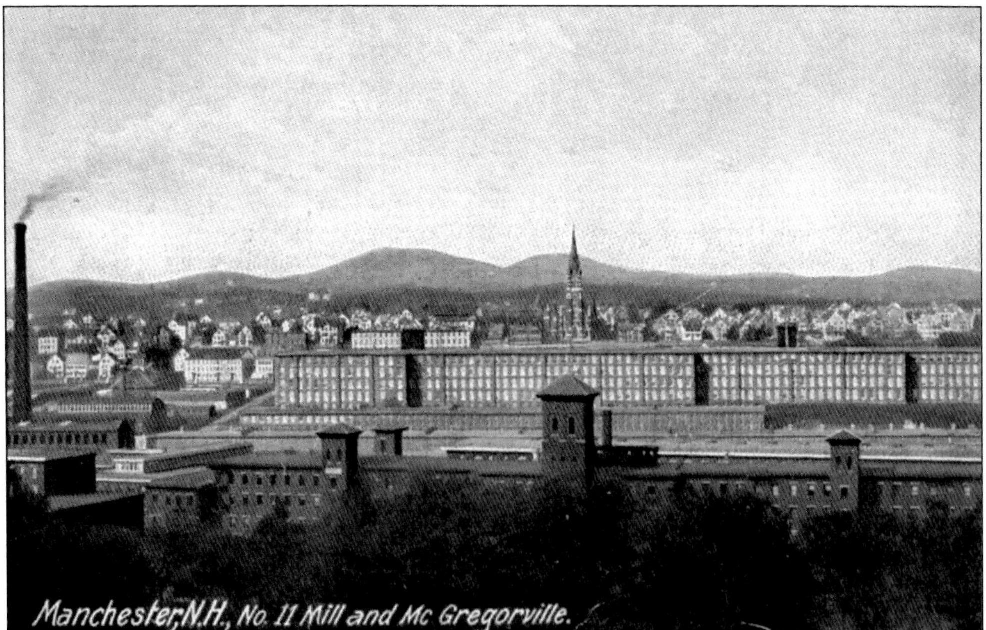

As they gazed toward the gargantuan mills of the Amoskeag Manufacturing Company and the steeple of Sainte Marie's Church dominating the western skyline, new arrivals to Manchester, especially farming families from quiet villages elsewhere in the United States, Québec, or Europe, probably stood in awe of what must have seemed to them a bustling metropolis. Beyond sit the Uncanoonuc Mountains, "maiden's breasts" in the language of the Penacooks.

Contents

ACKNOWLEDGMENTS

Without the assistance of the following individuals, this book would never have come about. Arcadia's former northeast publisher, Suzanne E. Guiod, initiated the project and invited me, through our mutual acquaintance, Kenn Walker of the Department of English at St. Anselm College, to take on the task. My editor at Arcadia, Erin M. Stone, patiently guided me through the actual production process, with the occasional collaboration of publisher Tiffany A. Howe.

Whatever information I could not obtain through my home library and private archives came to me mostly through Eileen O'Brien of the Manchester Historic Association; Cindy O'Neil of the Carpenter Memorial Library's New Hampshire Room; Judy Fosher of the Diocesan Museum; Constance Hébert and my cousin Constance Hamel, both of the American Canadian Genealogical Society; Dona Blais of the Manchester Fire Department; as well as many individuals too numerous to list herein. Novelist Ernest Hebert, also author of a book on postcards, *Greetings from New England*, went out of his way to give me valuable advice and support. My brother-in-law, Donald Ouellette, generously offered me indispensable computer assistance.

Whether or not they were aware of it, many relatives, friends, colleagues, and acquaintances, both living and deceased, have contributed directly or indirectly to this project by having shared with me, throughout the decades or very recently, their knowledge and memories of Manchester's past. Although space limitations do not allow for the listing of their names, they know that I very much appreciate their help. I do, however, wish to acknowledge my 91-year-old aunt, Lillian Perreault, whose keen recall of life in the Manchester of her youth I can only hope to possess should I ever reach her age. I also want to make special mention of the late Betty Lessard, librarian of the Manchester Historic Association for nearly 30 years, a veritable walking encyclopedia and gold mine of information on Manchester history, from whom I learned so much and whose absence I so deeply feel.

Finally, my son, Charles-Henri Perreault, and my wife, Claudette Ouellette-Perreault, lived through this project with me for many long months during which they offered me precious help and encouragement, most of the time with the utmost of patience and compassion.

My sincerest thanks and expression of deepest appreciation go out to all.

INTRODUCTION

A wise person once stated that we are not the veritable owners of our possessions but merely their temporary custodians. Be they something grand, such as the *Mona Lisa* housed at the Louvre, or something personal, such as the family albums lovingly preserved by a grandmother, our possessions are treasured for a time and then left behind in the care, and for the benefit of, future generations. For many years, I have enjoyed building a postcard collection of my hometown of Manchester, for which I am temporary custodian. Herein, I am given the chance to offer, in book form, a sample from that collection.

It all began in 1973. While working in a local print shop, I saw a photograph destined to appear in the Manchester Historic Association's annual report. It depicted our main thoroughfare, Elm Street, with huge elms, streetcar tracks down the middle, horse buggies, and people in Victorian-era clothing. Up to then, having had history courses limited to national and world events, I had never considered the concept of "Manchester history." Moreover, I encountered this photograph long before the practice, so commonplace today, of decorating public spaces with enlargements of archival images representing local history. For me, having seen this photograph ranks as a milestone that forever changed my life.

Subsequently, while employed as research assistant and oral-history interviewer for Tamara K. Hareven and Randolph Langenbach, authors of *Amoskeag: Life and Work in an American Factory-City*, I became acquainted with the Manchester Historic Association's rich collection, including archival photographs. Working daily in this environment further fueled in me a budding interest in my hometown's history. It inspired me to begin collecting the only images affordable to me at the time: vintage postcards. Thus began my days as a deltiologist with the purchase of a few postcards in 1974, two years before the U.S. bicentennial celebration rekindled people's interest in history.

The search for and discovery of such rare gems provide an entertaining way of familiarizing oneself with local history, as each image has a tale to tell. I cannot resist investigating the deeper story behind those postcards portraying an intersection that today is barely recognizable, a building that I never knew existed, or perhaps a disastrous event. Because postcards are relatively small, slowly scanning them with a photographer's loupe greatly enhances one's appreciation of the image. Doing so unveils details and isolates scenes that make up the total picture: facial expressions, clothing, signs, storefronts, and architectural features. It almost gives one the feeling of being able to transcend space and time by entering into the scene and exploring the terrain as if physically there.

Careful examination also reveals errors that publishers occasionally committed. Original black-and-white images by local photographers such as John G. Ellinwood and Ulric Bourgeois, who knew the city well, were often published elsewhere as postcards, especially high-quality colored ones printed in Germany until World War I. Consequently, their captions sometimes contained spelling errors or did not even correspond to the image in question. In the case of local photographers who published their own colored postcards or actual sepia-toned photo postcards, as did the Duclos Brothers, such errors proved rare. Wherever possible, I have endeavored to correct any inaccuracies.

While focusing primarily on their images, I wish to point out the alternate story that most postcards offer: the personal messages they bear. When the government first authorized them in 1898, "private mailing cards" had limited message space along their front edges, with writing on the back restricted to the address. Beginning in 1907, when the government permitted messages on the back, postcard mania gripped the country.

During the golden era of the postcard, when telephones had not yet caught on widely, people sent postcards for many reasons. Other than the usual greeting, "Im haveing a fine time in Manchester wish you was hear," complete with errors in spelling, grammar, and punctuation that make today's e-mails look Shakespearean by comparison, postcards were used to convey messages as mundane as "Lets meet at corner of Main & Wayne to-day at 2 o-clock." Locally, postcards could be mailed at dawn and reach their destination by noon.

When acquired as a lot, postcards might include messages written by the same individual over a long period. These provide glimpses into family stories and contemporary events, just as those from immigrants writing home paint colorful portraits of life and work through their eyes. Finally, there are messages written by the deltiologists of their day, who exchanged postcards and expressed their satisfaction upon receiving a much-desired image.

To historians, a vintage postcard with a captivating image and an informative message equals two valuable documents in one. I find it exciting to read someone's century-old message written in the person's own hand and then discover that individual's address and occupation in an old Manchester city directory. Such messages, along with strong images, provide a connection between us and our forebears, who lived in the same homes, walked the same streets, earned their livelihood in the same workplaces, and played in the same recreational areas as we do today.

Throughout the years, I have delighted in learning from my collection, which I have shared privately with family and friends and publicly through slide lectures and illustrated articles. I hope that this book will widen that audience, as the people of Manchester—old, young, natives, longtime residents, newcomers, and those who've moved elsewhere but who still care to reminisce—savor images of familiar landmarks as they originally appeared and of those that have since passed into history.

Today, long after Manchester's industrial heyday and the subsequent periods of decline and of collective soul searching, it behooves us to glance back one final time so that we might learn about and benefit from our past before moving ahead in our ongoing quest for Manchester's identity in the 21st century.

Welcome to bygone Manchester, where you are guaranteed to have a fine time.

One

Back to Derryfield and Early Manchester

For approximately 11,000 years, our area attracted Amerindians, who gathered here to fish, trade their wares, and commune with one another and their natural surroundings. Led by Chief Passaconnaway, the Penacooks left their toponymical imprint upon our landscape: the Merrimack and Piscataquog Rivers, Amoskeag Falls, Lake Massabesic, Cohas Brook, and, beyond city limits, the Uncanoonuc Mountains.

The 17th century brought the first (mostly itinerant) Caucasians, such as Rev. John Eliot, "Apostle to the Indians," who preached at Amoskeag Falls about 1650. Beginning in 1722, Scotch-Irish Presbyterians and English Puritans settled nearby, founding Derryfield in 1751. The town extended three miles from its western boundary, the middle of the Merrimack River, between Hooksett and Litchfield. It included vast farmlands, a settlement by Amoskeag Falls, and another, Derryfield Centre (known after 1810 as Manchester Centre), in the southeastern area along Mammoth Road, the old stagecoach route between Lowell and Concord.

Among the best-remembered names from this period, two stand out. A veteran of the French and Indian War and of the American Revolutionary War, Gen. John Stark played a major role in the struggle to establish this nation. He led American forces to victory at the Battle of Bennington in 1777. Samuel Blodget oversaw the construction of a canal around Amoskeag Falls, which enhanced the Merrimack River's status as a trade route. Moreover, his recognition of the river's waterpower potential shaped Derryfield's evolution, thus assuring its future as one of New England's premier industrial centers: Manchester.

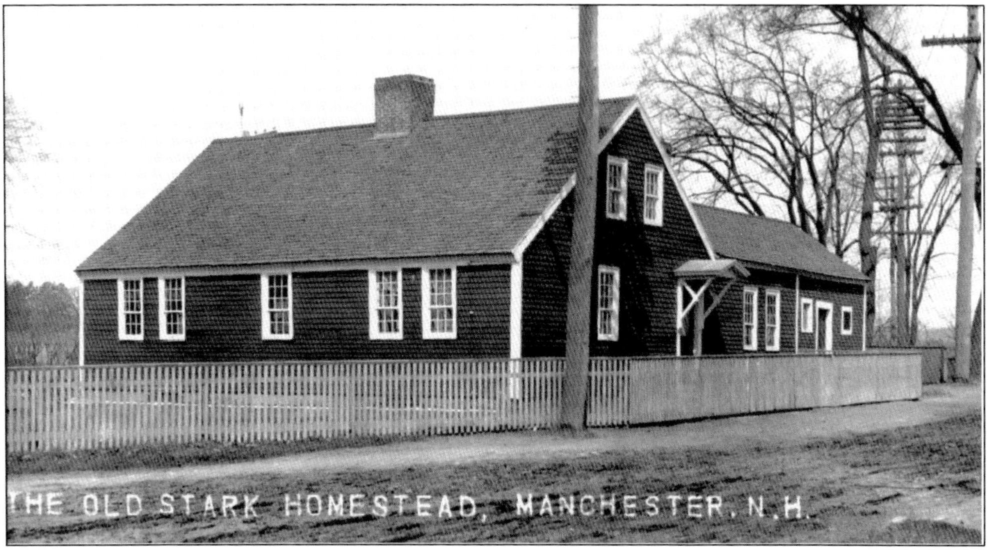

In 1736, Archibald Stark built what has become a relic of Manchester's Colonial era: the boyhood home of his son, Gen. John Stark. It stood immediately north of Amoskeag Falls on 800 acres of farmland along the Merrimack's east bank that extended from the falls to near the Hooksett line. John Stark lived here from age eight until his marriage to Elizabeth "Molly" Page in 1758, and again from 1761 to 1765.

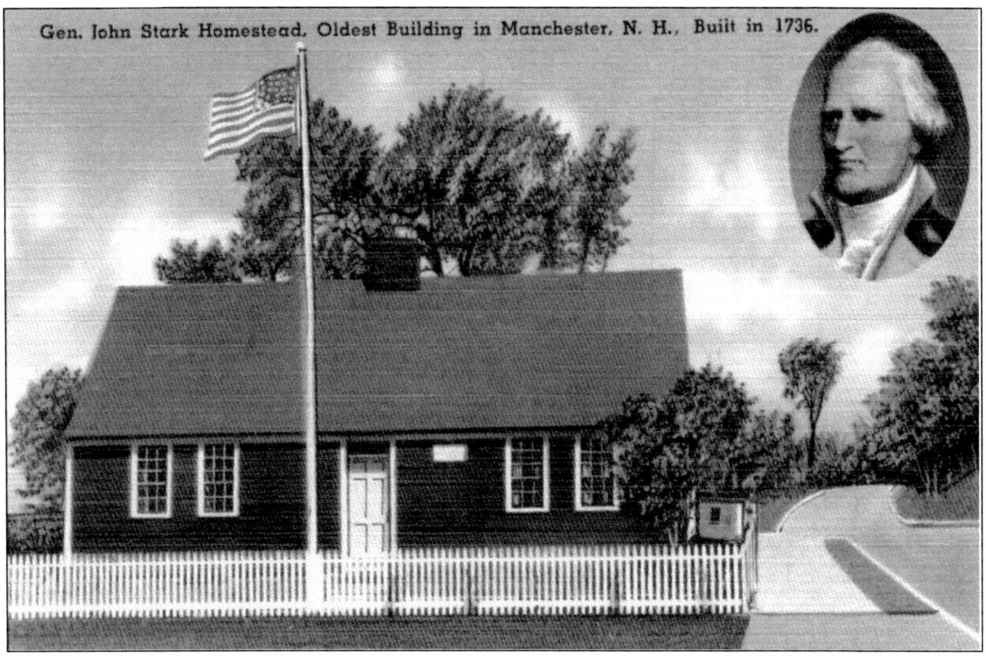

Having remained in the family until 1821, the Stark Homestead became property of the Amoskeag Manufacturing Company in 1835. After a century of changes and renovations, the Molly Stark Chapter of the Daughters of the American Revolution (DAR) acquired and restored it in 1937–1938. To prevent the home's demolition in 1968 upon the replacement of the Amoskeag Bridge, the DAR chapter had the house moved to its present location, 2000 Elm Street. Manchester's oldest structure is on the National Register of Historic Places.

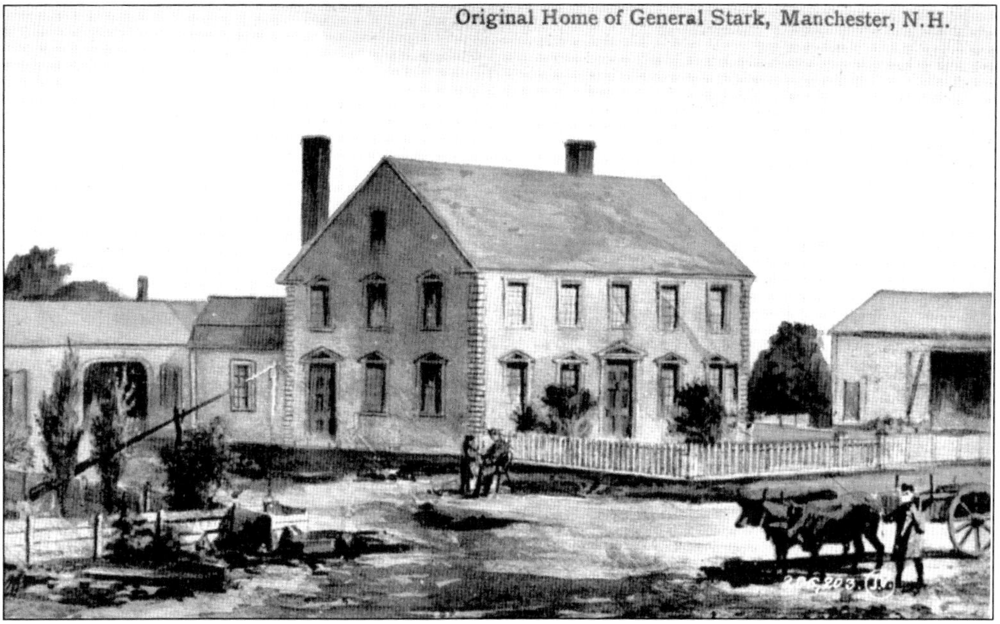

By 1765, because their small house had become inadequate, John and Molly Stark built a more spacious home on their farmland one mile north of Amoskeag Falls. There, they raised 10 of their 11 children to adulthood and lived out the rest of their years. In 1866, the century-old structure, by then the property of the nearby State Industrial School, burned, allegedly at the hands of youths from that institution.

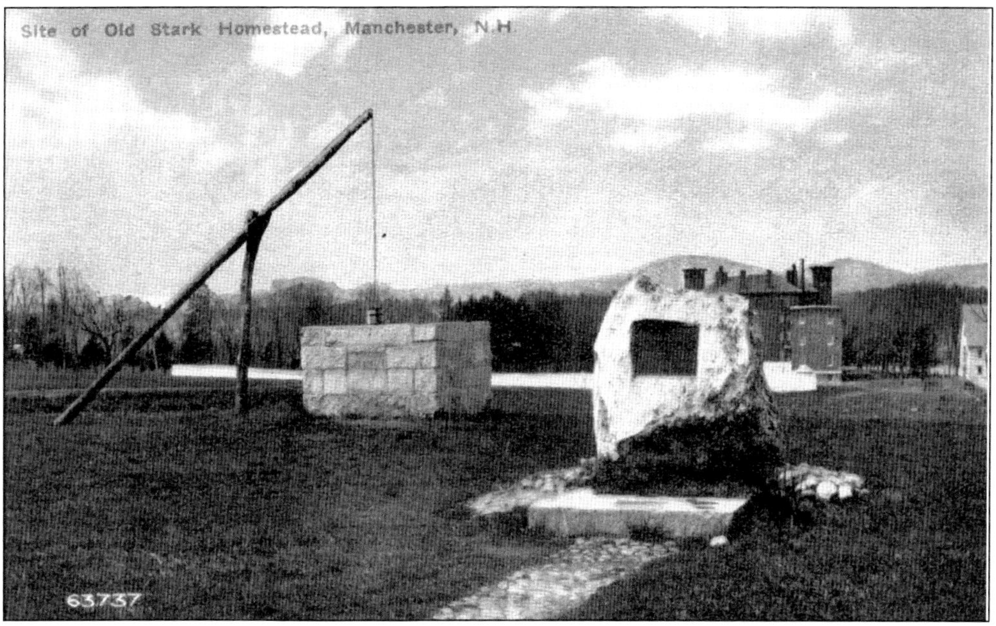

The only remnants of the Stark family's larger house, located along what has become River Road and facing the appropriately named Bennington Road, are the stone doorstep and the well. In 1906, the DAR placed a stone monument with a plaque to mark the site. Visible in the background are the buildings of the State Industrial School, also called the Reform School, now known as the Youth Development Center.

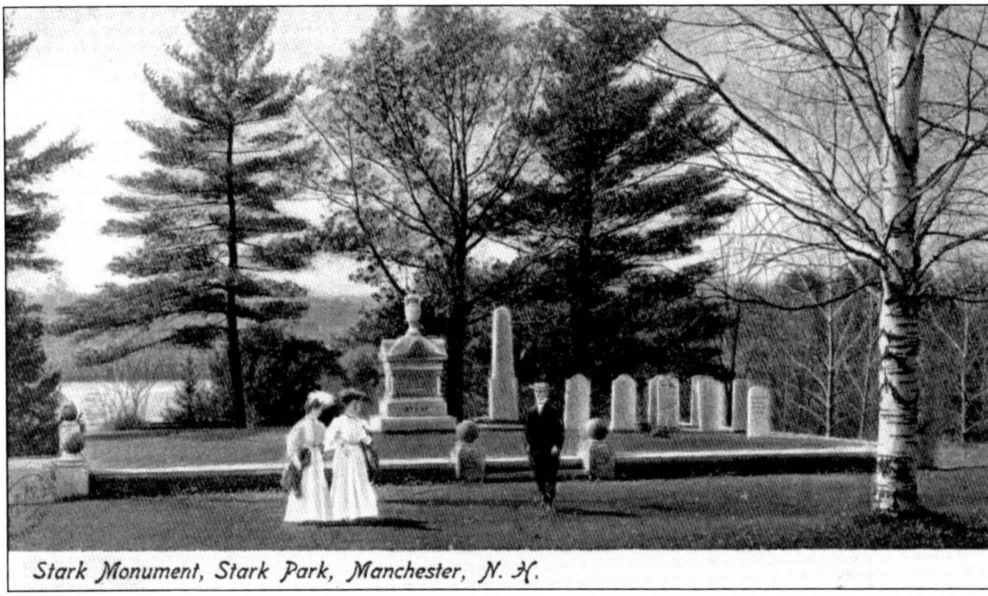

Gen. John Stark (1728–1822) and his wife, Molly, (1737–1814) rest with 27 relatives in the family cemetery, part of their 800-acre farm. In 1876, their great-grandchildren Elizabeth and Augustus Stark donated land, including the cemetery, to the city, which purchased another 30 acres to create Stark Park in 1893. New Hampshire owes its motto to General Stark, who wrote, "Live free or die: Death is not the worst of evils."

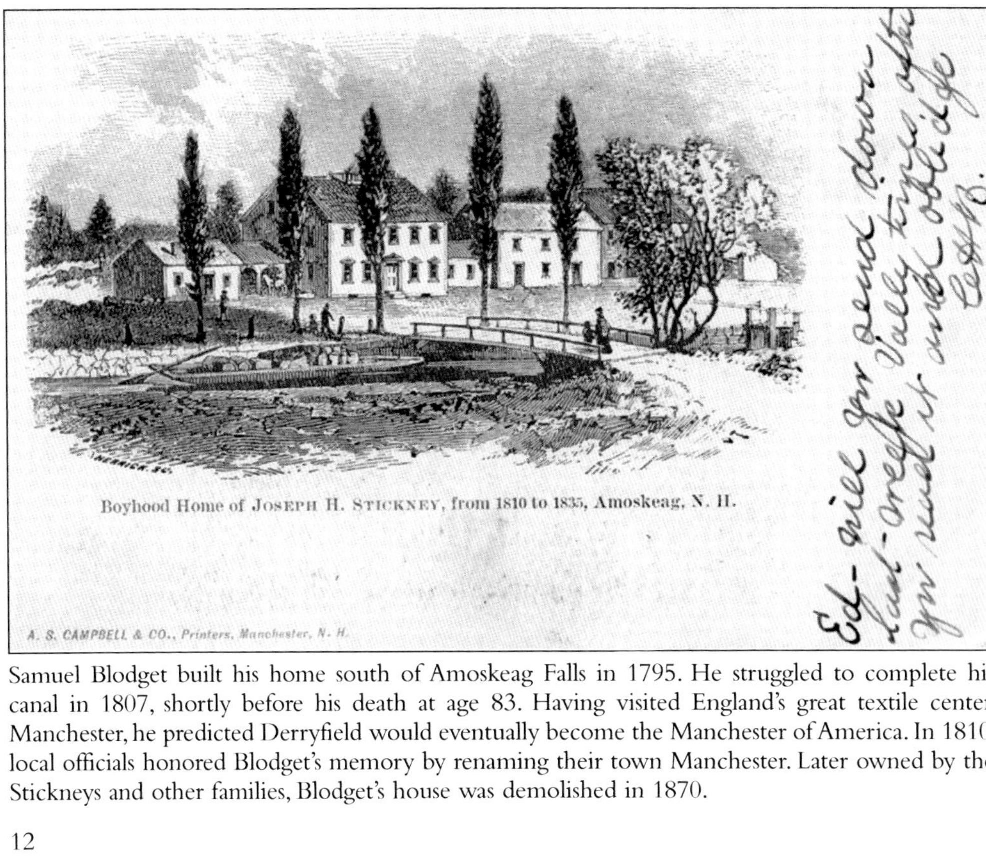

Samuel Blodget built his home south of Amoskeag Falls in 1795. He struggled to complete his canal in 1807, shortly before his death at age 83. Having visited England's great textile center, Manchester, he predicted Derryfield would eventually become the Manchester of America. In 1810, local officials honored Blodget's memory by renaming their town Manchester. Later owned by the Stickneys and other families, Blodget's house was demolished in 1870.

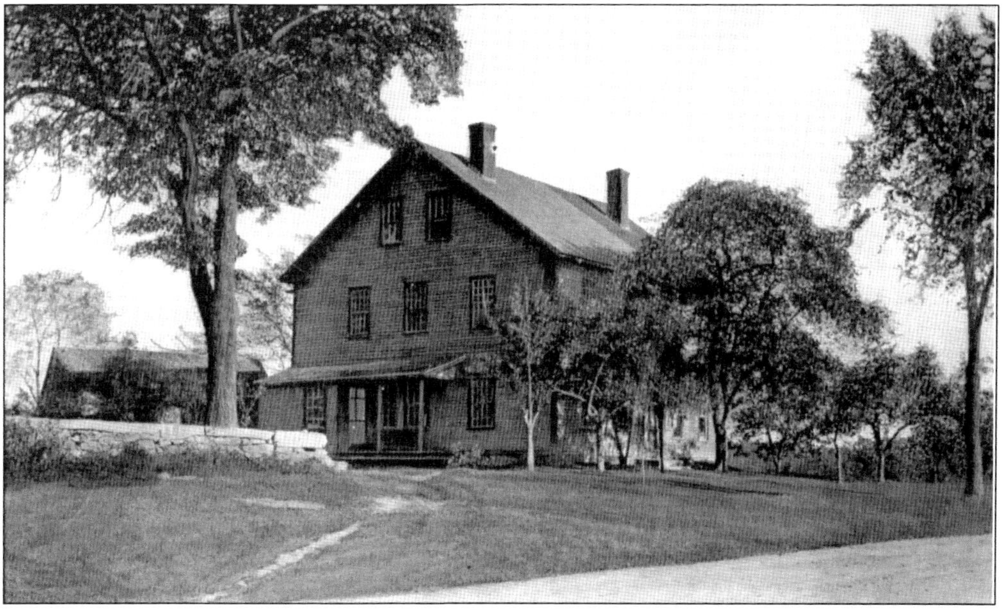

Built in 1759, Derryfield Centre's meetinghouse on Mammoth Road served as both church and town hall until 1840, when Manchester citizens voted to construct the Town House on Elm Street. In 1853, the meetinghouse was moved slightly south and transformed into a private dwelling. Vacant, it burned on August 12, 1973. Since 1978, Faith Baptist Church has occupied the lot. A marker at the Manchester Centre Cemetery indicates the building's original site.

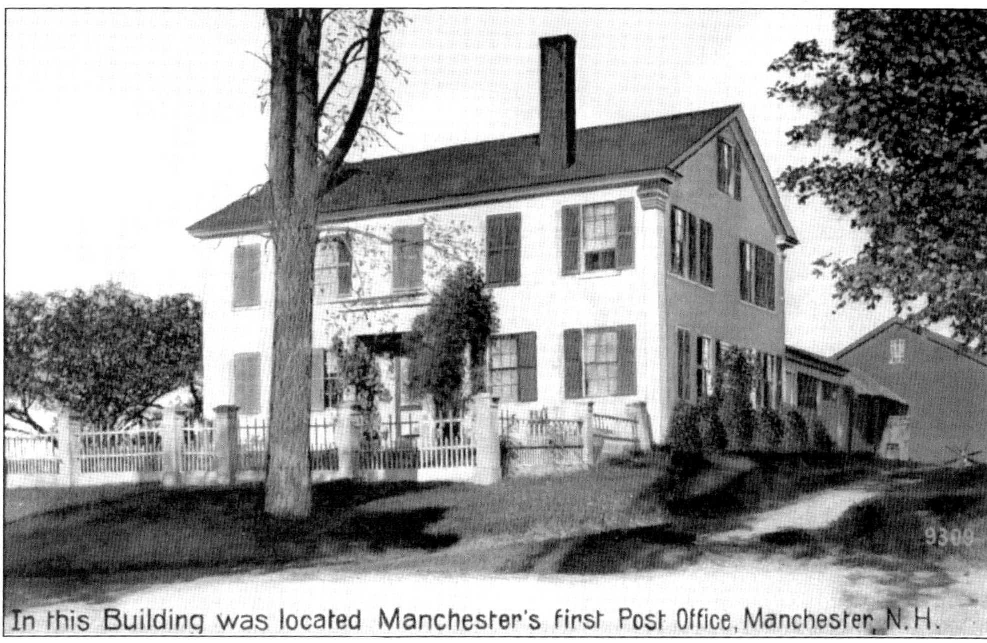

The town's first post office opened in 1831 on Mammoth Road in storekeeper Samuel Jackson's establishment. Upon arriving, stagecoaches had to wait while postmaster Jackson sorted through mailbags to find letters and parcels destined for Manchester addresses. In 1840, shortly after another post office opened in the rapidly developing downtown area, Jackson resigned, and his facility ceased operation. It later became a private residence, as it remains today.

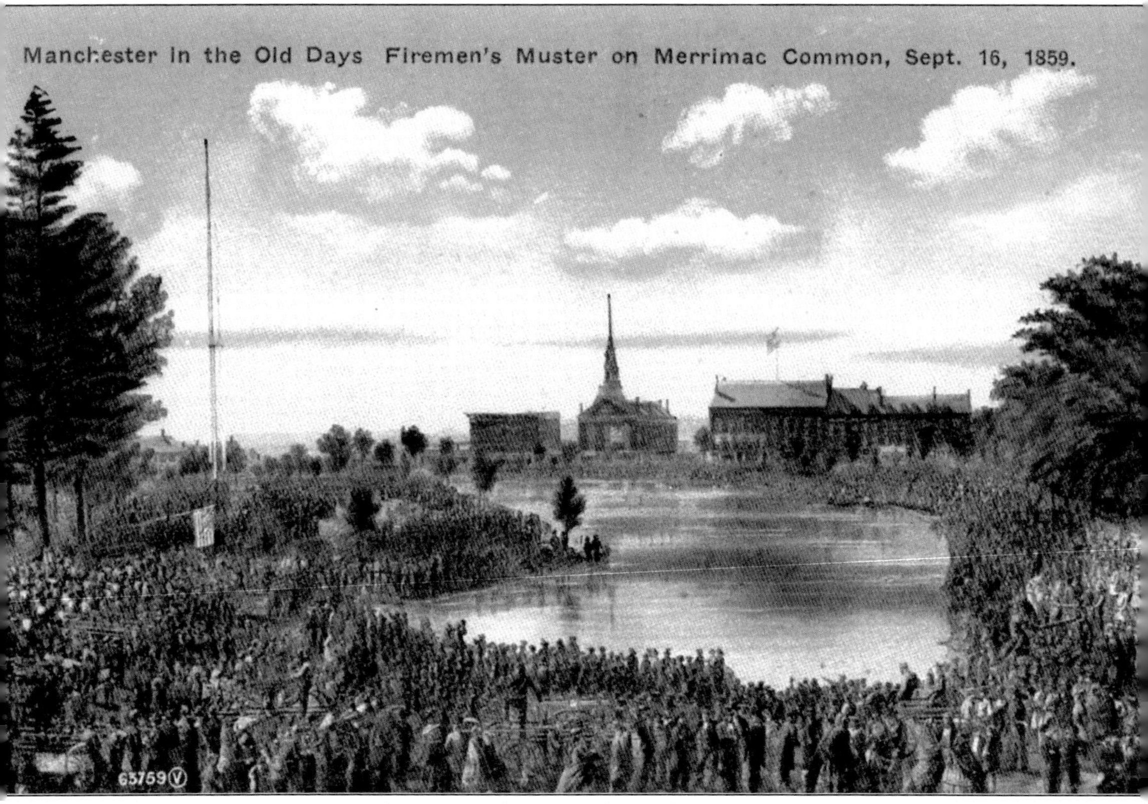

From the beginning, a rivalry existed between the settlements at Amoskeag Falls and Derryfield Centre. The onset of the Industrial Revolution and the town's renaming to Manchester foreshadowed the predominance of the small but growing manufacturing area near the falls and river. In 1840, plans laid out two years earlier for a new downtown began attracting businesses and government institutions from Manchester Centre to Elm Street and the vicinity. By 1846, the year of Manchester's incorporation, the downtown had acquired its modern urban image, with streets, parks, stores, and offices. Artist John B. Bachelder captured the flavor of early downtown in his famous lithograph depicting Manchester's last big firemen's muster in Merrimack Square on September 15 and 16, 1859. Merrimack Square, now Veterans' Memorial Park, provided an ideal location for these gatherings, in which 2,500 firefighters representing companies from all over New England competed for a cash prize. Bachelder neglected to show the rowdy, alcohol-fueled atmosphere, which spawned quite a riot.

Two

ALONG THE BANKS OF THE MERRIMACK

Without the Merrimack River, whose name, meaning "deep waters" or "strong current," was given by the Algonquian-speaking Penacooks, Manchester might never have existed. We love the Merrimack, yet we often mistreat it. Our river allows us to tame it, yet it occasionally rebels to remind us that we are not in charge. It also defines and divides us, as we call ourselves East Siders or West Siders. Yet it beckons and unites us for many reasons, as it has throughout time.

Drawn to its falls by an abundance of fish, the Penacooks also paddled along the river, their highway. Having opened it as a trade route, British settlers and their descendants later harnessed its waterpower for mills built of red bricks made from Hooksett's riverbank clay. Eventually, the mills converted to steam, then to hydroelectric power, further exploiting the falls.

Meanwhile, industrialization and urbanization polluted the river, rendering it unsuitable for most living creatures. Then came the decline of the textile empire and its fall after the great flood. A decaying millyard struggled to maintain itself by importing various new manufacturing enterprises.

Today, despite the loss to urban renewal of many superb examples of industrial architecture, a sparser but revitalized, more diversified millyard thrives. While the falls continue to supply part of our electrical needs, the cleanup of the river and the construction of a fish ladder at the Amoskeag dam have resulted in a riparian renaissance featuring the return of fish and numerous recreational and sporting opportunities.

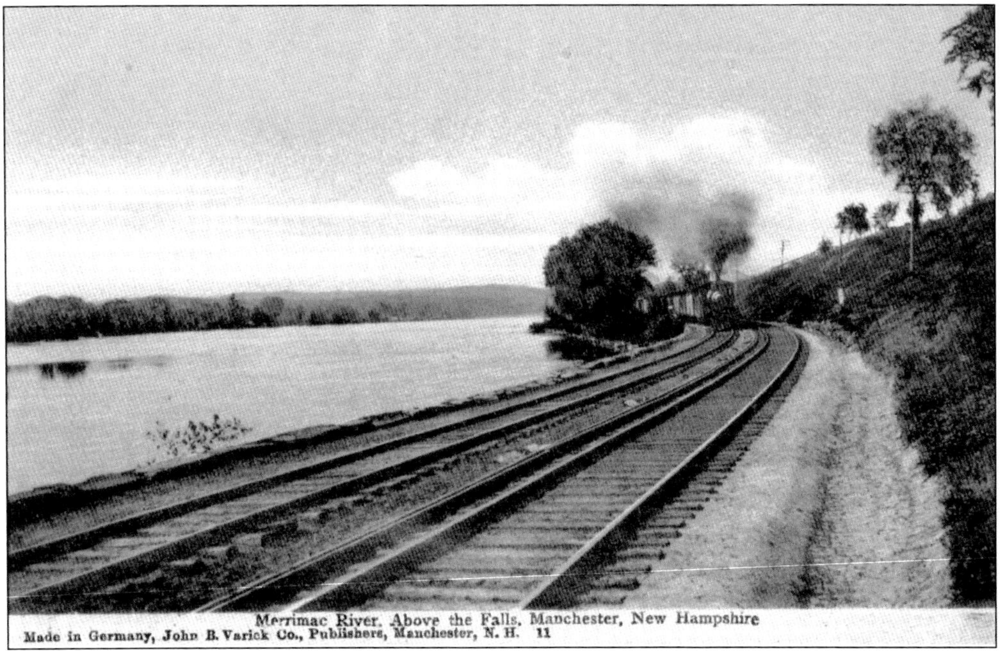

Amid protests that the coming of the railroad would antiquate travel by horse and shipping by barge, start fires from the locomotives' sparks, and create noise to drive people insane and cause hens to stop laying, the Concord Railroad inaugurated its line between Concord and Nashua for dignitaries on June 28, 1842. The first passenger train rolled through Manchester on July 4. Here, a locomotive steams south above Amoskeag Falls.

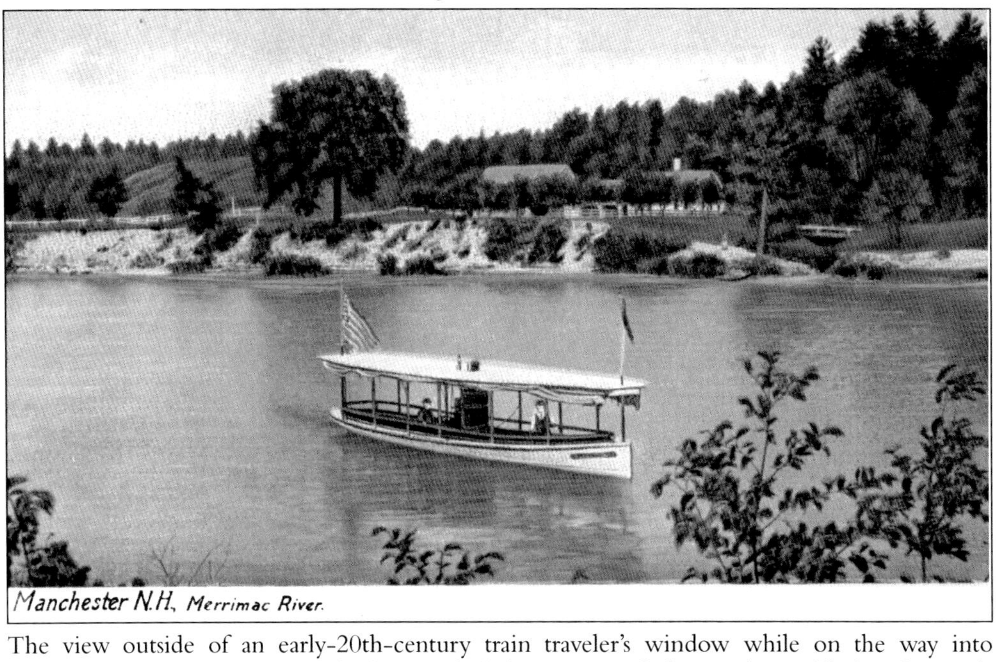

The view outside of an early-20th-century train traveler's window while on the way into Manchester from the north might have included a variety of pleasure boats filled with people enjoying the calm waters of the Merrimack River above Amoskeag Falls. Today speedboats roar past as they race up and down the river.

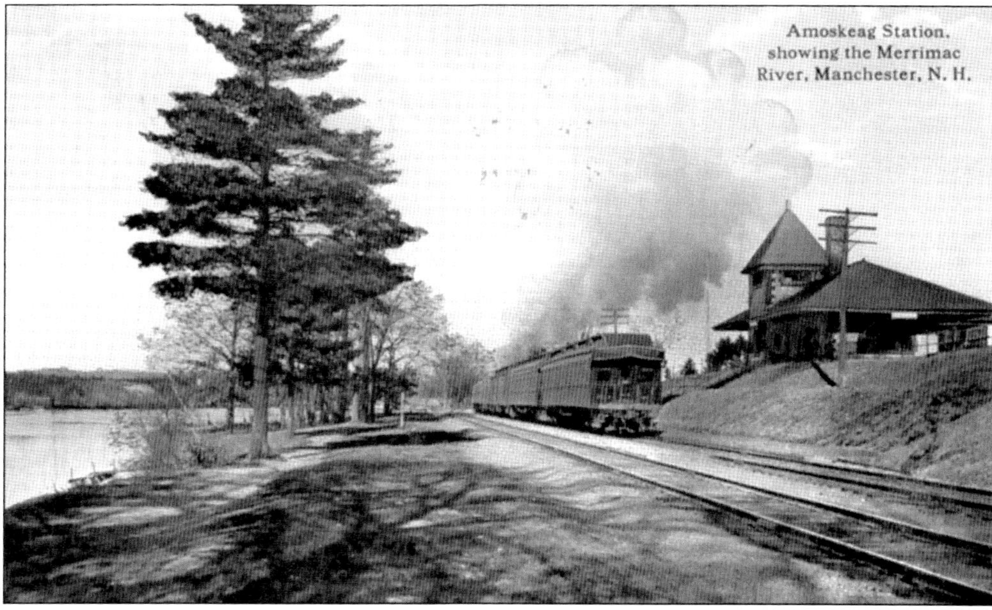

Despite clamor for a new main railroad station, the old one having become "a monumental disgrace" (as it was described in the *Journal of the Manchester Board of Trade* in 1892), the Concord & Montreal Railroad opened Amoskeag Station in 1892 to serve North End residents. Located at the foot of West Webster Street, it nearly bordered the property of former governor Frederick Smyth, who, coincidentally, was president of the Concord & Montreal Railroad. The station eventually became a private residence.

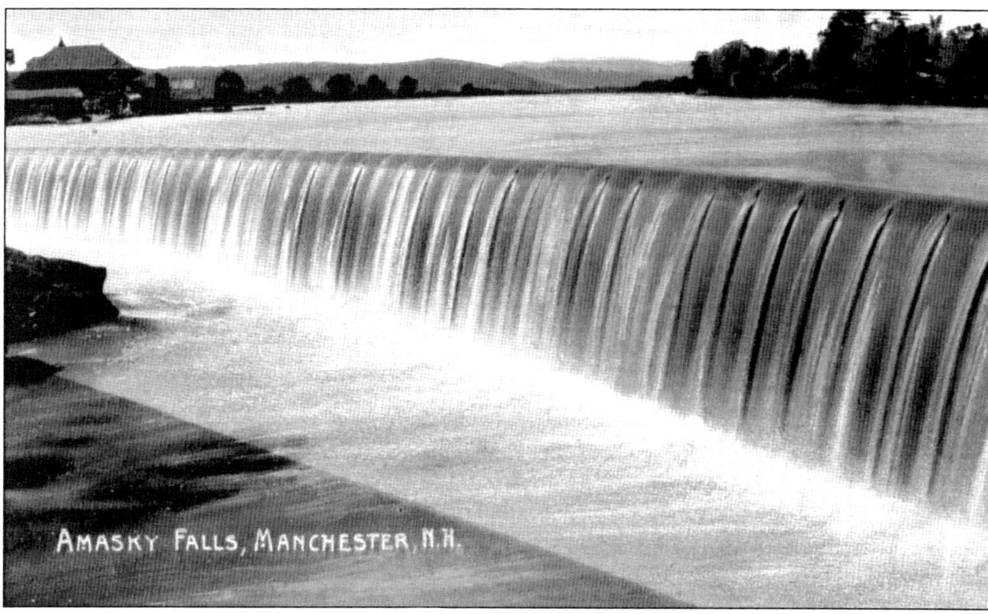

The Penacooks called Amoskeag Falls by several names, including Namaske and Namaoskeag, meaning "place of fish." Here, they caught salmon, shad, sturgeon, alewives, and what white settlers baptized "Derryfield beef": lamprey eels. In 1837, the Amoskeag company began constructing a dam to divert water into its Upper and Lower Canals, dug in 1837 and 1838, respectively. The company replaced the dam in 1871 and again, for hydroelectric power, in 1918–1923.

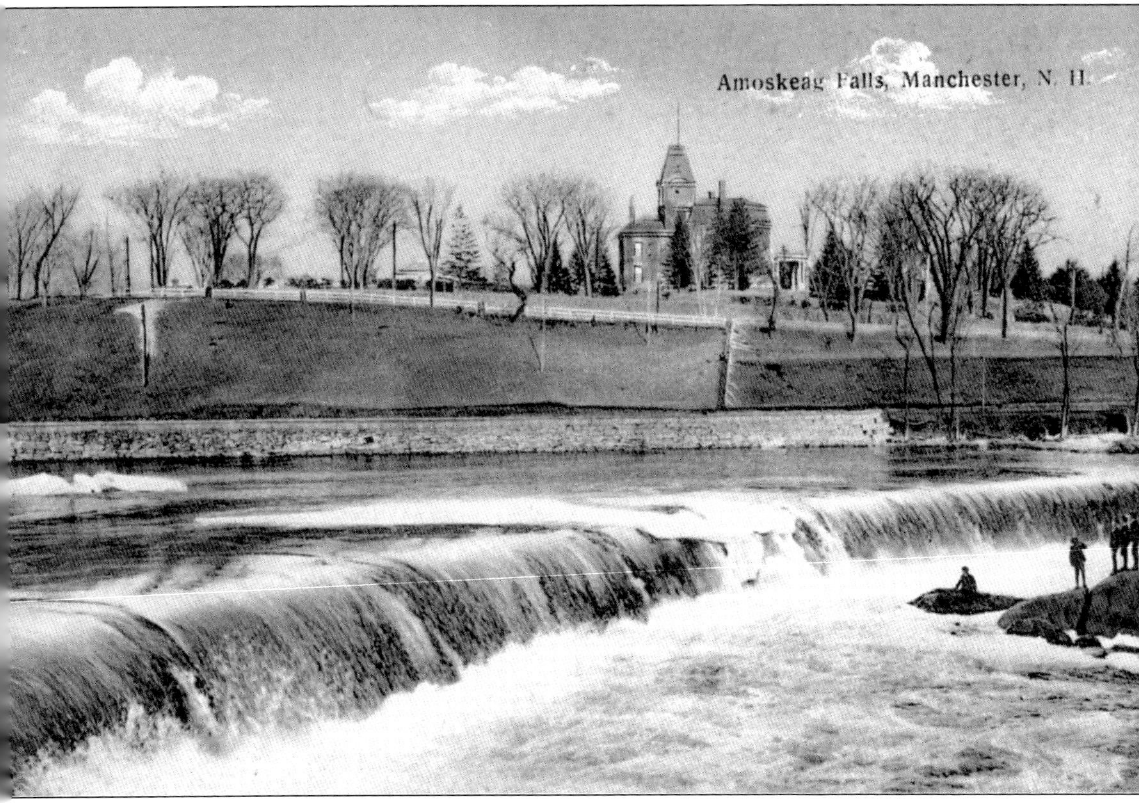

In 1872, former mayor and governor Frederick Smyth and his wife, Emily, moved into the Willows, a sumptuous red-brick mansion of their own design built on 10 acres overlooking Amoskeag Falls that were once the site of a Penacook village. The home featured frescoed ceilings, marble fireplaces, woodwork from native trees, an elevator, and a mansard roof with tower. In 1877, it had the city's first residential telephone line, connected to Smyth's Elm Street bank office in Smyth's Block. On Thursday, August 23, 1877, Rutherford B. Hayes, a guest at the Willows, became the first president to try Alexander Graham Bell's recent invention. Upon returning to Washington, Hayes had the first telephone installed in the White House. Widowed in 1885, Smyth remarried shortly thereafter. Following his death in 1899, his widow, Marion, lived on at the Willows for many years. Vacant after World War II, it later housed the Sunny Hill Nursery School. Its demolition in 1969 provoked *Life* magazine's "Parting Shots" to comment stingingly, "What Manchester, N.H. really needs is another parking lot." The Brady Sullivan Tower now occupies the site.

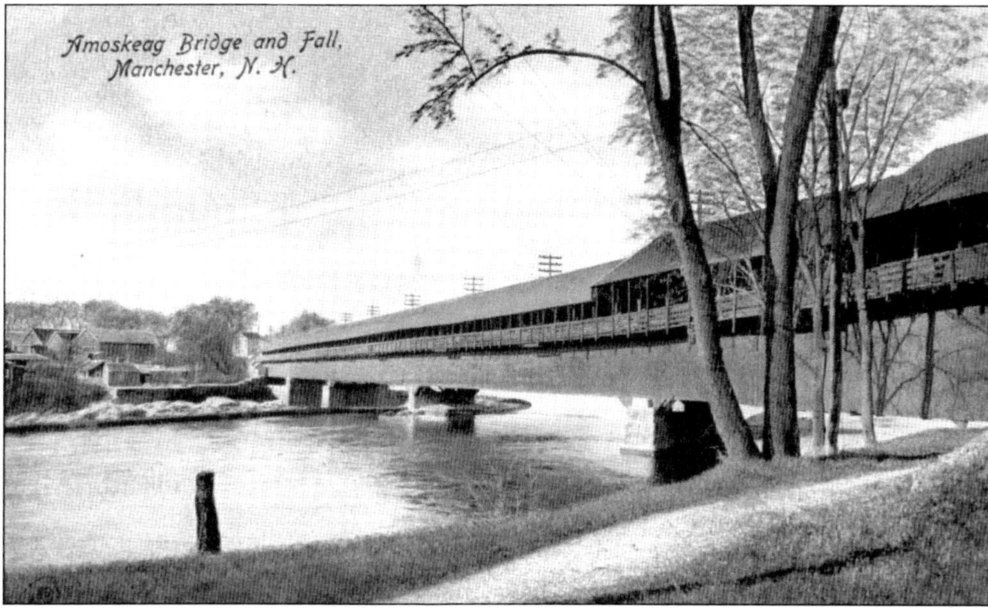

Built in 1854 to replace its freshet-doomed predecessor (1842–1853), the second Amoskeag Bridge measured 450 feet long. Having withstood freshets and floods, it became unsafe and was closed completely by 1919. In the wee hours of Sunday, August 15, 1920, wrote author Grace Holbrook Blood, it "slowly and without commotion or violence settled and sank into the river." Its two successors were constructed in 1921 and 1969.

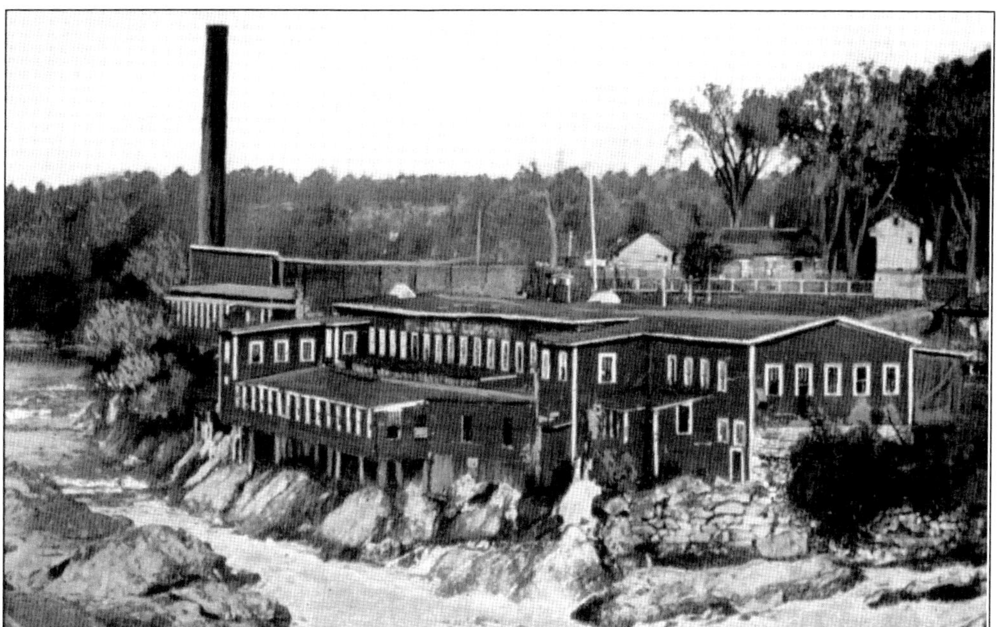

Located near the west end of Amoskeag Falls on the site of the area's earliest textile mills, the P. C. Cheney Paper Mills operated from 1871 until shortly after the death of proprietor Person C. Cheney in 1901. In addition to his business activities, Cheney served as mayor of Manchester (1872), governor of New Hampshire (1875–1877), U.S. senator (1886), and U.S. envoy extraordinary, minister plenipotentiary to Switzerland (1892–1893).

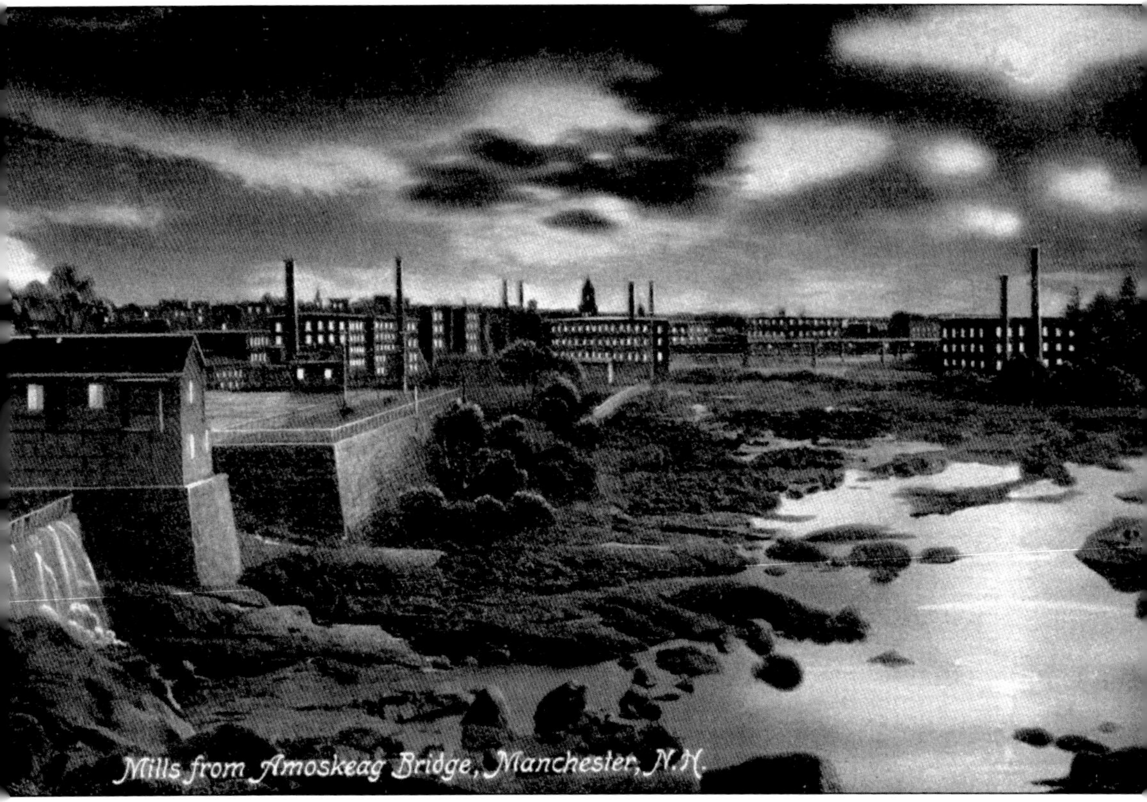

Although the roots of Manchester's textile industry reach to 1804–1805, when Benjamin Prichard constructed his cotton mill west of Amoskeag Falls, the area's transformation from an agrarian village to an urban center began in 1831 with the incorporation of the Amoskeag Manufacturing Company. As a land and waterpower developer and producer of textiles and other goods, including mill machinery, steam locomotives, and steam fire engines, the Amoskeag acquired water privileges and real estate on both banks of the Merrimack. There, from 1838 to 1915, the company built mills and workers' housing for itself and for other textile manufacturers. At age 18, Ezekiel A. Straw, Amoskeag's engineer and future agent, created Manchester's street plan, plotting land for commercial, residential, and recreational use. Over time, the Amoskeag absorbed its sister corporations to become the largest textile manufacturing company in the world; at its peak, its labor force was estimated at 17,000. For 105 years, until its closing in 1936, Amoskeag was synonymous with Manchester, which evolved into one of New England's quintessential planned industrial cities.

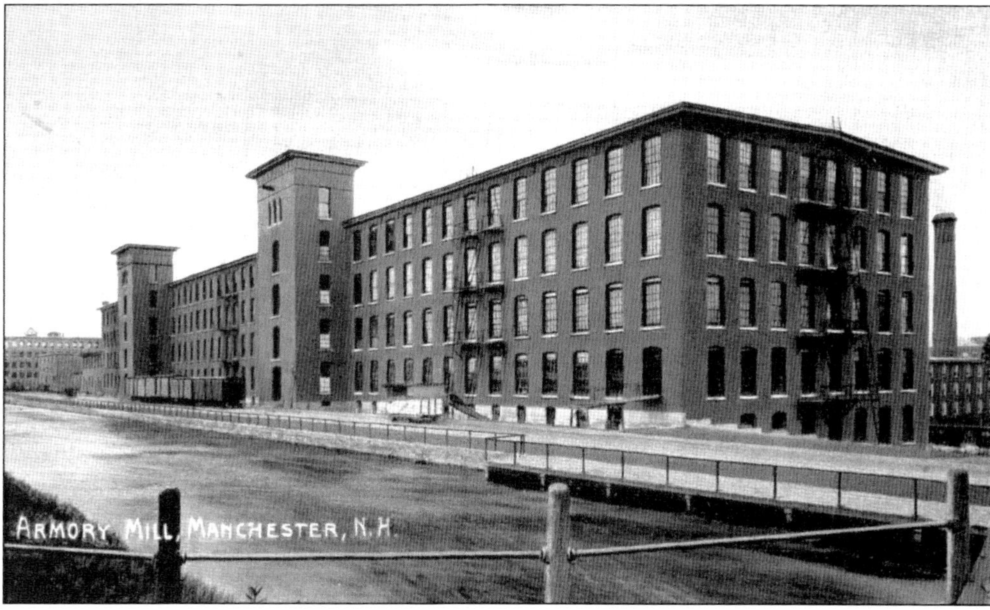

Flowing past the Amory Mill, the Upper Canal measured slightly more than one mile before turning west just south of the present-day Millyard Museum and emptying into the Lower Canal. Water also flowed through penstocks beneath the mills, turning turbines connected to an ingenious system of gears, pulleys, and belts that powered mill machinery above. The 1975 relocation of Boston & Maine's (B&M) railway included the filling in of the Upper Canal.

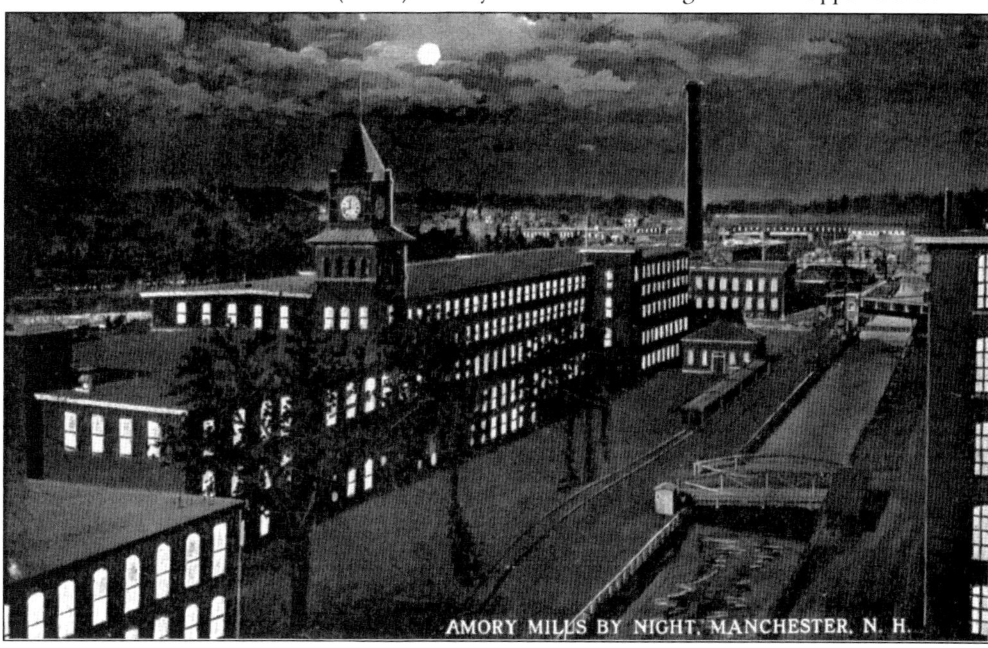

The Jefferson Mill, named for Thomas Jefferson, great-grandfather of Amoskeag's treasurer, Thomas Jefferson Coolidge, was built in 1886 during the company's steam-power era. Admired for its handsome clock tower, it also proved Amoskeag's commitment to Manchester at a time when its competitors had begun moving south due to lower production costs. Below, at right, flows the Lower Canal, where, since 1977 when the canal was filled in, traffic zips along Commercial Street.

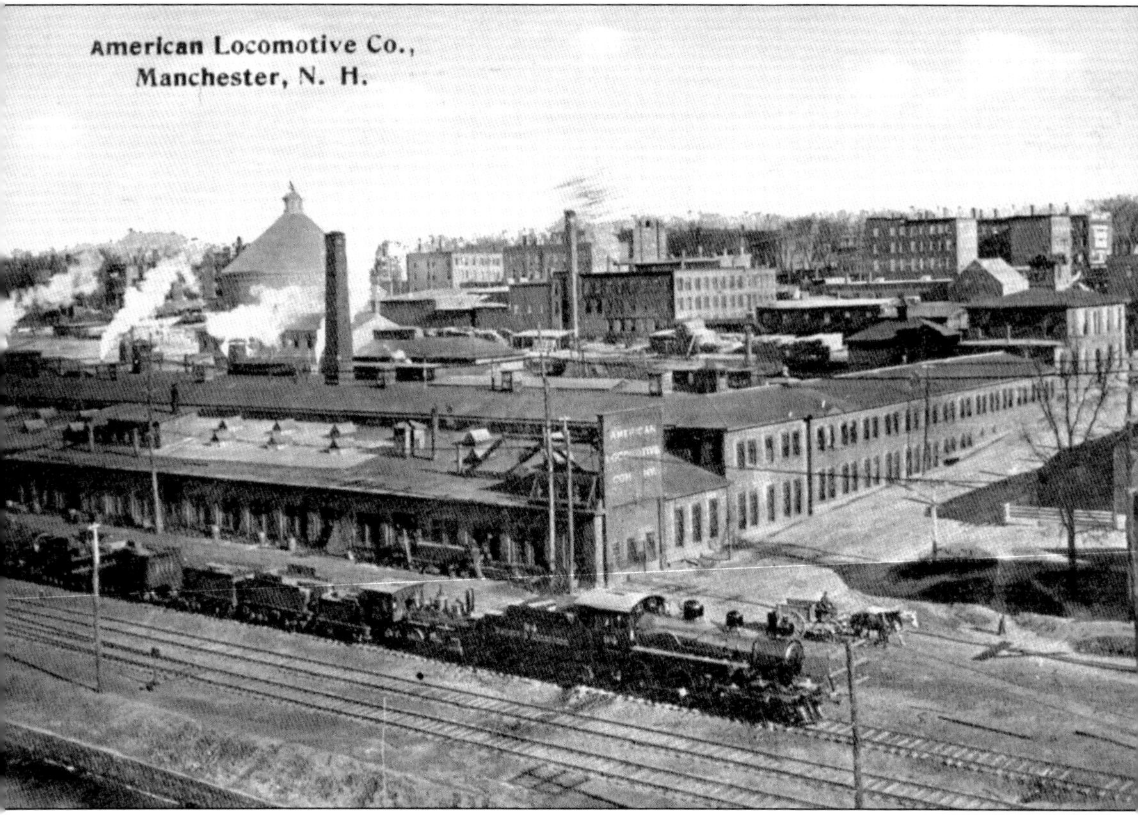

Between 1849 and 1859, the Amoskeag Machine Shop manufactured 232 steam locomotives. It then retooled to make 550 steam fire engines. The company sold its locomotive branch to the Manchester Locomotive Works, incorporated in 1854 and managed by Aretas Blood, which began manufacturing 20 locomotives annually. Later employing up to 700 men, it eventually turned out 14 locomotives monthly. In 1876, it assumed Amoskeag's discontinued production of steam fire engines. After Blood's death in 1897, the American Locomotive Company of Schenectady, New York, absorbed the company in 1901. Seen here about 1910 from the roof of the Amory Mill, in front of the plant on Canal and Hollis Streets, is Engine No. 94, made for the Bangor & Aroostook Railroad. After World War I, the building became a garage for Amoskeag's vehicles. With its Hollis Street wing largely demolished, it has since housed many businesses, including the Pandora Factory Store, which closed about 1990 after three decades. In the background sits a gasometer built about 1880 by the Manchester Gas Light Company and demolished in 1937.

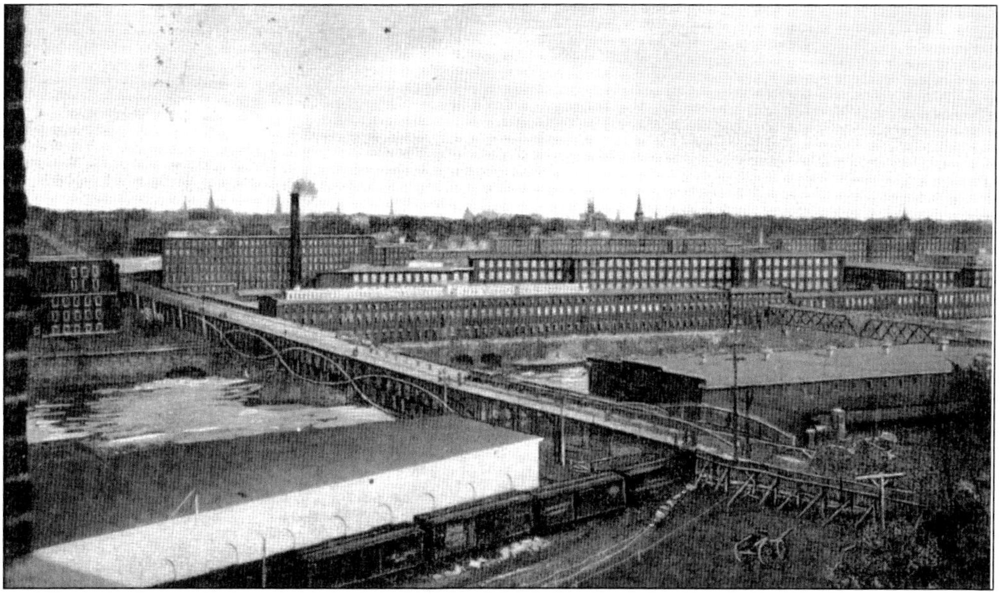

Five bridges have spanned the Merrimack River at Bridge Street, beginning with Robert McGregor's own McGregor Bridge in 1792, which led straight to his farm on the West Side. Upon its completion in 1881, the third McGregor Bridge ranked in New England as the largest iron bridge and the only two-tiered bridge. Its upper level accommodated public traffic, while the Amoskeag Manufacturing Company had private use of its lower level.

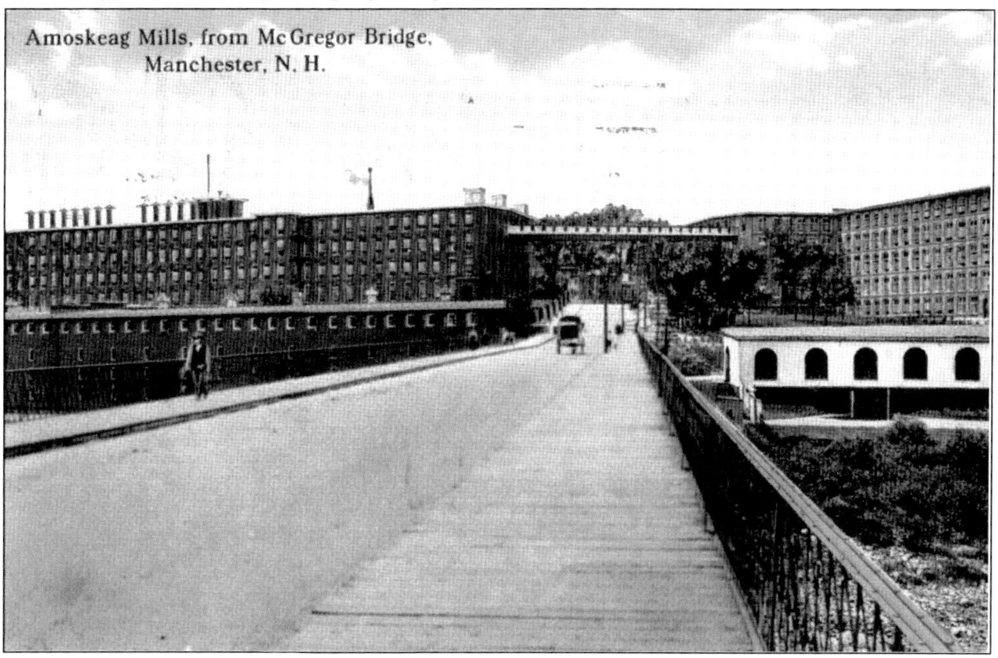

Prior to the opening in 1881 of the McGregor Bridge, Mayor Horace B. Putnam decided to test its strength. At a given signal, city teams and watering carts, having loaded up at full capacity and weighing an estimated 60 tons, crossed the bridge simultaneously from opposite directions at a lively pace. The bridge passed the test. It also withstood the flood of 1896, but not that of March 1936. This view looks west.

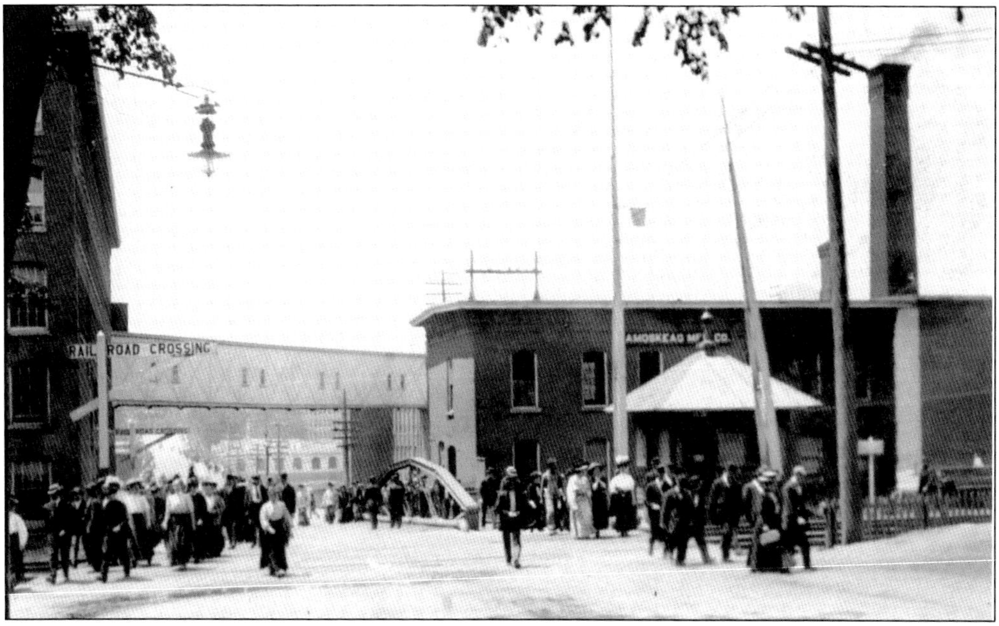

Prior to 1937, no bridge that spanned the river at West Bridge Street ever carried traffic above Canal Street and the railroad tracks. Here, at noontime on a summer day about 1909, Amoskeag mill workers cross the intersection of Canal and West Bridge Streets. Immediately beyond the tracks is a bridge over Amoskeag's Upper Canal, and in the distance is the upper deck of the McGregor Bridge.

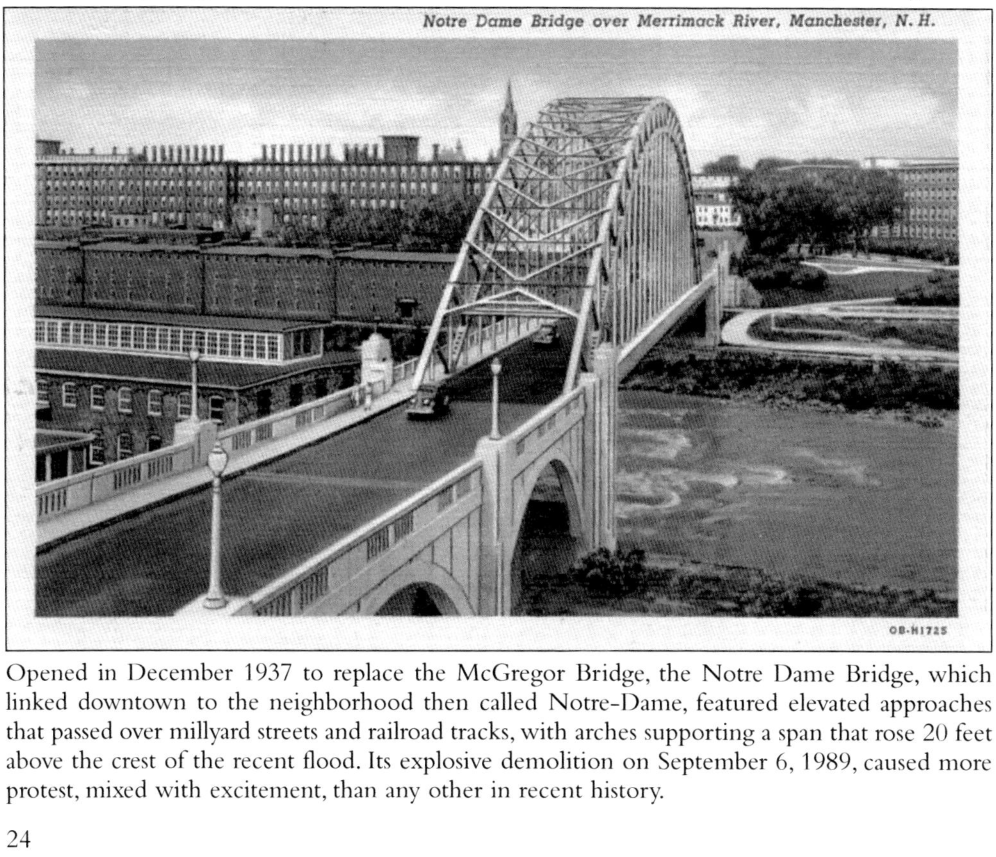

Opened in December 1937 to replace the McGregor Bridge, the Notre Dame Bridge, which linked downtown to the neighborhood then called Notre-Dame, featured elevated approaches that passed over millyard streets and railroad tracks, with arches supporting a span that rose 20 feet above the crest of the recent flood. Its explosive demolition on September 6, 1989, caused more protest, mixed with excitement, than any other in recent history.

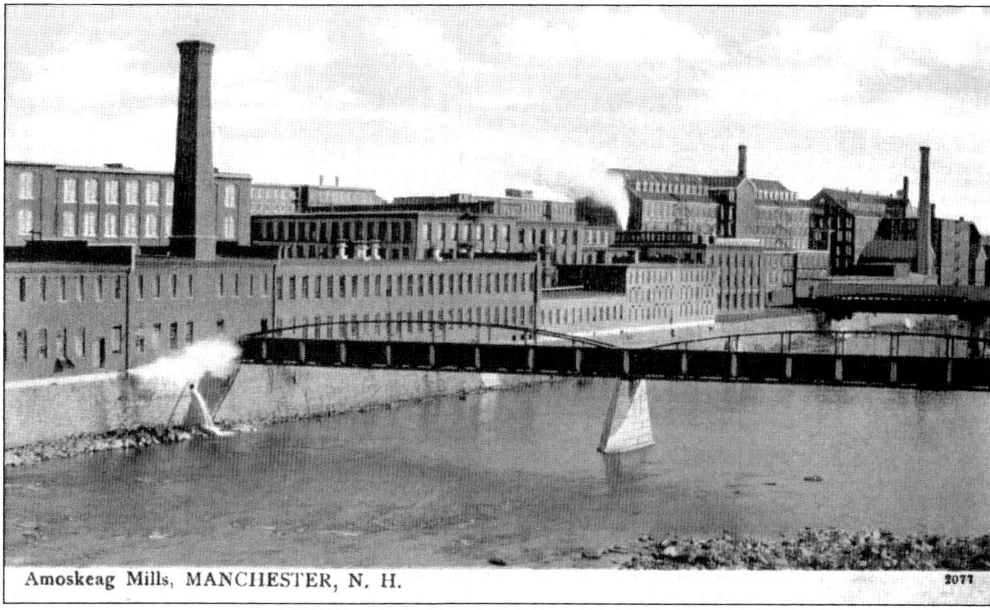

Until 1880, the Amoskeag's machinery operated entirely on waterpower. The introduction of steam power resulted in the company's expansion to the river's west bank and the construction of private bridges. Here, on the east bank, sit a steampipe bridge and, in the right background, a pedestrian bridge. The flood of 1896 swept both bridges downriver, just as the flood of 1936 carried away their replacements, whose piers remain intact to this day.

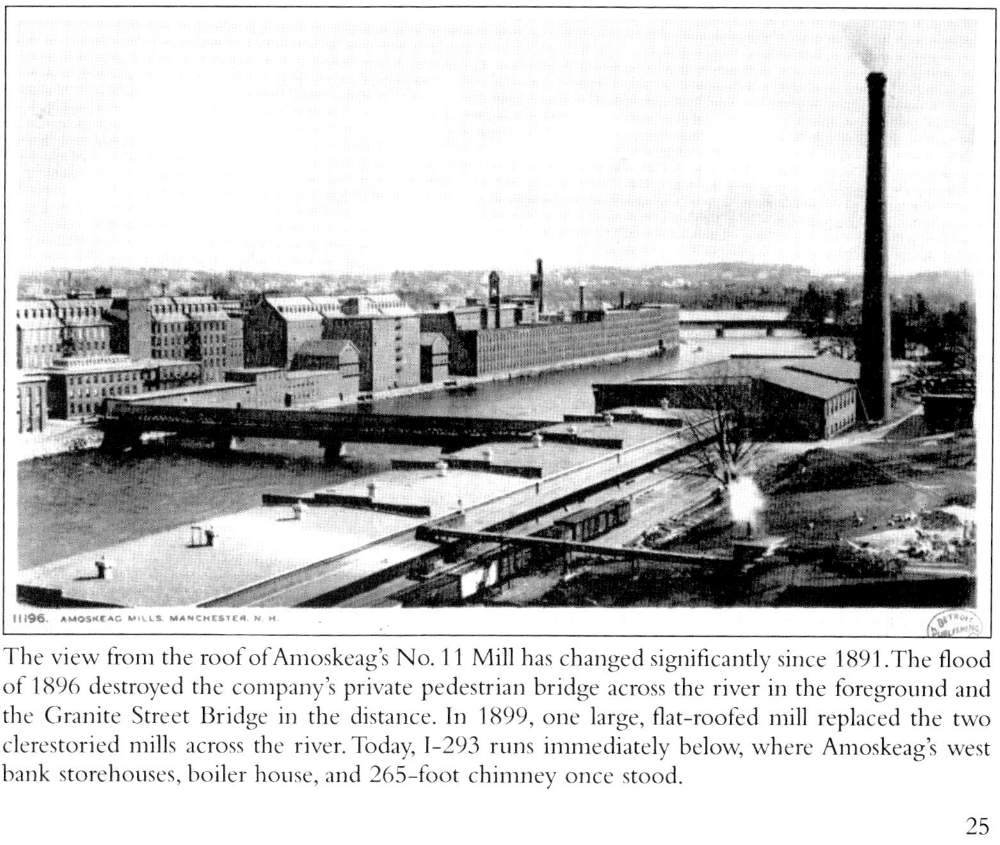

The view from the roof of Amoskeag's No. 11 Mill has changed significantly since 1891. The flood of 1896 destroyed the company's private pedestrian bridge across the river in the foreground and the Granite Street Bridge in the distance. In 1899, one large, flat-roofed mill replaced the two clerestoried mills across the river. Today, I-293 runs immediately below, where Amoskeag's west bank storehouses, boiler house, and 265-foot chimney once stood.

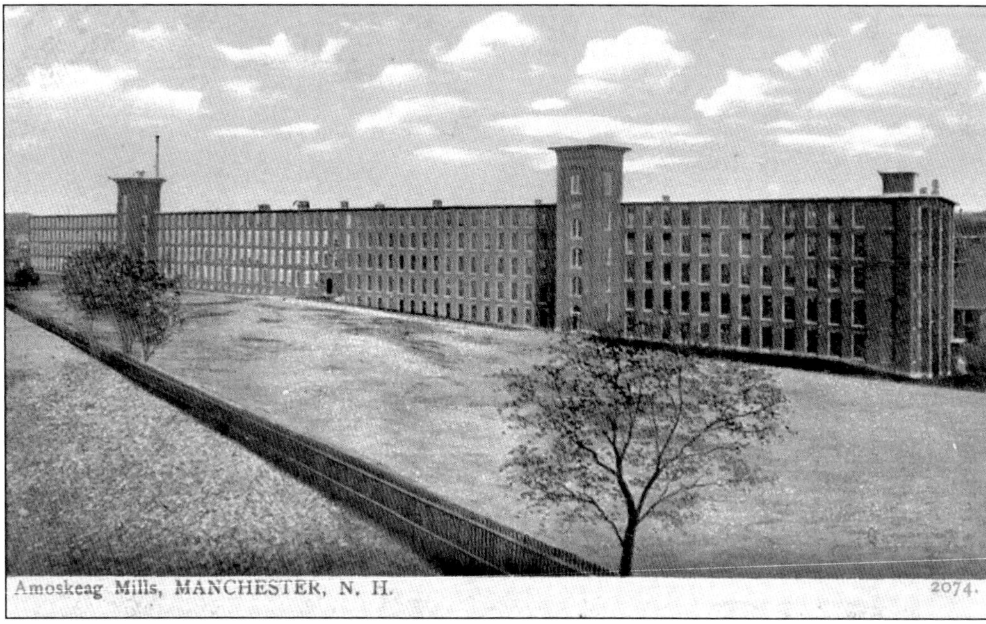

Located on McGregor Street between West Bridge and Foundry Streets, Amoskeag's No. 11 Mill took from 1889 to 1891 to construct. Once the largest cotton mill building in the world, it measured 900 feet by 103 feet and contained 4,000 looms. Beginning in 1913, its cloth room produced American flags, including the "Great Amoskeag Flag" of 1914, which measured 95 feet by 50 feet. Renamed Mill West, today it houses various businesses.

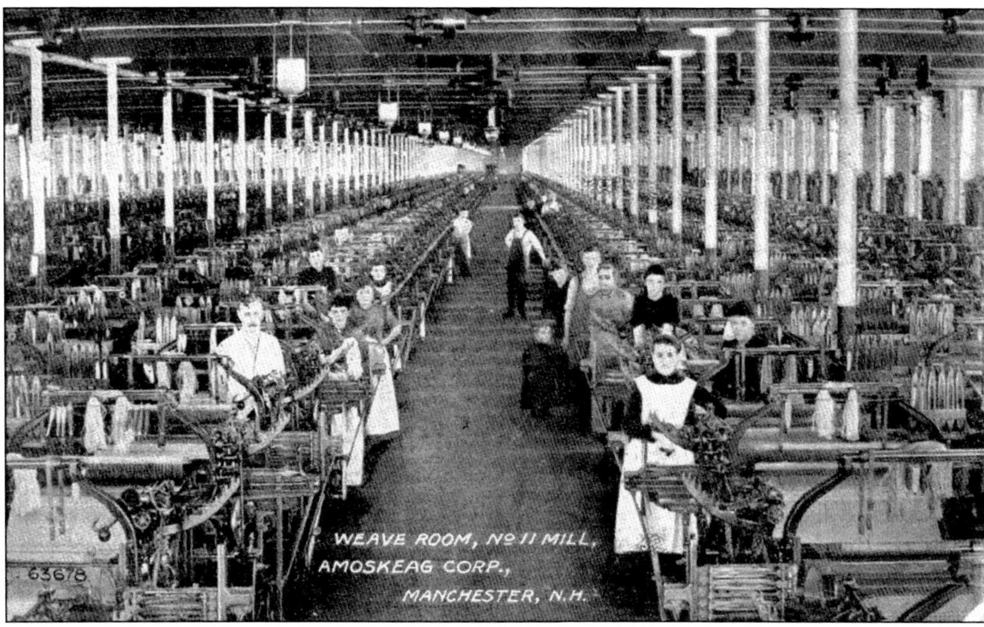

Without ever having visited a weave room such as the one seen here in No. 11 Mill, it is difficult to imagine the ambiance that reigned within. Even before entering the building, putting one's hand against the outside brick wall revealed the trembling of 4,000 looms running simultaneously. Inside, seemingly never-ending rows of looms repeatedly made their deafening "click-clack" noise, and the air was thick with humidity, cotton dust, and, in summer, stifling heat.

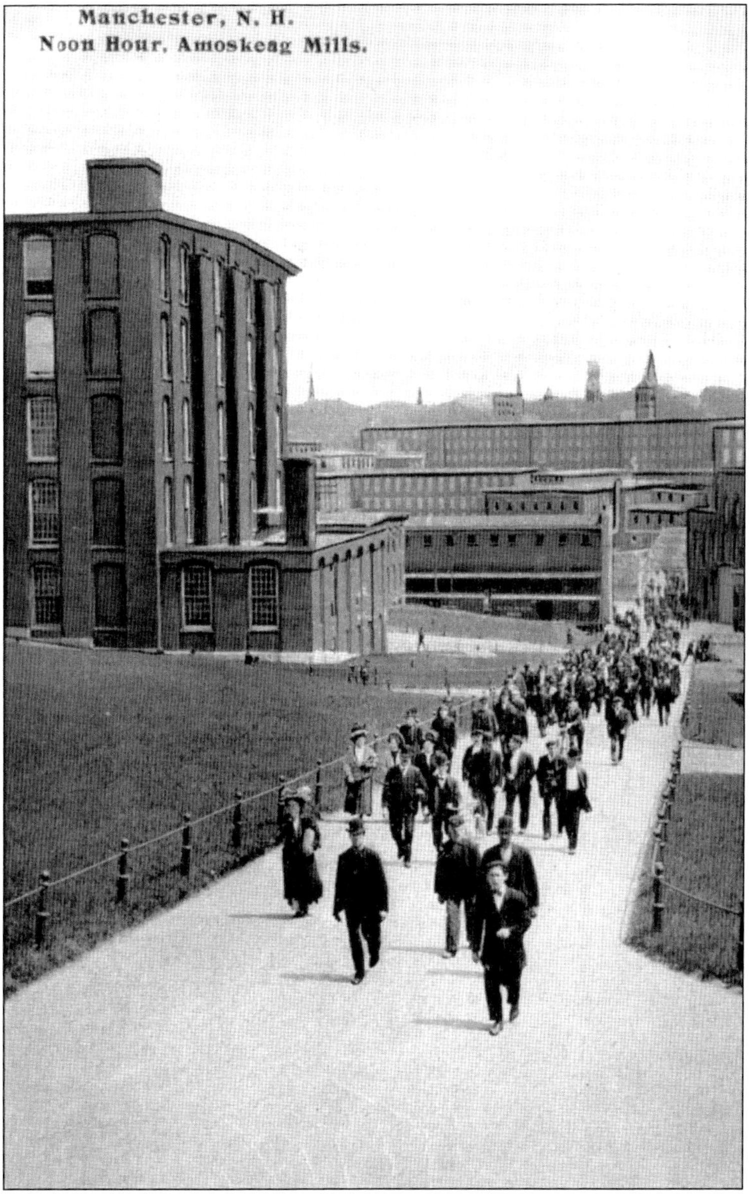

Operatives living near the millyard could take their noon meal at home. Although small at lunchtime, crowds grew enormous when work let out at 6:00 p.m., as thousands heading in every direction emerged simultaneously from the millyard. The audio effect of such a multitude could further enhance the visual, as sounds of not only English speaking but also of French, German, Swedish, Polish, Greek, Hungarian, Russian, Portuguese, and many more languages from nearly 30 lands could be heard, according to one contemporary newspaper account. Here, about 1910, workers walk west on what today is Foundry Street, just south of Mill West. The company's pedestrian bridge, seen in the distance at the foot of the incline, crossed over to the Merrimack's east bank at this point. A system of bridges, overhead passageways, and walkways linked many buildings in the millyard. Theoretically, a person could walk from one end of the millyard on one side of the river and arrive at the other end on the opposite bank without ever leaving Amoskeag property.

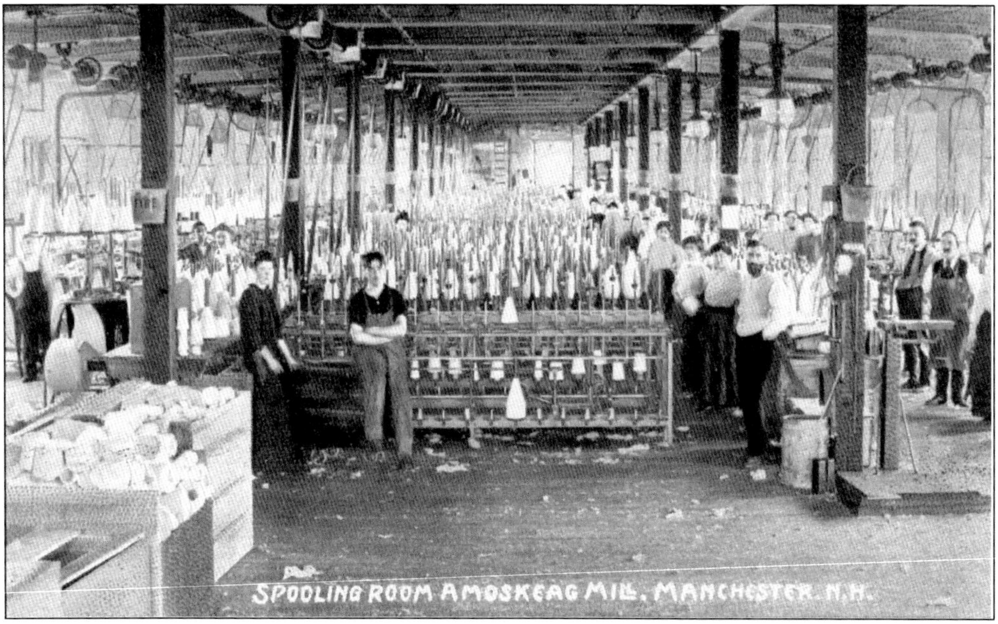

Spooling, along with carding, spinning, warping, and other operations, was but one step in the lengthy pre-weaving stage. According to statistics published by Amoskeag in 1912, its 8,500 men and 7,000 women produced 50 miles of cloth per hour and earned a total weekly payroll of $150,000. Amoskeag's acquisition of the Stark Mills in 1922, despite an ongoing strike at both companies, increased its work force to about 17,000.

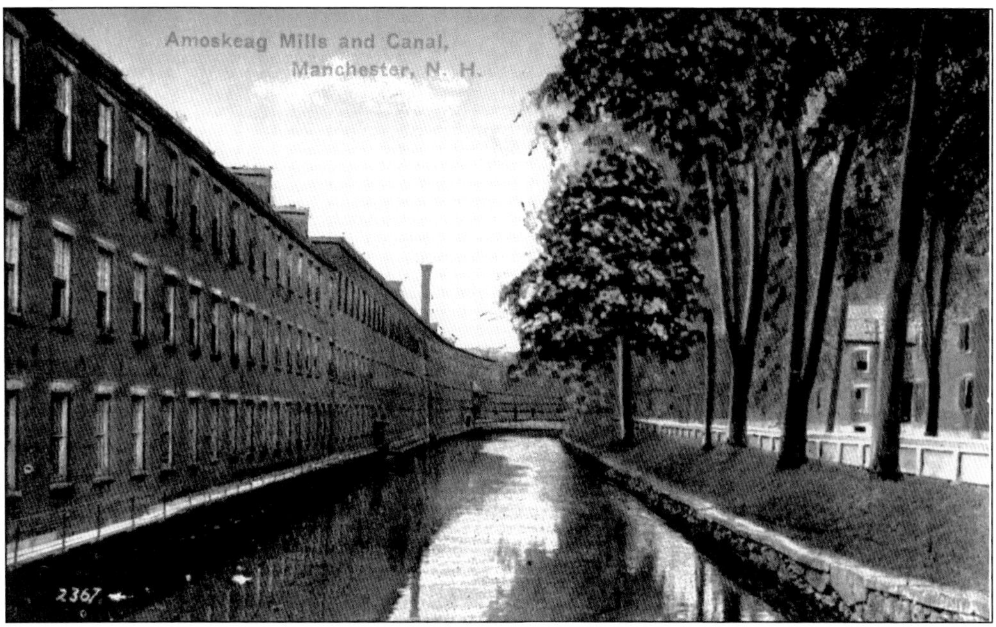

To offset the image of factory life as one of drudgery, Amoskeag's architects and engineers always endeavored to blend beauty with function by creating as pleasant and practical an environment as possible. A fine example of this concept once existed in the millyard's Southern Division: No. 4 Mill gently curved along the Lower Canal facing a fenced and tree-lined State Street, with its rows of corporation housing.

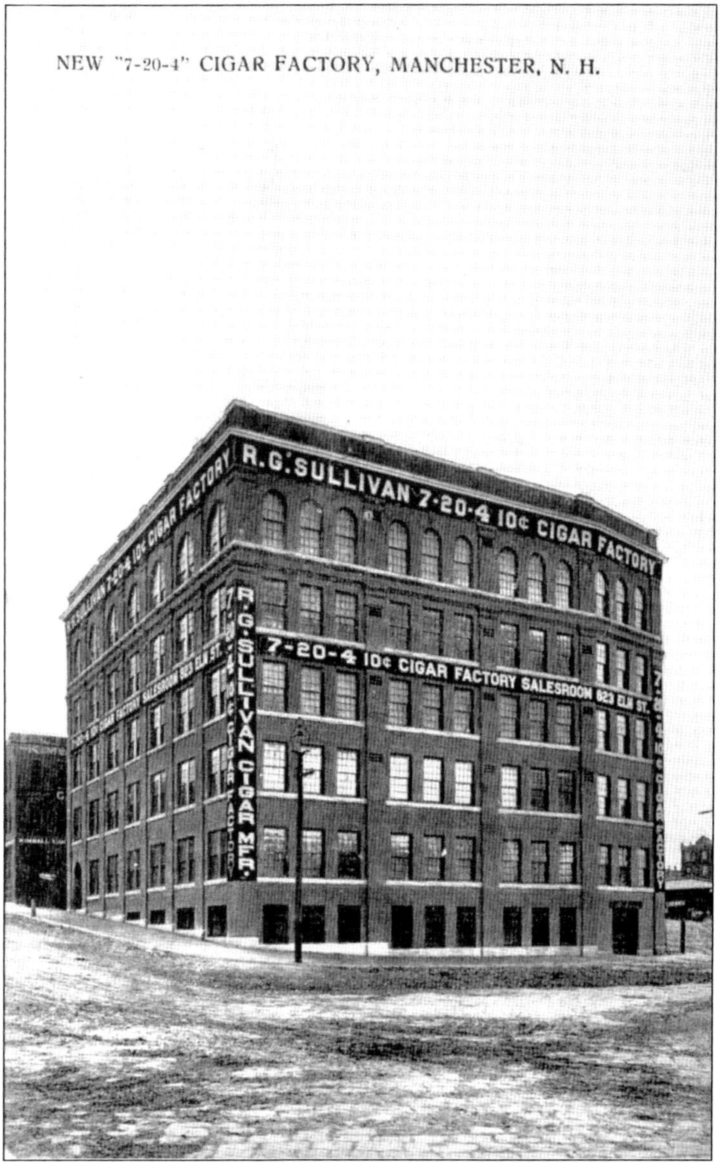

In 1874, at age 19, Roger G. Sullivan began manufacturing cigars and selling tobacco products with Nicholas Stuber at 10 Amherst Street. Subsequently alone, Sullivan moved to 724–726 Elm Street, where he created his "7-20-4 Cigar," named after his business address. In 1908, he opened his factory on West Central and Canal Streets, where 1,500 to 2,000 skilled cigar makers, many from Belgium, hand-rolled 200,000 to 225,000 cigars daily. According to the company's marketing materials, the Manchester facility became "the largest union cigar factory in the world making 10 cent cigars," paying $20 million in annual taxes. As sole proprietor, Sullivan was reputedly the country's largest individual taxpayer, contributing $500,000 annually. After his death in 1918, family members oversaw operations for many years. Beginning in 1928, the building attracted attention for having the only aviation beacon north of Boston. After the company closed in 1961, the factory housed the Indian Head Shoe Company until 1977 and Indian Head Athletics until 1983. Renovated in 1985, it now houses offices. Viewers of NBC's *Saturday Night Live* might recall that during the 1970s its stage set featured a 7-20-4 Cigar sign.

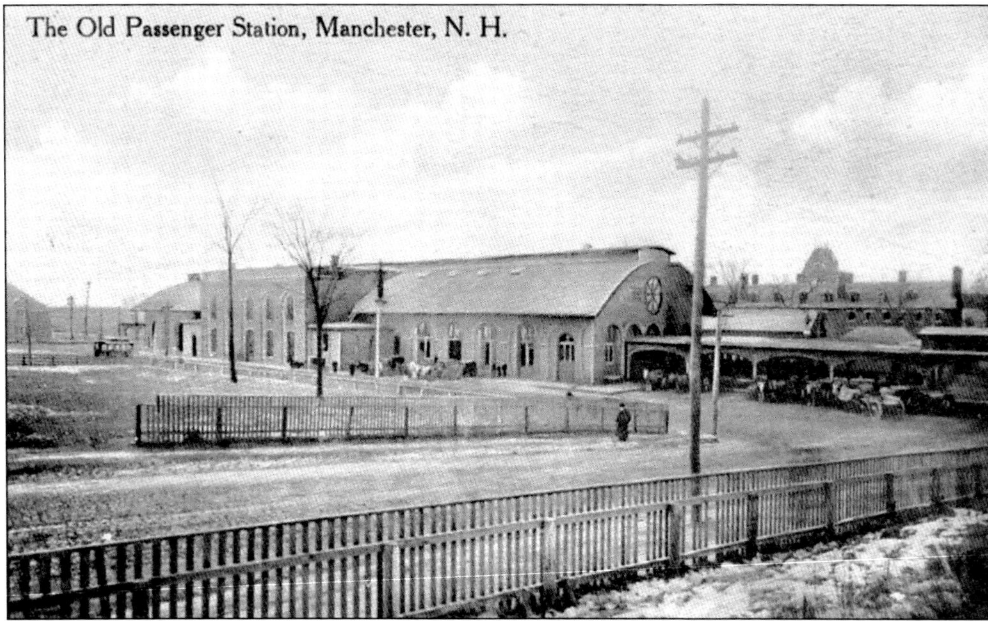

Train travel had increased so rapidly after barely more than a decade of service through Manchester that, by 1855, a new, larger red-brick passenger station replaced the original one from the 1840s. The station, seen here looking southwest from near the foot of West Central Street at Canal Street, stood at the northwest corner of Canal and Granite Streets. Until 1898, it was where many newcomers, especially immigrants, first set foot in Manchester.

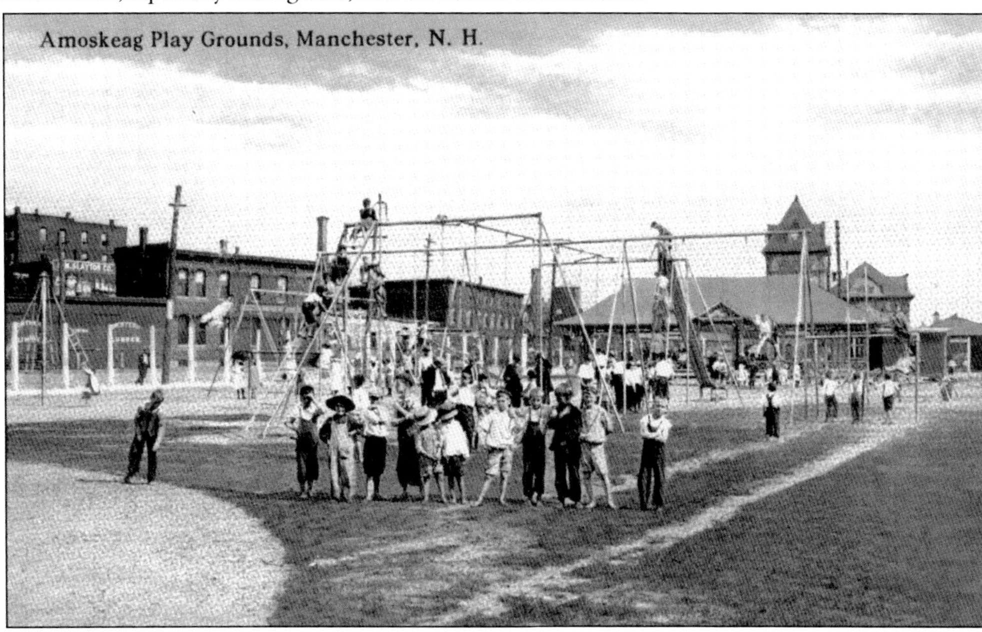

Constructed in 1911 on the site of the old passenger station, whose successor appears here in the distance, the Amoskeag playground served children of the company's workers, especially those living nearby in corporation housing. Along with the children's gardens, medical and dental offices, cooking and textile schools, and other benefits, it belonged to the Amoskeag's new program of corporate paternalism that attempted to foster employee loyalty while avoiding labor unrest.

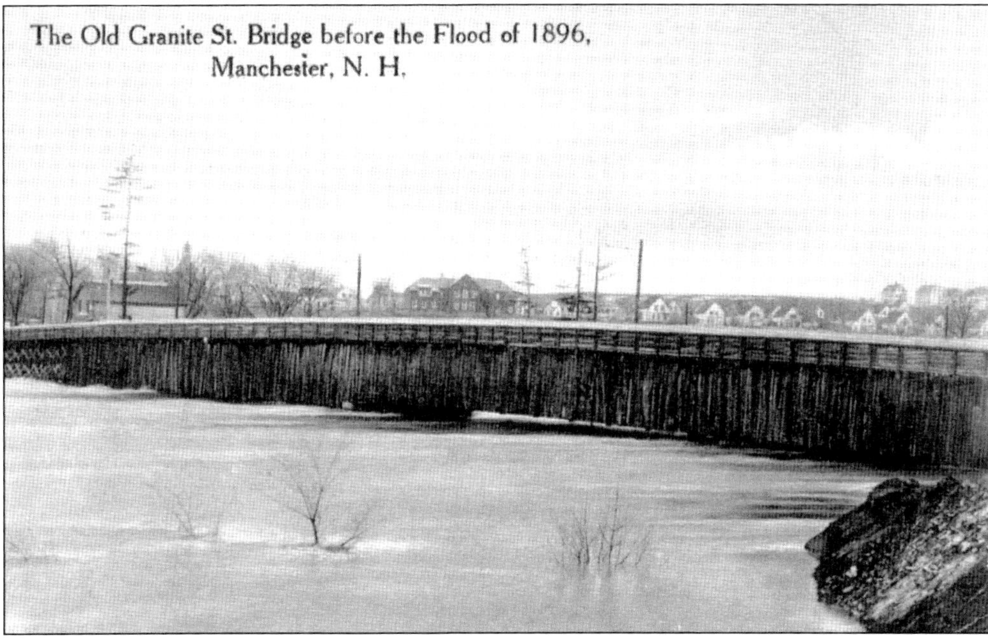

Before 1853, the middle of the Merrimack River constituted Manchester's west boundary. After the freshet of 1851 destroyed the first Granite Street Bridge, the city and its neighbor at this precise location, Bedford, disagreed over reconstruction plans. Unwilling to compromise, each proceeded independently. Bedford's lattice work appears at extreme left, in contrast with Manchester's solid plank design. The middle pier, hidden here at high water, bore the letters "B" and "M."

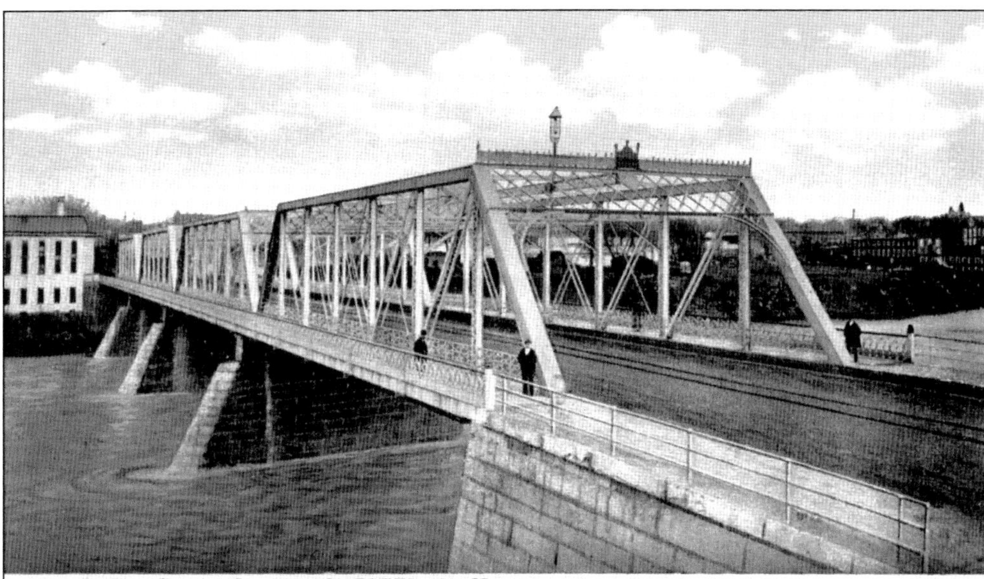

The third Granite Street Bridge, seen here looking toward the east bank, opened in November 1896. The city's worst flood up to that point had carried part of its wooden predecessor away the previous March. The city dismantled this bridge in 1954 to replace it with another bridge, which, in 1979–1980, gave way to a fifth Granite Street Bridge.

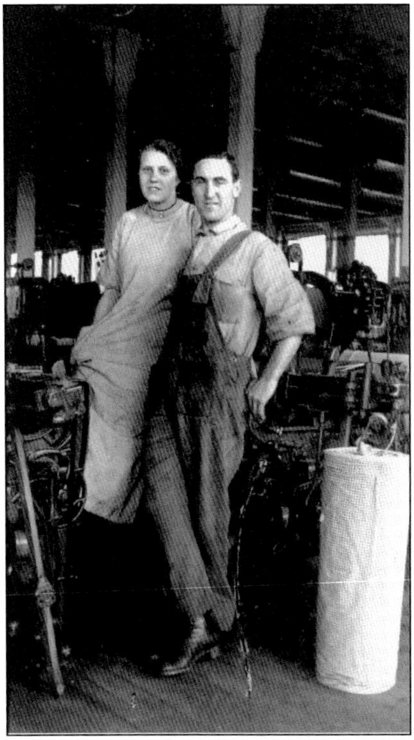

During the great postcard craze of the early 20th century, private citizens sometimes had their family photographs made into postcards. Here, an unidentified couple who were friends of the Wilfrid Labarre family had themselves photographed in the mills. Judging by their smiles, it would appear that working with relatives or friends helped relieve some of the less desirable aspects of their jobs.

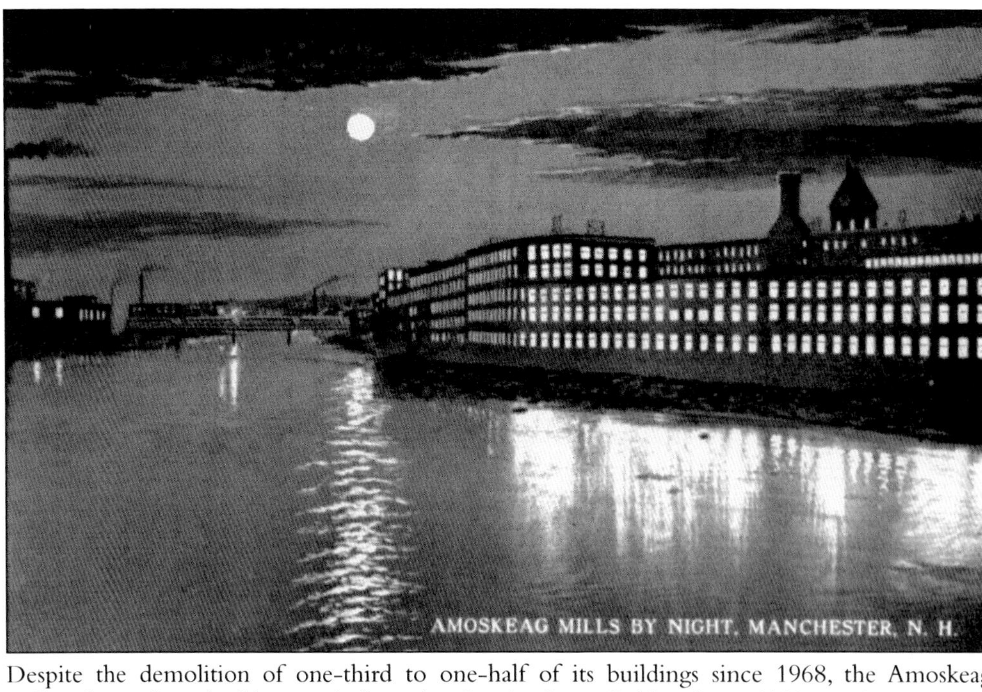

Despite the demolition of one-third to one-half of its buildings since 1968, the Amoskeag Millyard, seen here looking north from the Granite Street Bridge about 1910, continues to awe modern-day lovers of historical architecture. Since a typical work day lasted from 6:00 a.m. to 6:00 p.m., in winter the mill operatives had little time to contemplate the ambiance that Amoskeag's management had created, supposedly for their benefit.

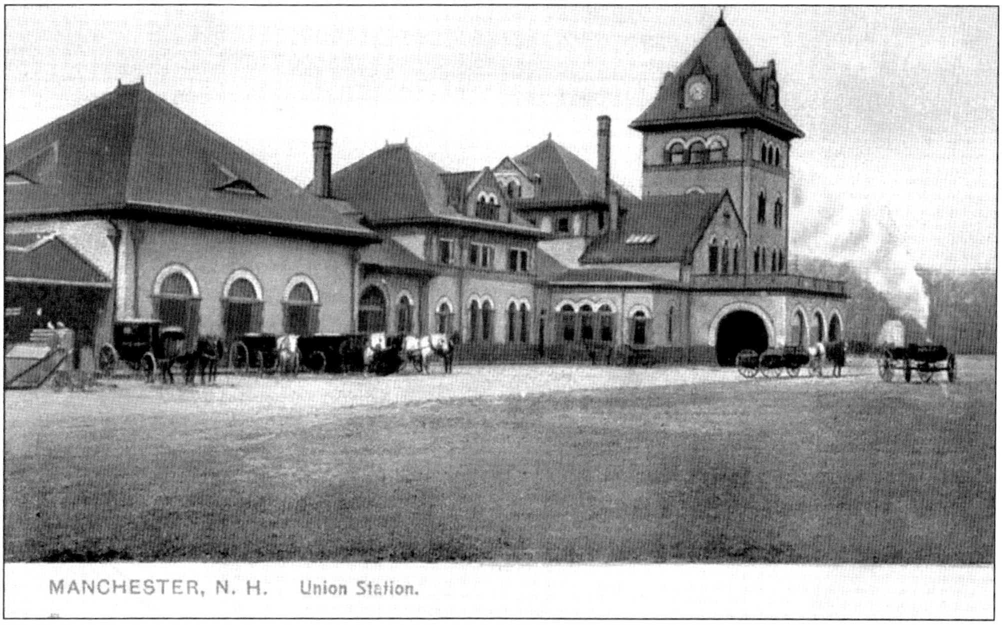

Opened on March 6, 1898, the B&M Railroad's yellow-brick Union Station, located near the southwest corner of Canal and Granite Streets, served Manchester's passengers longer than its two predecessors put together. Undoubtedly, it must have awed several generations of visitors, new arrivals, and lovers of railroad architecture. With the decline of passenger travel by rail came the demolition of Union Station in the fall of 1962.

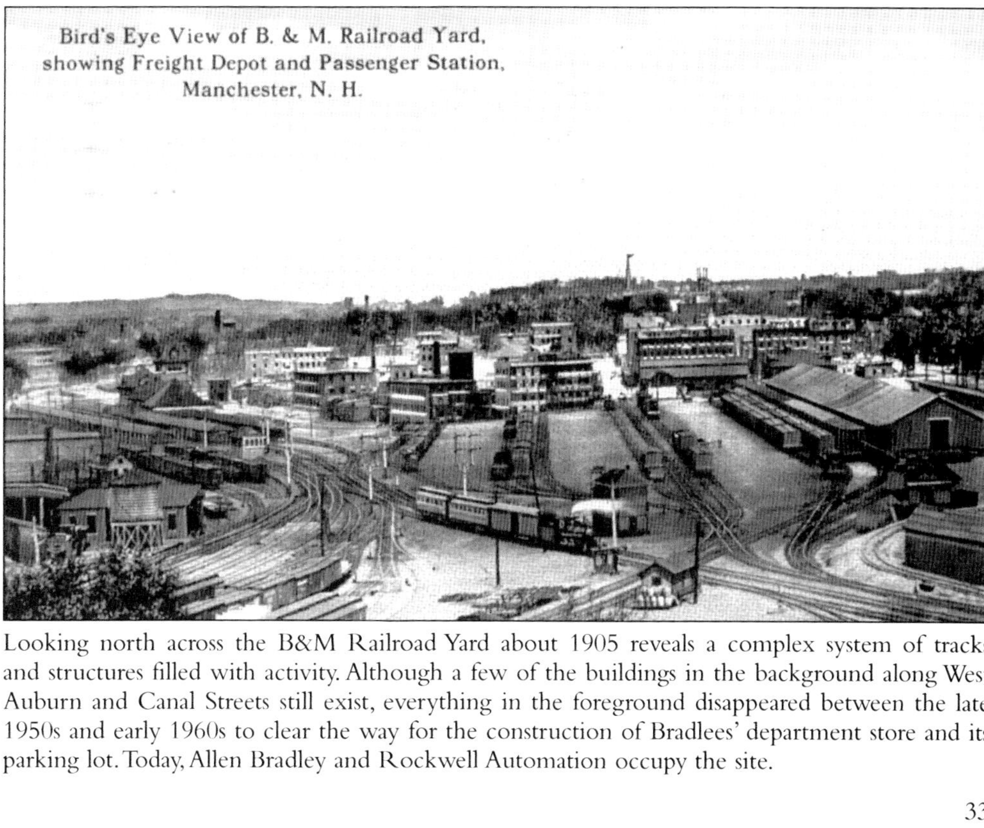

Looking north across the B&M Railroad Yard about 1905 reveals a complex system of tracks and structures filled with activity. Although a few of the buildings in the background along West Auburn and Canal Streets still exist, everything in the foreground disappeared between the late 1950s and early 1960s to clear the way for the construction of Bradlees' department store and its parking lot. Today, Allen Bradley and Rockwell Automation occupy the site.

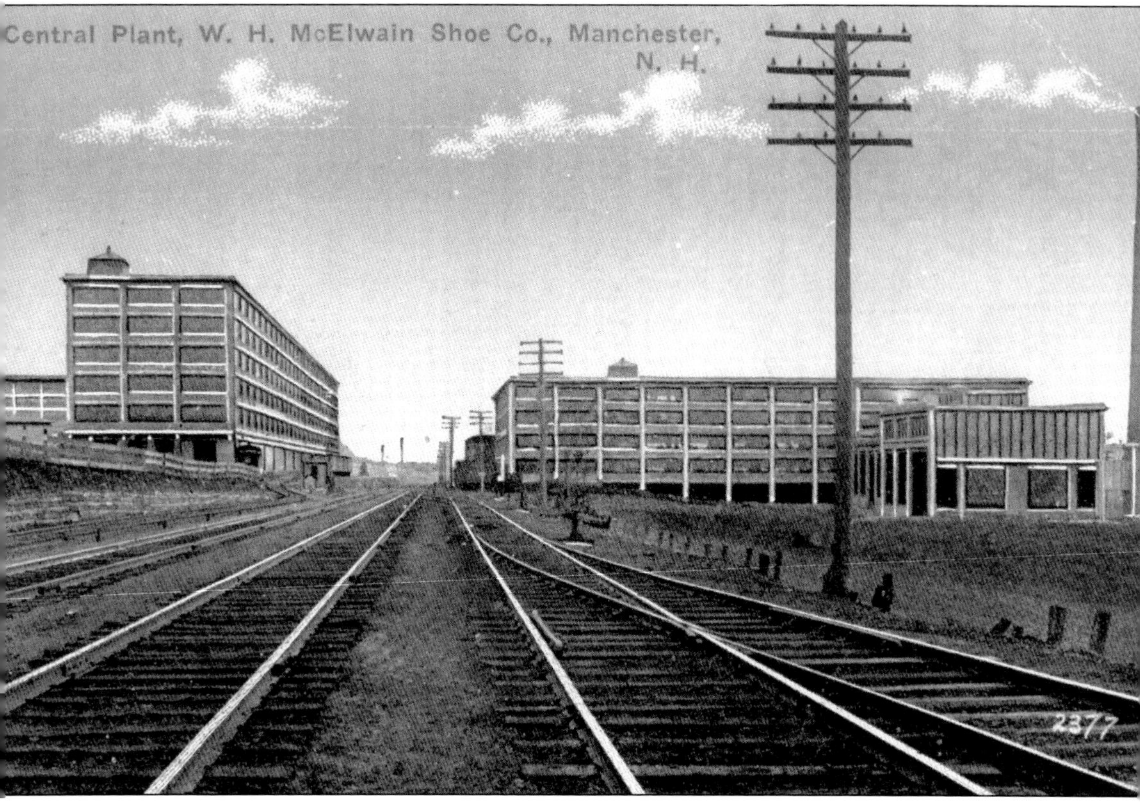

In 1902, William H. McElwain built a factory at the southeast corner of Valley and Hall Streets in East Manchester's shoe manufacturing district. Due to his death in 1908 at age 41, he never saw his company spread into another eight locations around Manchester. In 1912, under his brother, J. F. McElwain, the W. H. McElwain Company's Central Plant opened as the country's largest shoe factory under one roof. This held true even before the addition of its northern wing in 1917, which was not yet built when this photograph was taken. The view looks south before the Queen City Bridge crossed overhead. In 1921, the International Shoe Company absorbed the McElwain plant and flourished along with Manchester's other shoe manufacturers, including J. F. McElwain, who had resigned and started a company under his own name. Gradually, shoes replaced textiles as the city's primary industry. By the 1960s, shoe manufacturing had begun to decline. Various firms have come and gone since the International left. Today, among others, Hesser College, which moved in as of January 1990, occupies the entire south wing and part of the west.

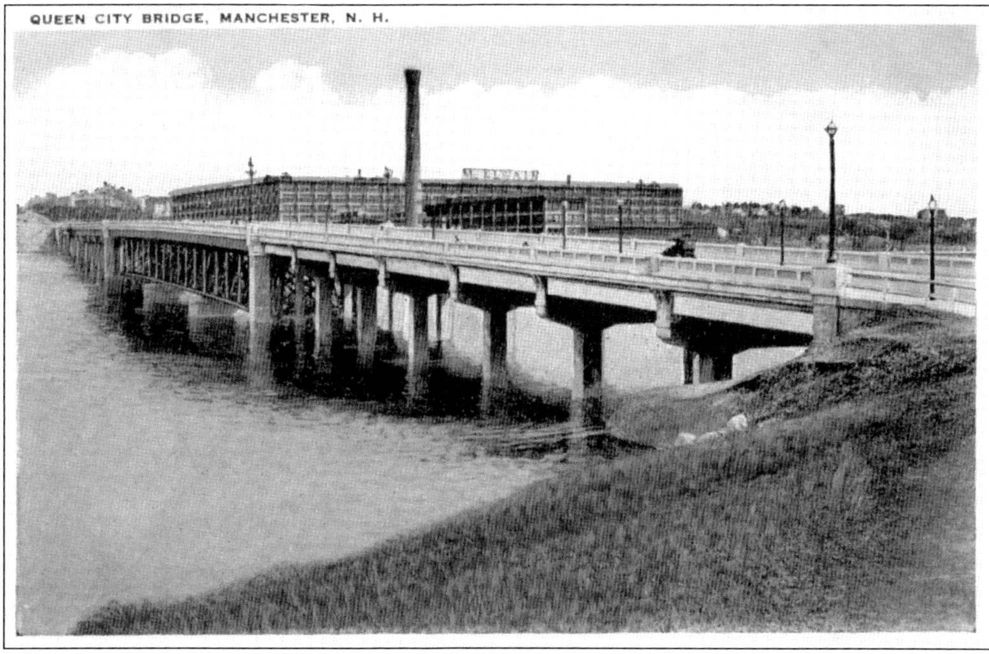

From the early days of Derryfield, when they relied on ferries, up to the era just after World War I, when the bridges that spanned the Merrimack were all within or near the millyard, residents well to the south had always managed without a bridge. In 1923, the Queen City Bridge opened in response to increased development of the area. In 1974 and 1992, two other bridges replaced the original one.

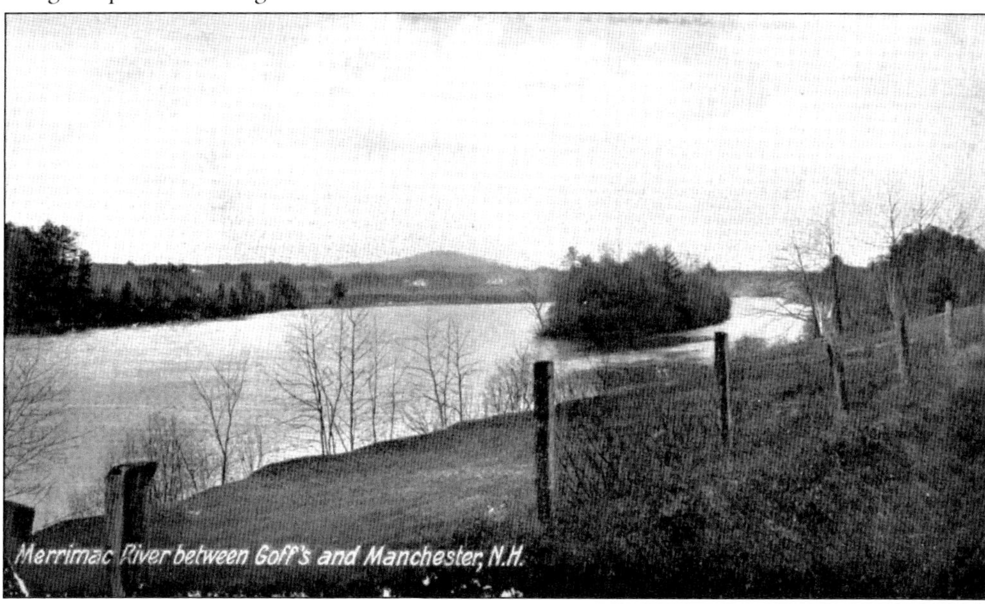

By 1900, the terrain along the banks of the Merrimack near Goffe's Falls, seen here looking northwest, had changed but little from the description that Henry David Thoreau offered in his account, *A Week on the Concord and Merrimack Rivers* (1849): "We passed a large and densely wooded island this forenoon, between Short's and Griffi[n]'s Falls." Today, Thoreau would easily recognize Carthagina Island. As for the rest, one can only wonder.

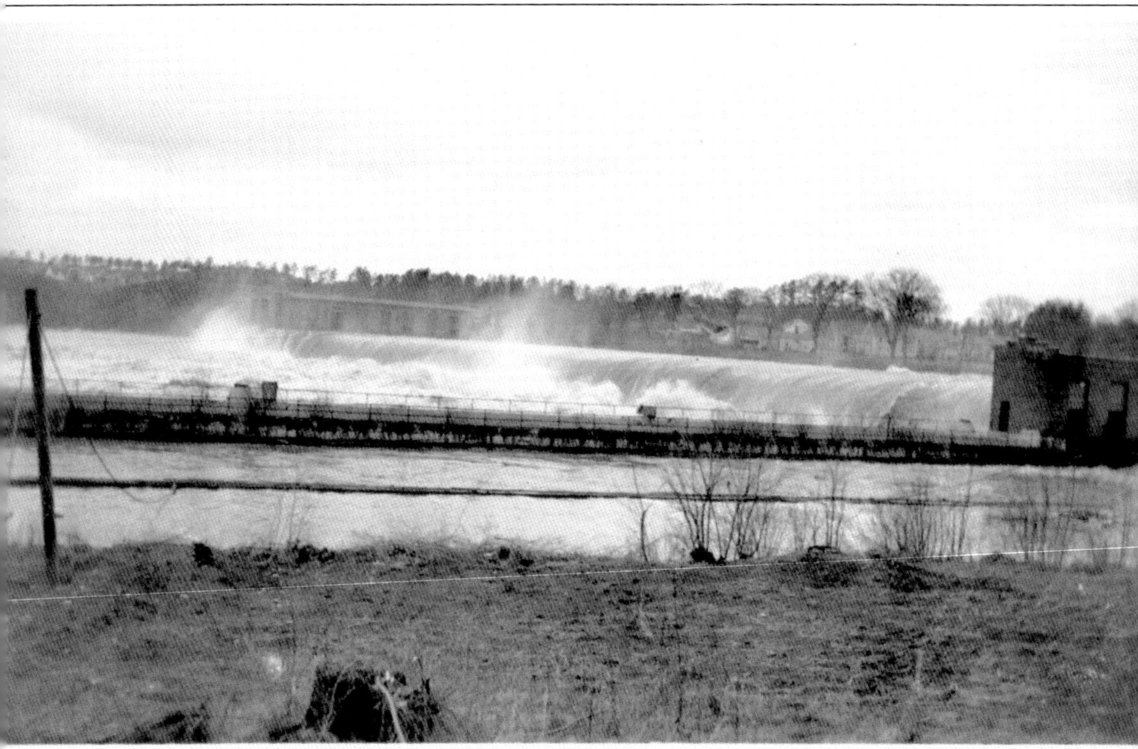

Throughout history, Manchester and the Northeast in general witnessed spring freshets or floods, a few of which did incredible damage. These events usually resulted from several factors: increased winter snowfall, prematurely mild temperatures causing rapid thawing, and unusually rainy springs. Each time, it appeared as if water levels at the Amoskeag Falls dam rose higher than before: a record 9 feet 6 inches in 1878, 10 feet 2 1/2 inches in 1895, 11 feet in 1896, and 11 feet 2 1/2 inches in 1927. None, however, even compared with the flood of 1936, when the water level over the Amoskeag dam peaked at 17 feet 2 inches. The most devastating flood in New England history came to Manchester in two surges. The first occurred from Thursday, March 12, to Sunday, March 15. A period of calm was followed by heavy rain that produced the more violent surge between Tuesday, March 17, and Friday, March 20. The flood not only caused several million dollars' worth of damage along the river but also went well beyond, destroying much of a neighborhood.

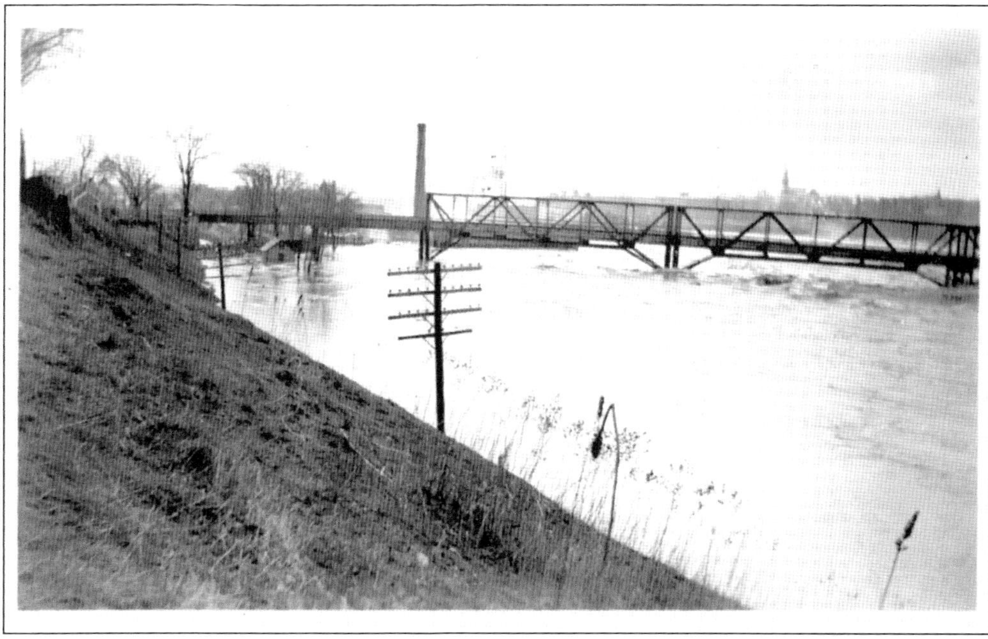

Looking south along the east bank of the Merrimack just above Amoskeag Falls, the water has completely inundated the B&M railroad tracks. In the distance, the third Amoskeag Bridge, which replaced the old wooden covered bridge in 1921, resisted the strength of the flood waters. It was demolished in 1969 to make way for the present two-span Amoskeag Memorial Bridge.

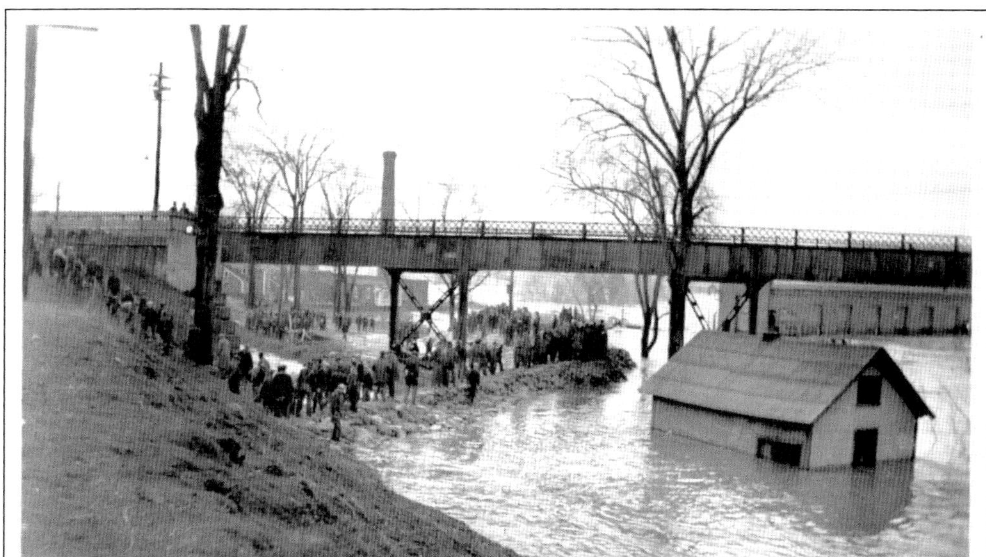

Here, as flood waters continue to rise at a rate of one-tenth of a foot per hour over the Amoskeag dam, 500 men risk their lives and pile 25,000 sandbags to protect the Amoskeag company's hydroelectric plant. Twice they fled for safety as large sections of the Suncook railroad bridge came crashing into the Amoskeag Bridge. But, their efforts paid off, as the plant was spared.

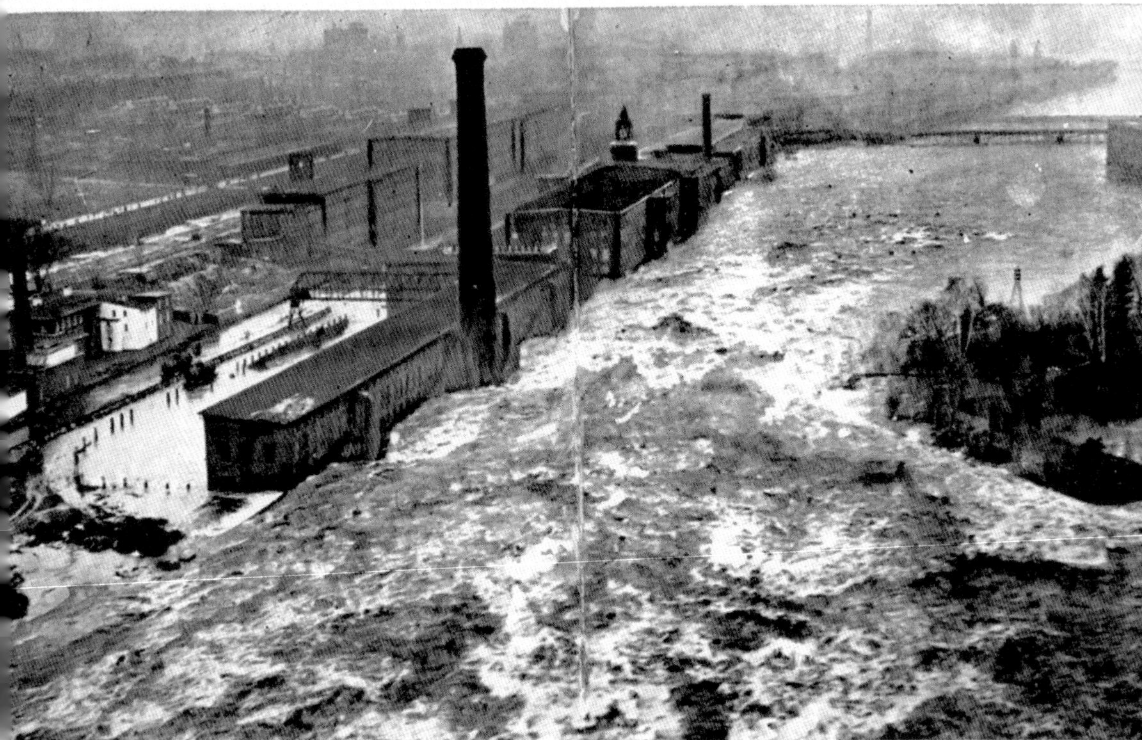

FLOOD SCENE. AMOSKEAG MILLS, MANCHESTER, N. H.

Following the Civil War, competition from Southern mills, where cotton grew locally, caused their Northern counterparts to implement cost-cutting measures that inevitably led to labor unrest. At first, unlike elsewhere, Manchester remained relatively calm, due in large part to Amoskeag's paternalistic programs. Then came Amoskeag's nine-month strike of 1922, briefer strikes in 1933 and 1934 during the Great Depression, its shutdown in September 1935, and its declaration of bankruptcy the following Christmas Eve. The flood of 1936 merely added to the chaos. Here, looking south, an aerial photographer has captured a scene showing the north end of the Amoskeag Millyard, with the ground floor of the Jefferson and other mills under water. When the river finally receded, leaving sand and silt in and around mill machinery and damages amounting to $2.5 million in the millyard alone, all hope of reorganizing and reopening the Amoskeag came to an abrupt halt, and with it, the end of an era in Manchester's history. Never again would one company dominate so many aspects of life in the Queen City.

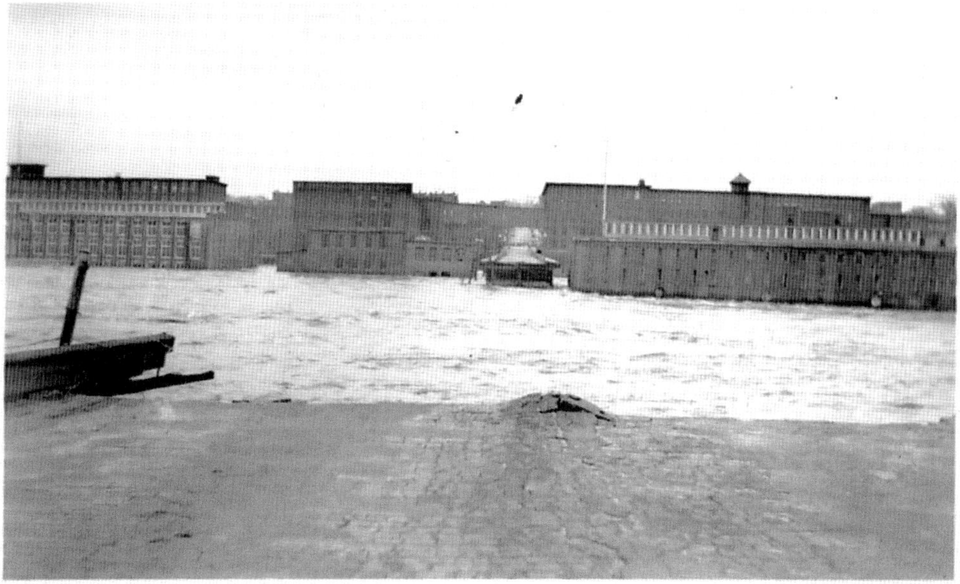

On Thursday, March 19, 1936, the McGregor Bridge trembled and roared as the current finally overpowered it, sending its middle section sailing southward. Its debris then collided with Amoskeag's steampipe bridge, which broke apart, as had the company's pedestrian bridge earlier. The B&M's North Weare bridge had given way the previous Friday, just as a train was about to cross over it.

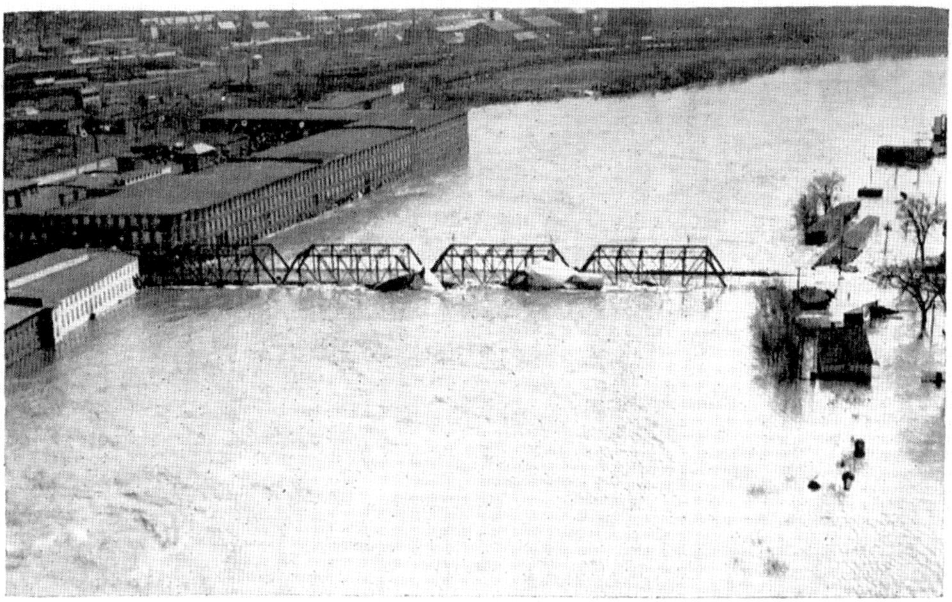

FLOOD SCENE ON MERRIMACK RIVER AT MANCHESTER, N. H.

Farther downriver, the Granite Street Bridge became entangled with debris from two large oil tanks that once stood on Grand Island, just below the Amoskeag dam. The swift and forceful rapids swept them from their moorings shortly before midnight on Thursday, March 19, 1936. Because the flood cut off communication between the East and West Sides, amateur radio operators helped keep emergency personnel, the press, and the public in contact.

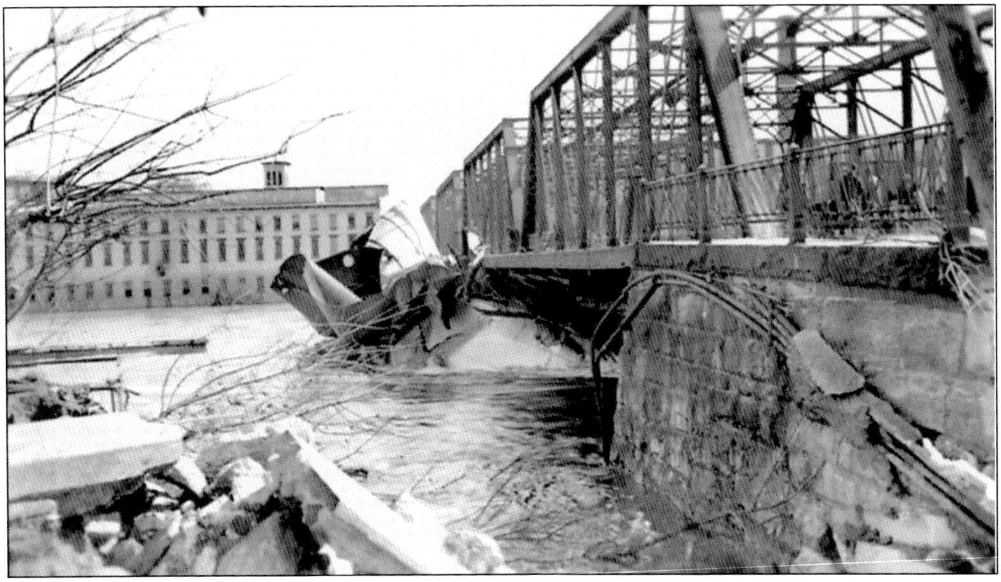

Despite having endured constant bashing by debris from every broken structure upriver, the Granite Street Bridge, seen here looking from west to east after flood waters had begun to recede, held firm. Manchester, too, managed to stay strong and recover. Community and business leaders formed Amoskeag Industries, which paid $5 million for the Amoskeag's mills and equipment for subsequent resale. This guaranteed to fill the millyard with many small, individual, and diversified manufacturing firms.

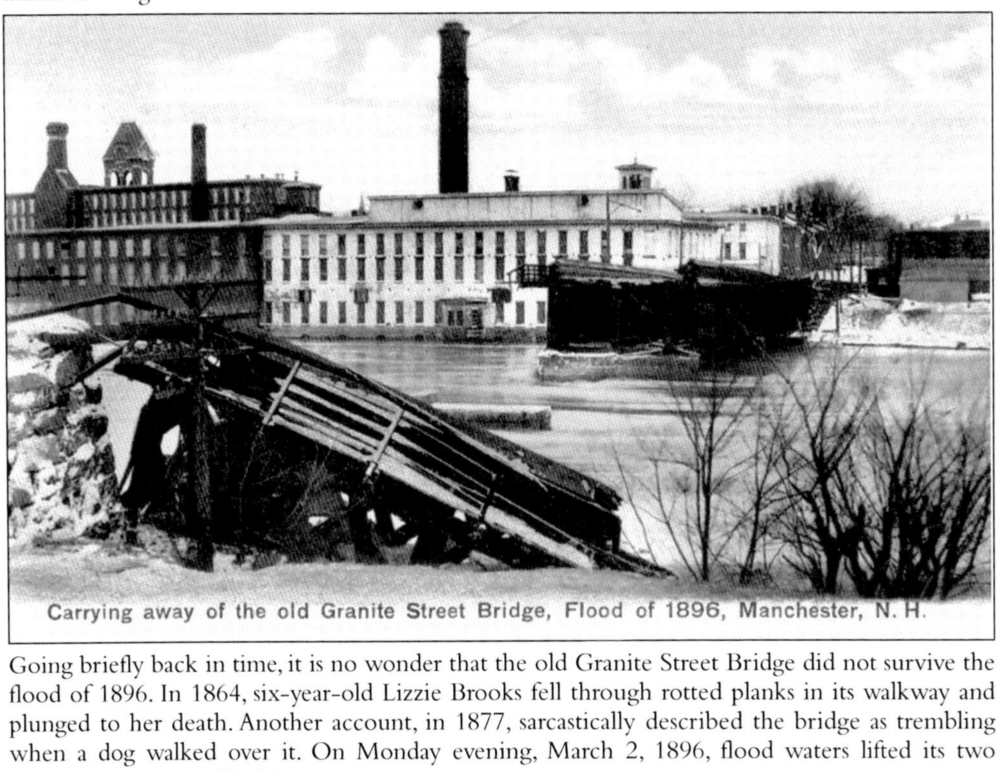

Carrying away of the old Granite Street Bridge, Flood of 1896, Manchester, N. H.

Going briefly back in time, it is no wonder that the old Granite Street Bridge did not survive the flood of 1896. In 1864, six-year-old Lizzie Brooks fell through rotted planks in its walkway and plunged to her death. Another account, in 1877, sarcastically described the bridge as trembling when a dog walked over it. On Monday evening, March 2, 1896, flood waters lifted its two westernmost spans off of their piers.

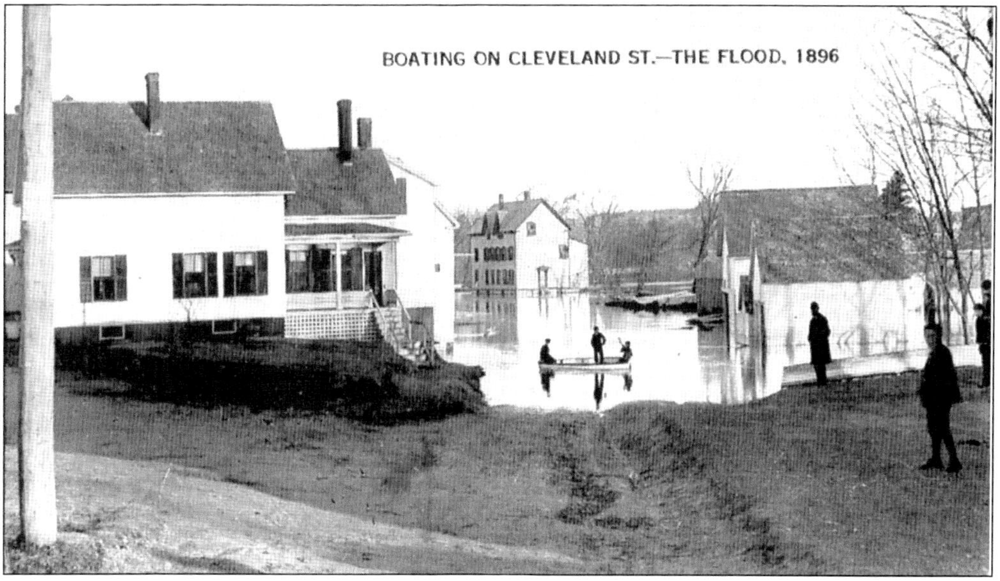

During every tragic event, some resourceful and imaginative souls, either through absolute necessity or simply for sheer pleasure, find ways of alleviating some of the pain. This spirit is quite evident here in 1896, as some adventurous residents of old Squog Village on the West Side go boating not in their neighborhood river, the Piscataquog, but on Cleveland Street, just along the river's north bank, near Blaine.

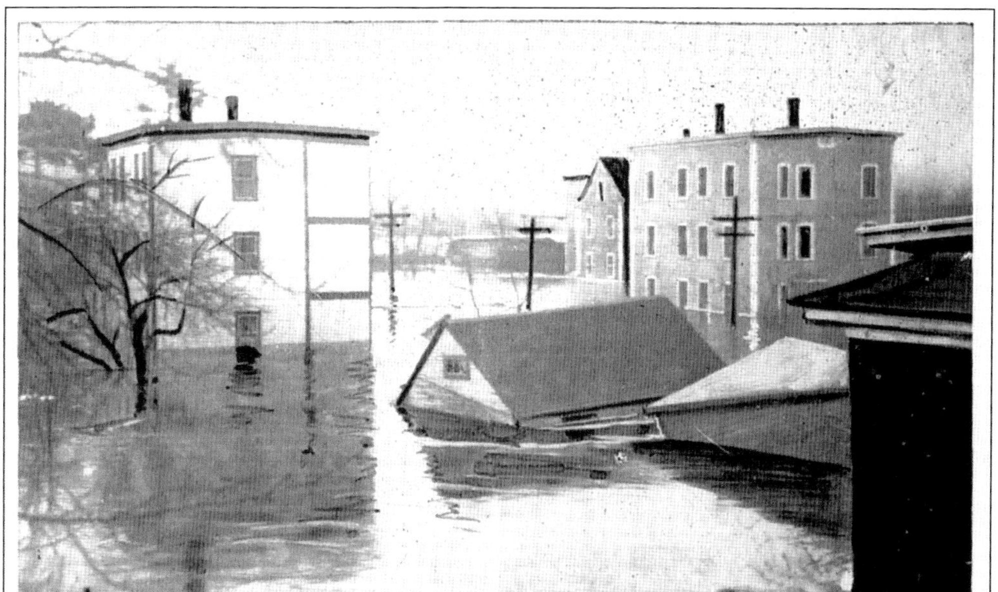
FLOOD SCENE ON MERRIMAC RIVER AT MANCHESTER, N. H.

The flood of 1936 proved far more destructive, especially in Piscataquog Village, than the flood of 1896. In those areas of the neighborhood where the land lies low along both the Merrimack and the Piscataquog, especially on Turner, Second, and Cleveland Streets and nearby side streets, the rivers combined to cause 2,000 people to flee their homes and businesses, which suffered an estimated $1.8 million worth of damage.

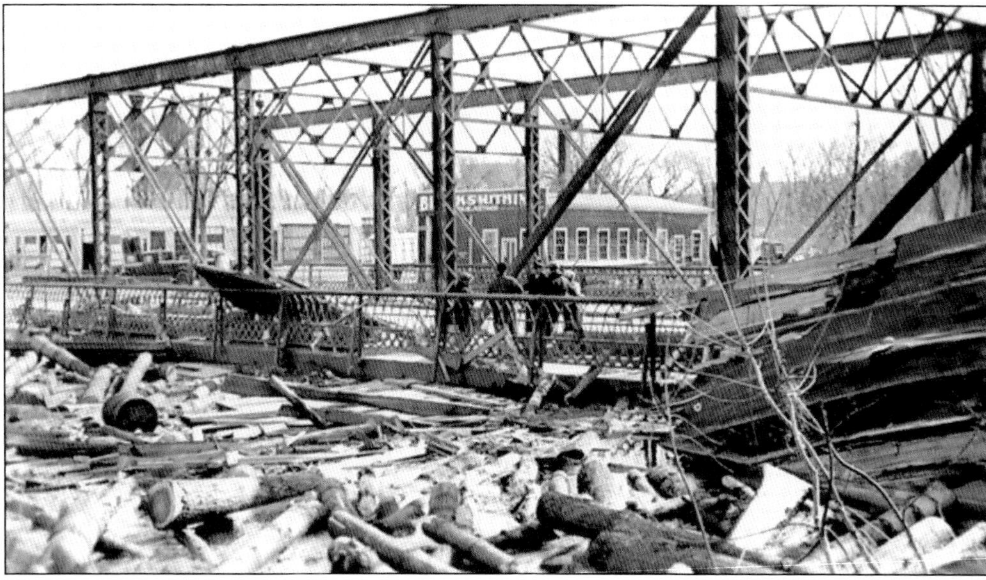

Although the flood brought unimaginable hardship, the swift response of emergency personnel and volunteers, who even rescued 32 people from rooftops, guaranteed the safe evacuation of the affected area's entire human population. Meanwhile, near the Second Street Bridge, residents of the Manchester Zoo fared less well. A rather moving account in the *Manchester Union* says that all of the animals perished, while alternate sources list a lone survivor, a bear.

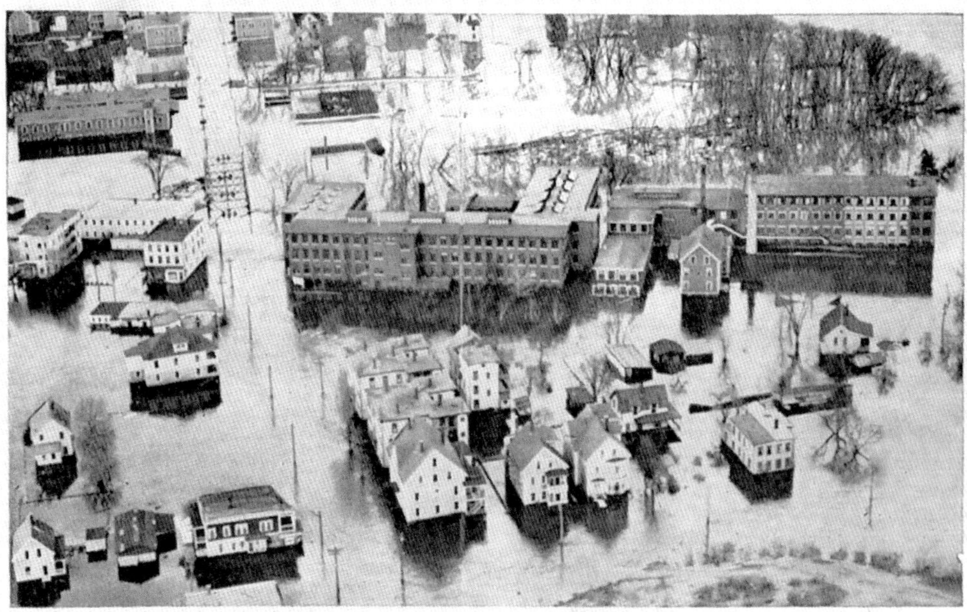

BAD FLOOD SPOT IN MANCHESTER, N. H.

From the air, looking north toward the intersection of Second and West Hancock Streets, the long since demolished homes in the foreground resemble boathouses in a harbor. Nearby sit the buildings that housed the N.H. Heel Company, G. P. Crafts, and Morse & Malloy Shoe Companies, including the one recently renovated by Families in Transition. Since 1936, flood control has improved. A more recent freshet, mild by comparison, occurred in April 1987.

Three

Rambling through the Streets of Downtown

Where *is* our downtown? In 1650, Chief Passaconnaway would have replied, "Namaoskeag." In 1751, residents of Derryfield Centre would have boasted, "Along the Mammoth Road," whereas in 1807, Samuel Blodget would have retorted, "Here at my canal," thus bringing the downtown back to Amoskeag Falls. By 1846, Manchester's recently elected first mayor, Hiram Brown, would have insisted that it was "by our new City Hall, on Elm from Merrimack to Bridge Street." Then again, German-speaking residents of Piscataquog Village in 1880 might have found everything they needed in their downtown along South Main Street, as would their French-speaking counterparts in 1900, who lived one mile farther north on McGregorville's Main Street.

Twentieth-century urban growth added numerous definitions and locations of downtown. To some, downtown meant Elm Street between Lake Avenue and Salmon Street. Those at the opposite extreme spoke of "the inner city," meaning everything west of Mammoth Road. To the youngest Manchesterites, the question might be answered simply, "Where else? The Mall of New Hampshire."

Regardless of how we define downtown, there has long existed a core in and around Elm Street. It was nurtured at first, then later neglected and abused, resulting in the loss of some of our most precious architecture and homegrown businesses. Revitalization has since come to the area, with mixed results. At the dawn of the 21st century, it remains a downtown in search of itself. This chapter is a look back at an era when, to all Manchester residents, downtown still constituted the heart and soul of our city.

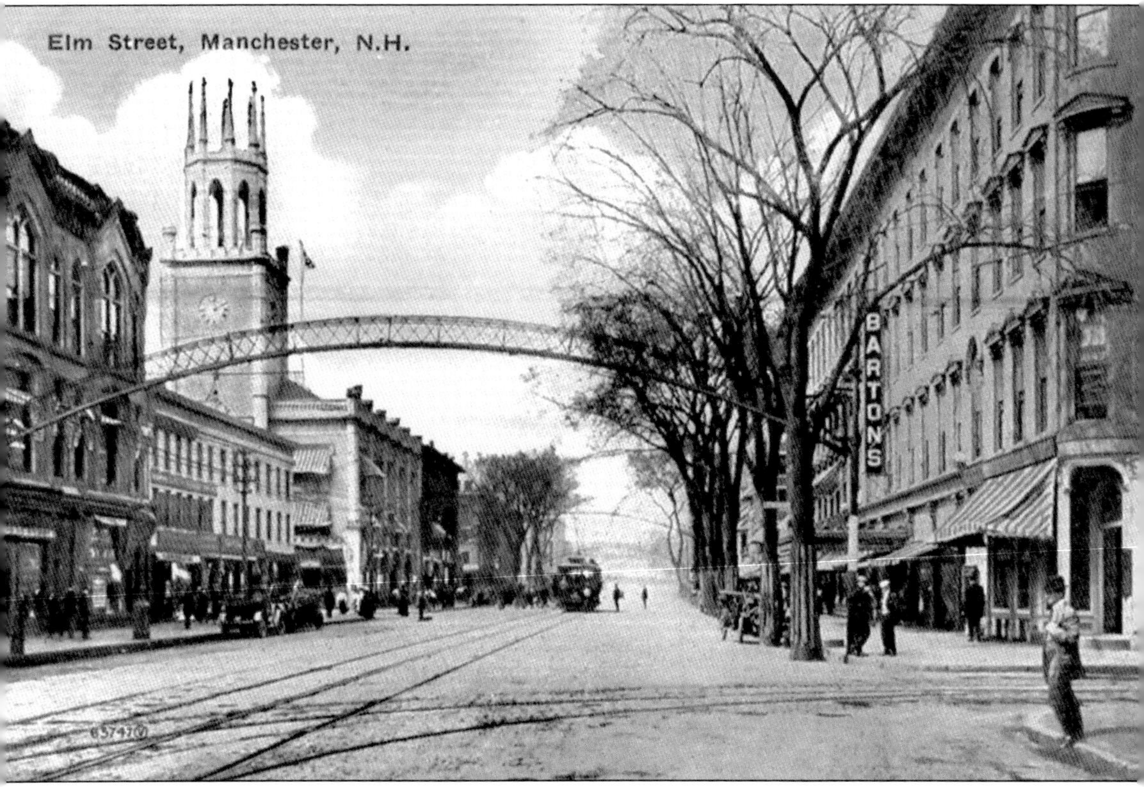

Laid out in 1838 according to the Amoskeag company's plan, Manchester's main thoroughfare supposedly took its name from a large elm tree that stood at what became the corner of Elm and Spring Streets. Early on, the town planted a row of elm trees down the street's center; they all died after gas pipes were installed in 1852. Mayor Frederick Smyth had them replaced along both sidewalks for approximately one mile, but the new trees eventually died of Dutch elm disease. Elm Street boasted several impressive business blocks, most featuring local red bricks or granite. Later, granite paving stones and trolley tracks appeared. Running nearly parallel to the Merrimack River, with a slight bend just south of Bridge Street, Elm Street was once among New England's widest principal avenues, stretching 100 feet across until the late 1990s, when the city widened certain sections of its sidewalks and narrowed its busiest portion for diagonal parking. It terminates in a cul-de-sac at both ends and is a mere 3.4 miles long.

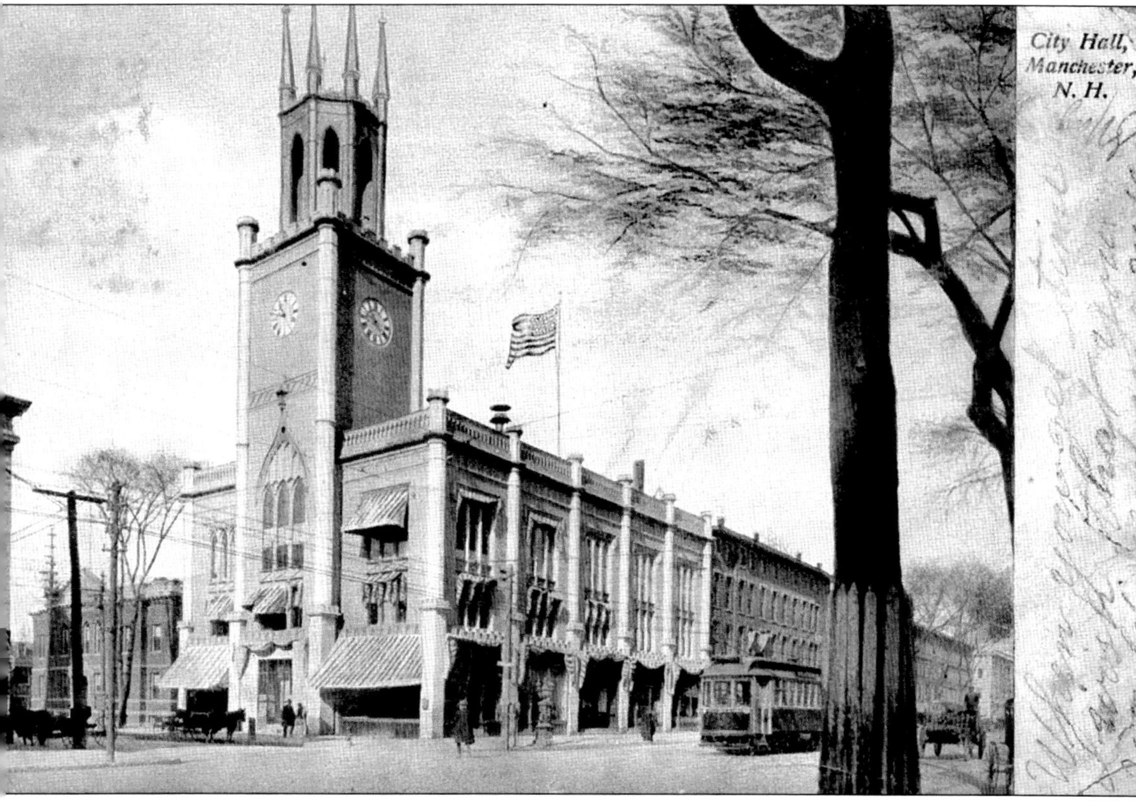

Manchester's City Hall was designed in a unique form of the Gothic style by Edward Shaw. It was completed in 1845 at a cost of $35,000 and replaced the Town House, which had burned in 1844 after a three-year existence. The new City Hall originally featured a stucco exterior finish. The first floor consisted of stores and the Common Council chamber, the upper floors included the mayor's office and other offices and committee rooms, and the southwest corner of the basement housed the city prison. In 1895, after a debate over its proposed demolition, City Hall underwent extensive renovations. The main entrance and stairway were relocated from Market Street to Elm Street, and the stucco finish was removed to expose its red-brick walls. Having later lost its spires, it survived more demolition attempts and further renovations. City Hall was listed on the National Register of Historic Places in 1975, but Manchester citizens' true crowning achievement, literally, occurred in 1980 when the Queen City's foremost government building received new spires. In 1999, major renovations returned the main entrance and stairway to Market Street.

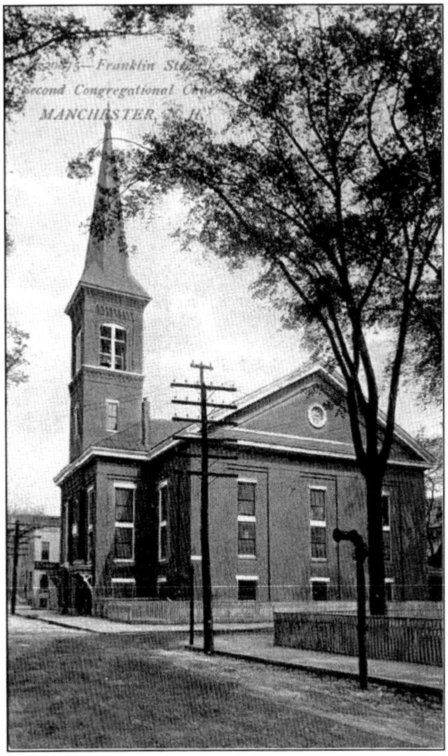

The Franklin Street Church stood at the southeast corner of Franklin and Market Streets. It was organized in 1844 and built in 1847 to alleviate crowding in the First Congregational Church's earlier building, which was located where the Opera House Block now sits. Renovations in 1878 included the addition of the spire and the relocation of the front entrance to Market Street. After the society moved into the Brookside Congregational Church in March 1960, the old church was demolished.

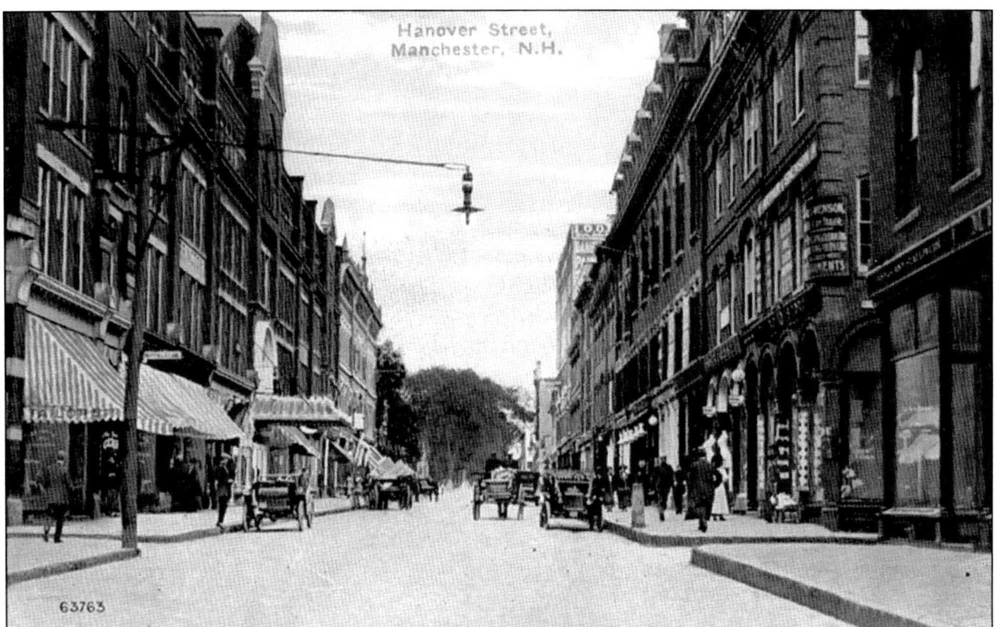

What many considered Manchester's second principal downtown avenue, Hanover Street, has managed to retain its Victorian flavor despite the demolition, especially along its south side, of several buildings. It is seen here looking east near Nutfield Lane about 1912. During the late 1980s, its north side, especially the Opera House Block and the Mirror Building, underwent a major facelift to reveal exquisite red-brick façades that decades' worth of paint had kept hidden.

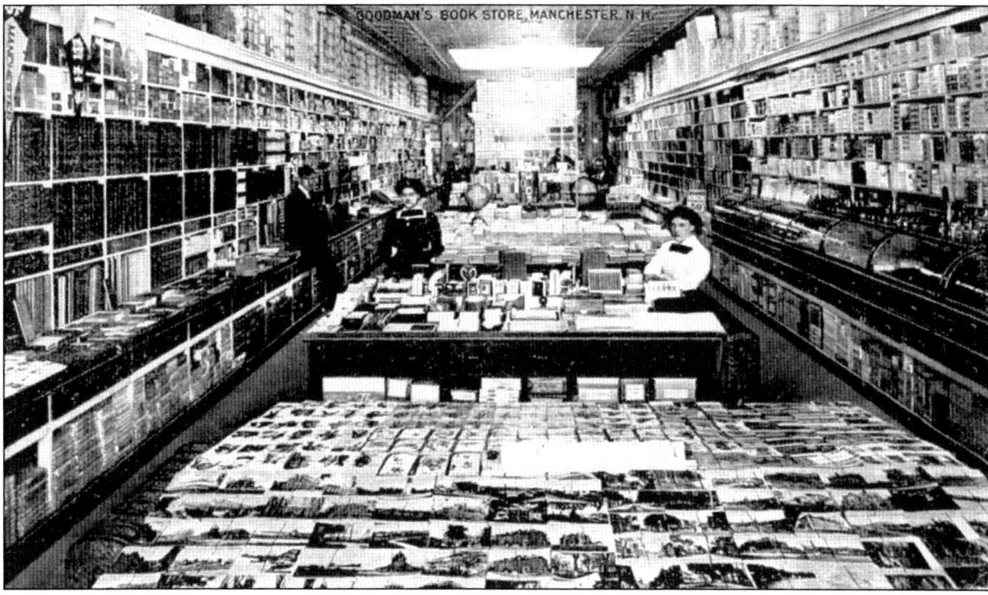

Before the era of malls and chain stores, shoppers relied upon their city's commercial backbone, local family-owned businesses. Beginning in 1881, Goodman's Bookstore served at various locations in downtown Manchester for nearly 110 years. It is seen here at 25 Hanover Street about 1910. Through a photographer's loupe, some Manchester postcards appearing in the present volume become clearly visible in the display case at the bottom.

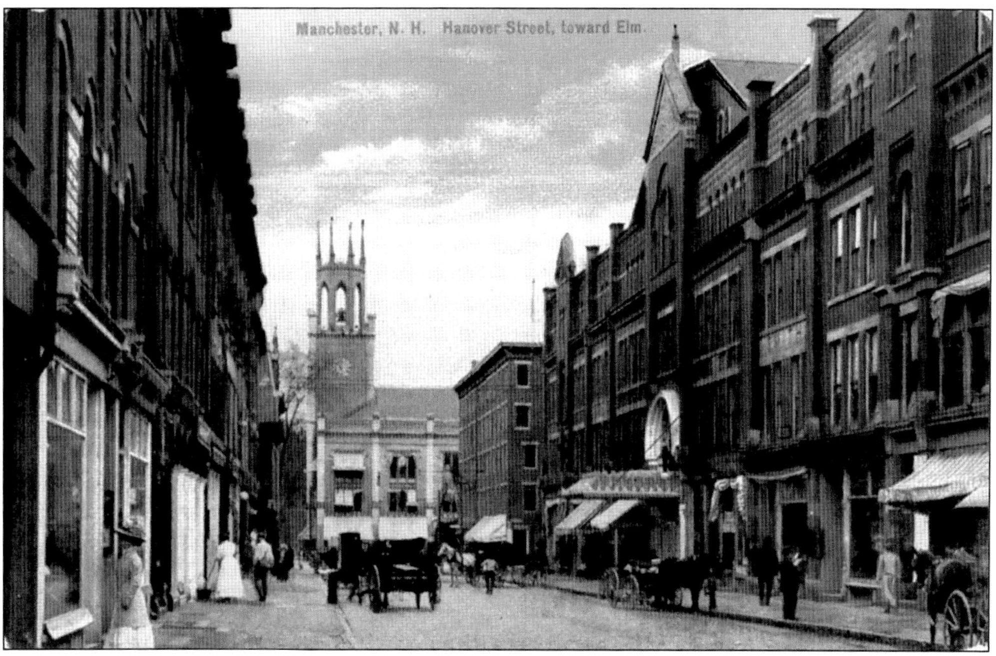

Opened on January 24, 1881, the Manchester Opera House, seen at right about 1895, had a luxurious auditorium with two balconies. World-famous personalities, such as Edwin Booth, Maurice Barrymore, Sarah Bernhardt, and Buffalo Bill Cody, graced its stage. It later served as a vaudeville house and then under various names as a cinema, most recently the Strand Theatre. Fire destroyed the auditorium on March 10, 1985, leaving the façade intact.

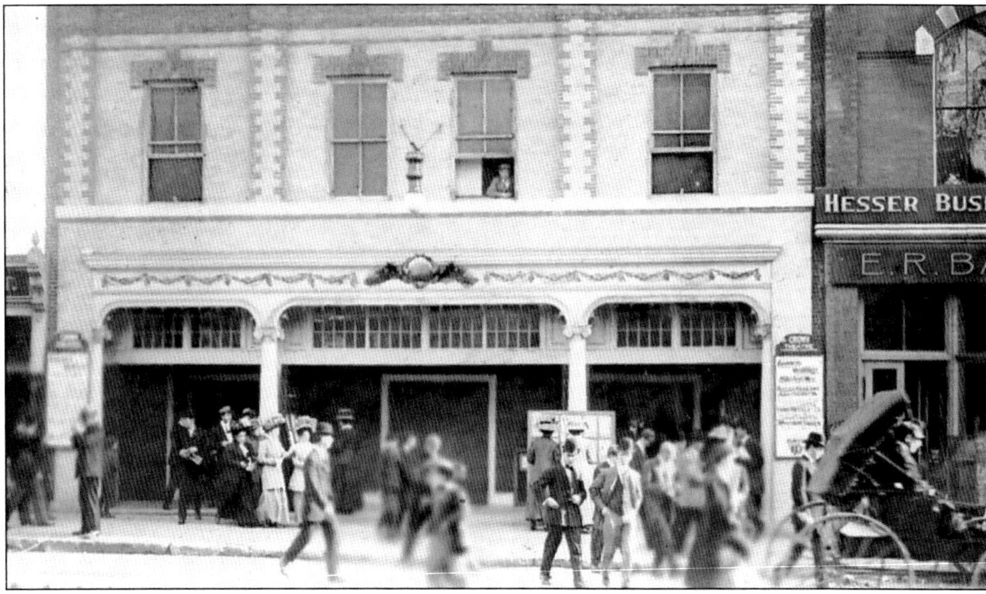

In this *c.* 1912 image, people walk past the Crown Theatre at 97–99 Hanover Street, seemingly unaware that a Duclos Brothers' Studio photographer is capturing them for posterity. Only the boy in the upstairs window looks directly toward the camera. The Crown, whose sign at right advertises "Advanced Vaudeville," eventually showed films and became the Variety (1955–1961). Subsequently a clothing boutique, it has housed Child and Family Services of New Hampshire since 1971.

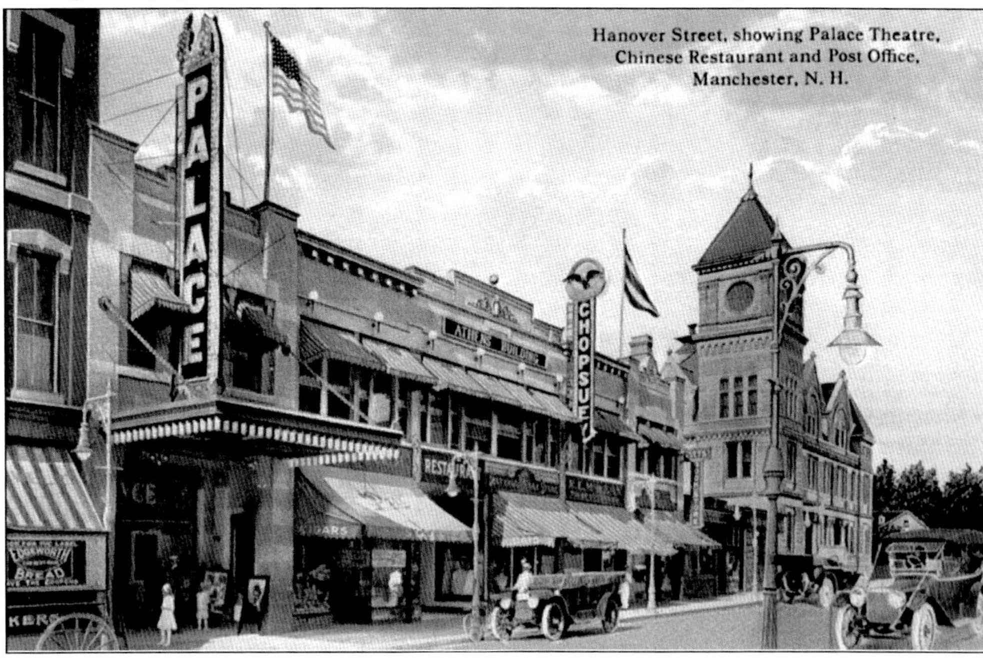

Built in 1915 by Greek immigrant and Lyric Theatre owner Victor Charas, the Palace stands out as the only original downtown theater still in operation. As did some of its contemporaries, the Palace eventually began showing films. The theater continued to operate into the 1960s before finally closing. Despite certain setbacks since its restoration and reopening in 1974 for live performances, it survives and even thrives, remaining a rare jewel in the crown of downtown.

Manchester has had a combined total of 37 downtown and neighborhood theaters occupying 19 buildings. The heyday of local theaters lasted roughly from 1915 to 1929, when no fewer than 11 operated simultaneously. Four of these were located on the Great White Way, Hanover Street, seen here looking west between Elm and Chestnut Streets. They were the Auditorium/Strand in the Opera House, the Palace, the Lyric, and the Crown, whose sign is visible at the upper left.

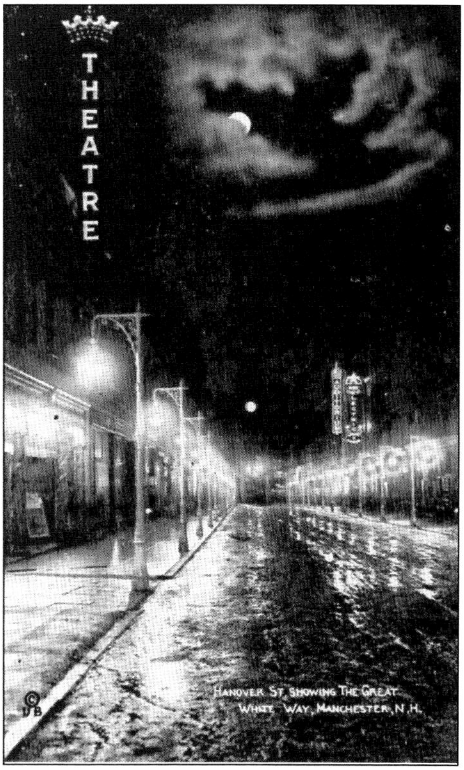

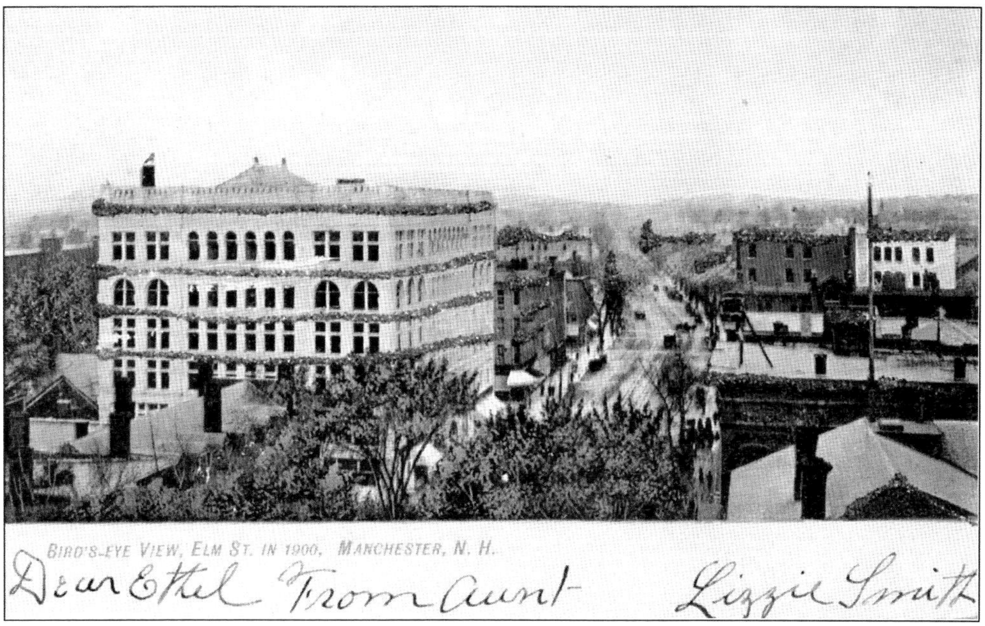

The celebration of Manchester's semicentennial as a city in 1896 inspired photographers to document the architectural growth of downtown that had taken place during the 19th century. Evidence of that growth is seen in this bird's-eye view, looking north along Elm Street from the roof of the six-story Pickering Building. The Kennard, rising well above its neighbors at left, ranked among New England's outstanding modern business blocks.

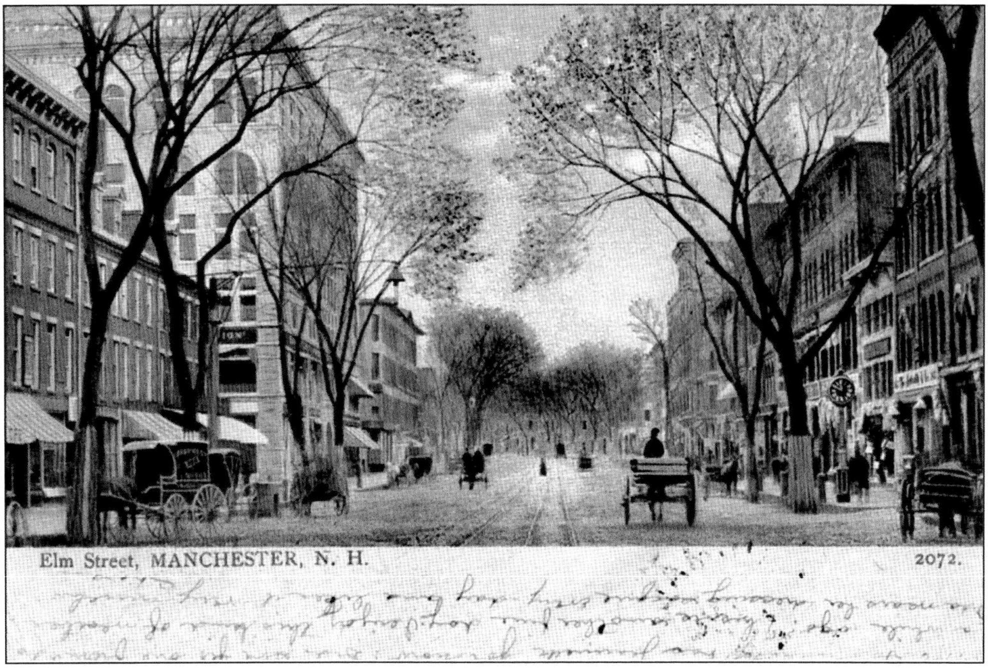

Manchester grew from fewer than 1,000 inhabitants in 1810 to 10,000 by 1846, when it went from town to city status. By 1896 it was home to about 55,000. At that time, Elm Street, seen here looking north, still boasted many elms. In December 2004, the owner of Dunlap's Block, at the northeast corner of Elm and Amherst Streets, replaced the clock, seen here at right, with a close replica.

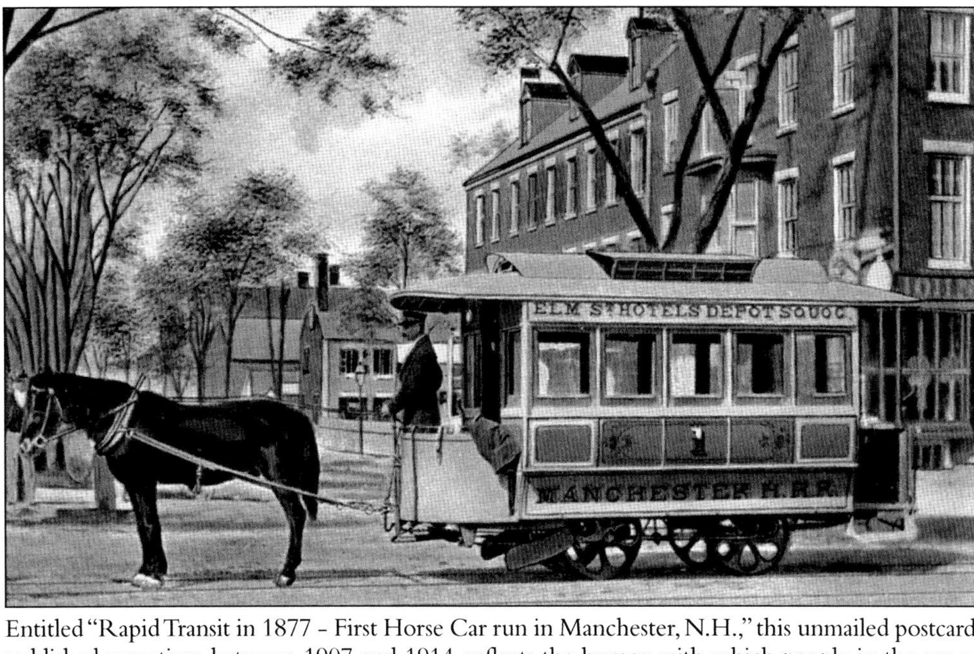

Entitled "Rapid Transit in 1877 - First Horse Car run in Manchester, N.H.," this unmailed postcard, published sometime between 1907 and 1914, reflects the humor with which people in the era of the electric streetcar and relatively new automobile viewed the transportation methods of a mere generation earlier. The Manchester Horse Railroad inaugurated its line of public transportation, seen here on Elm Street looking west toward Stark Street, on September 15, 1877.

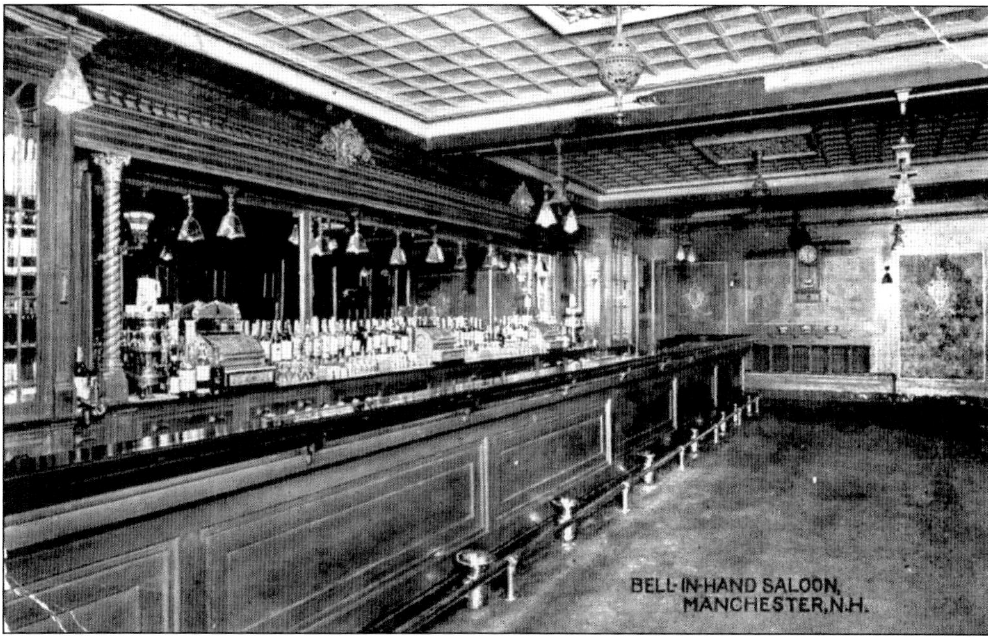

At one time, downtown Manchester had many back-street businesses. When Richards & Thornton liquors' Bell-In-Hand Saloon, located at 147 Nutfield Lane, south of Amherst Street, first appeared in the Manchester city directory in 1904, it was one of 56 such establishments listed. Eventually, many more saloons opened. Meanwhile, the Anti-Saloon League, having worked diligently since 1895, finally won when Prohibition went into effect in 1920.

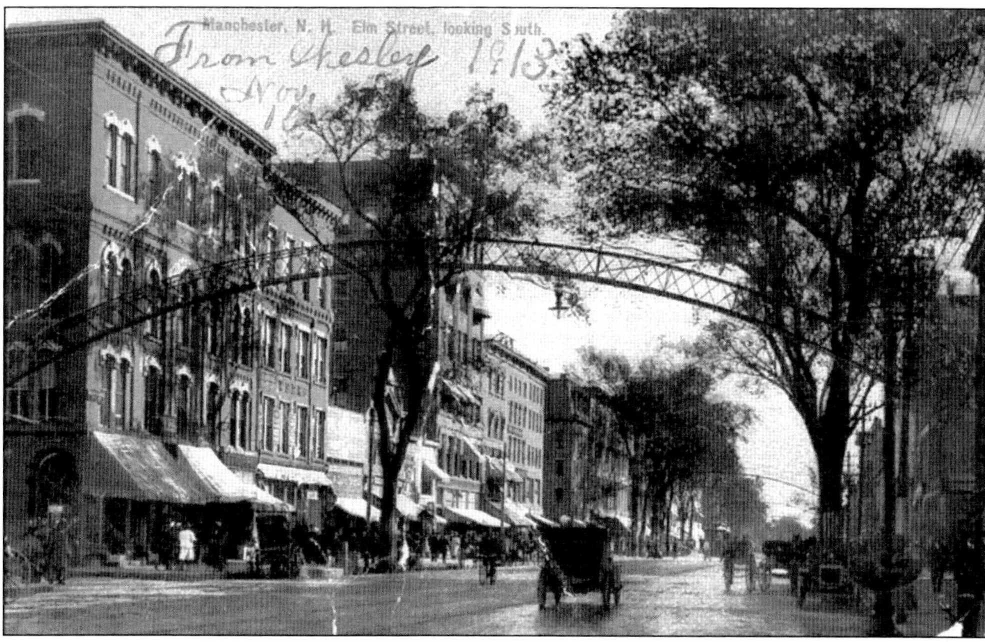

An automobile—which people would have called a horseless carriage just a few years earlier—rides south on Elm Street near the corner of Amherst Street about 1910. By then, people had become accustomed to such a sight, though many still drove horse buggies. At left, along the east side of the street, sits a row of large business blocks, including the tallest, the six-story Pickering Building.

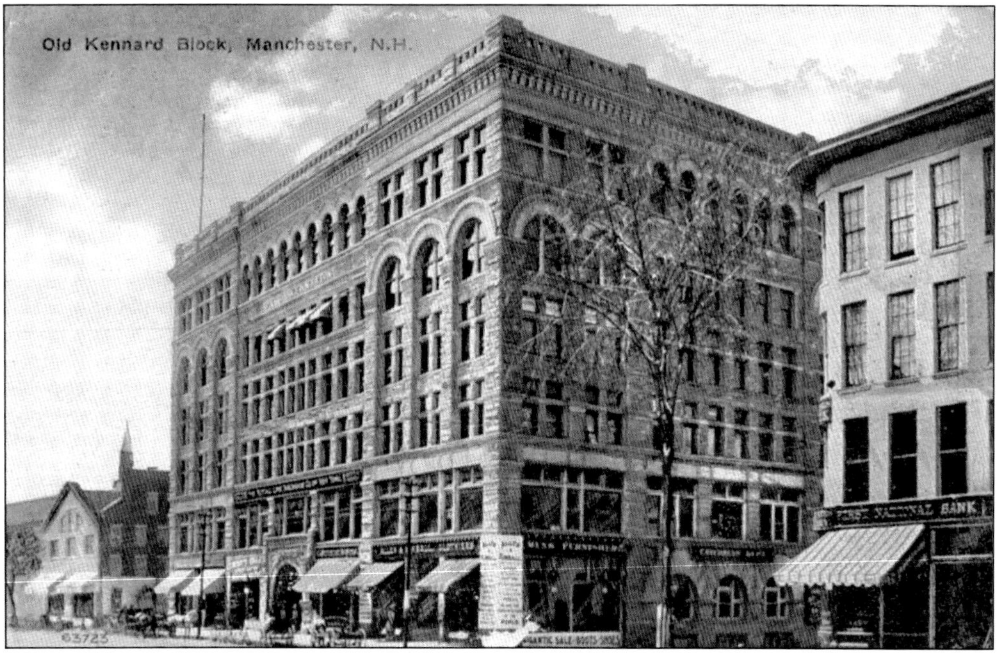

The Kennard Block's grand scale and modern construction made an impact in 1892, especially by comparison with its predecessor, the Stark Block, which resembled mill housing. It also established the reputation of its architect, William M. Butterfield, who went on to design hundreds of buildings and homes throughout New England. Located on the west side of Elm Street between Mechanic and Water Streets, it contained 120 stores, offices, and rooms.

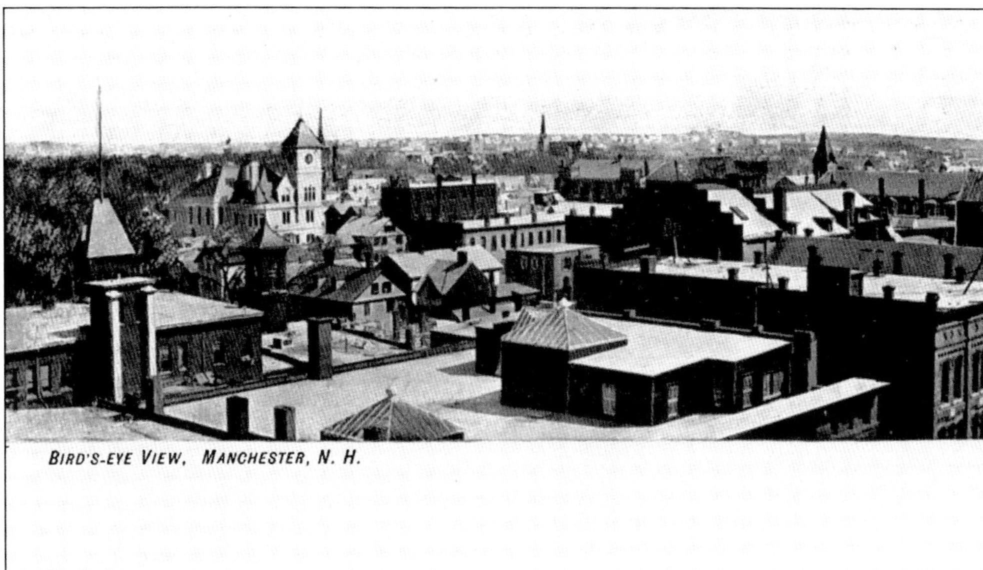

In its day, the roof of the Kennard Block offered a spectacular panorama of downtown, as seen in this *c.* 1896 image, which looks southeast. The prominent buildings seen here, clockwise from the extreme left foreground, are the rear of the Central Fire Station, the Old Post Office Building, the barely visible spire of St. Anne's Church immediately to the right of the Old Post Office Building's tower, St. Augustin Church, the First Free Baptist Church, and the rear of the Opera House.

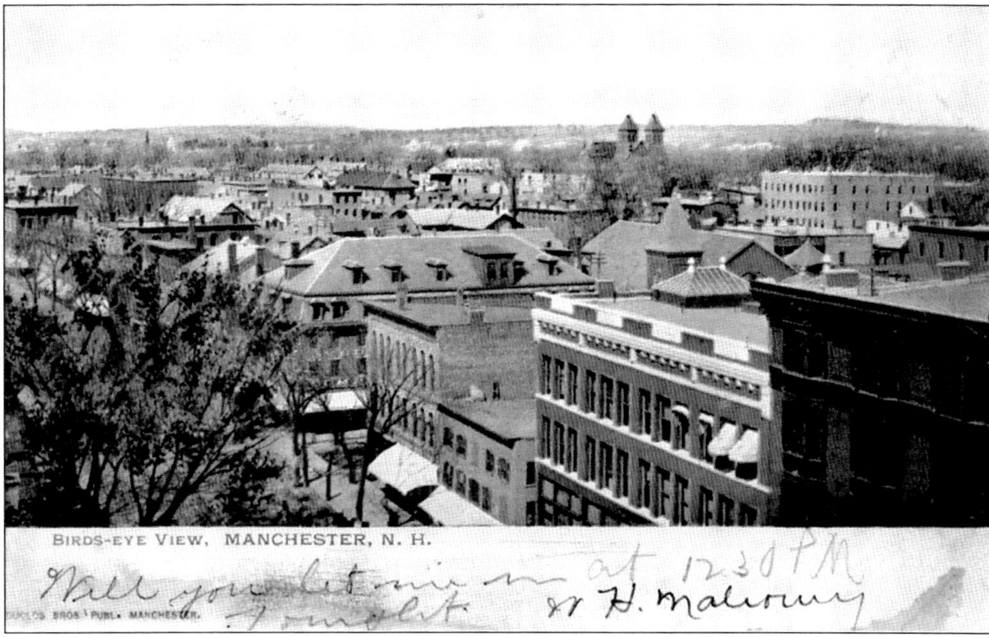

Looking northeast, the City Hotel, with its mansard roof, sits at the center of this image. Immediately to its right, on Lowell Street, is the First Universalist Church. Built in 1839, it was downtown's oldest surviving church building for decades. It became the Star Theatre about 1913, and later housed the Cocoanut Grove Ballroom, Krazy Market, and other establishments before finally sitting vacant. It was demolished in June 1984. St. George Church's twin towers rise in the background above.

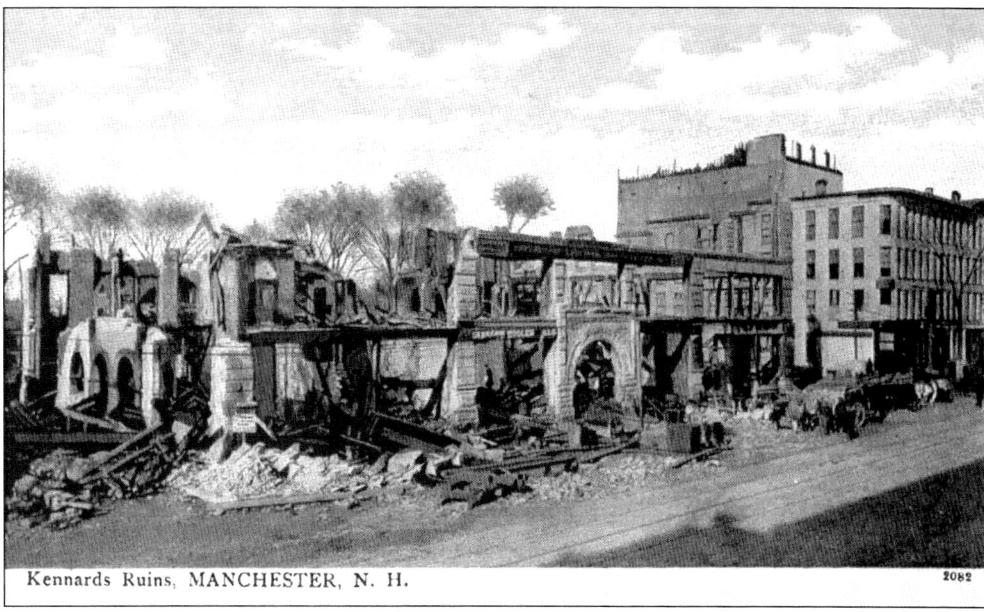

However modern for its time, the Kennard Block had one major flaw: its fireproof construction was limited to the first floor. On January 14, 1902, fire destroyed the building and all of its contents except for a bicycle that attorney Allan Wilson had left in the basement. The Manchester Institute of Arts and Sciences lost its nearly complete collection, 82 pieces, of the famous Rogers' Groups by sculptor John Rogers.

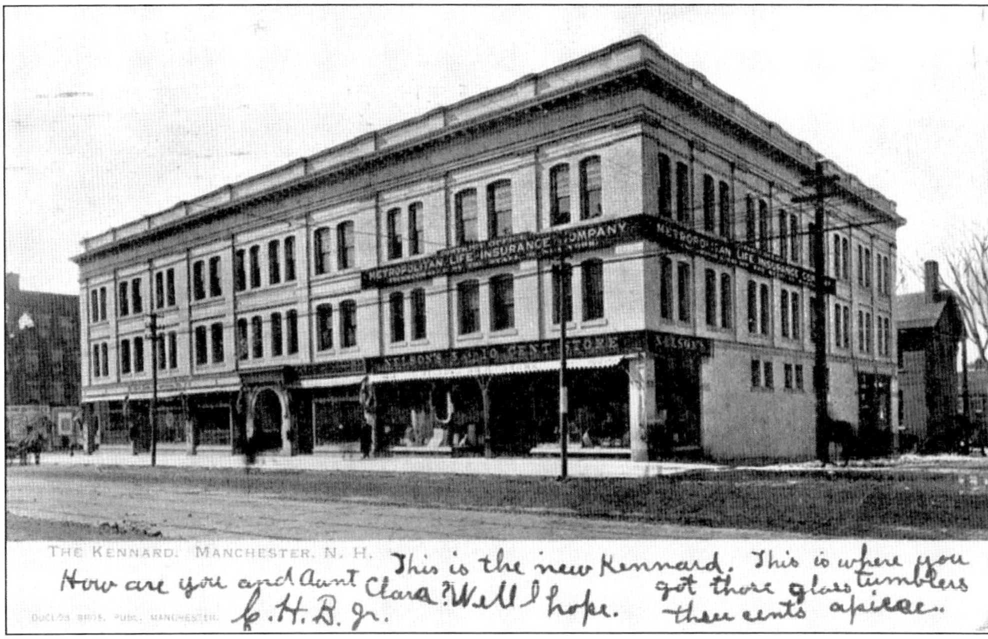

Here, someone wrote in 1906, "This is the new Kennard. This is where you got those glass tumblers three cents apiece." For many years, the new Kennard Block was home to Nelson's 5 and 10 Cent Store, publisher of many Manchester postcards. Having later housed J. J. Newberry's, the block was demolished in 1971 to make way for the Hampshire Plaza Mall and its 20-story office tower, which also did away with Water Street.

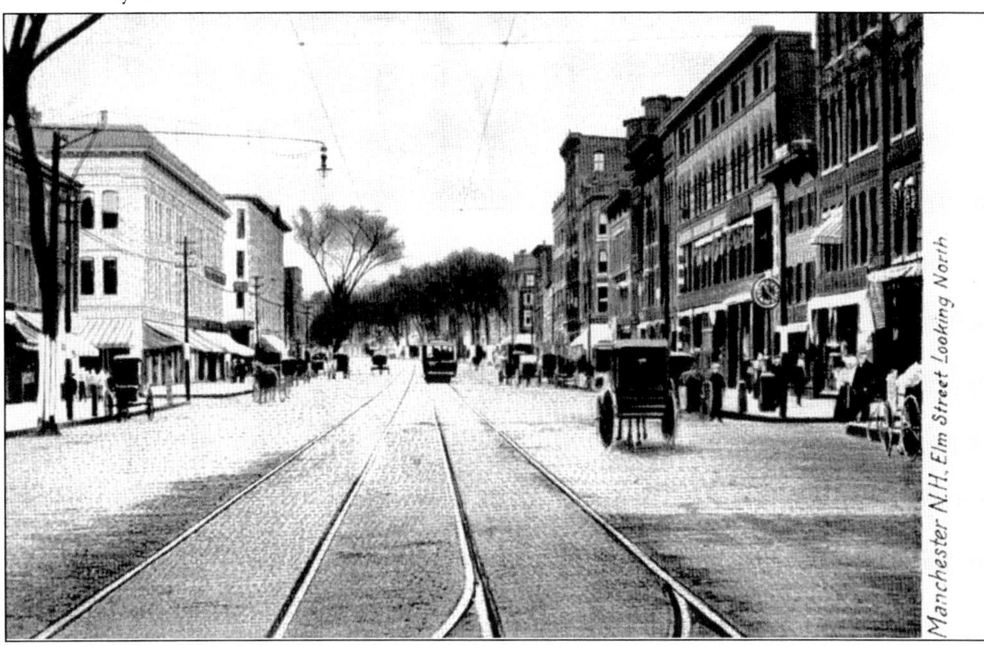

Looking north on Elm Street from near Amherst Street, the scene has changed dramatically within just a few years (see page 50). The new, more modest Kennard Block, which replaced its predecessor in 1903, no longer towers over its neighbors. Also, far fewer elm trees line the street than previously.

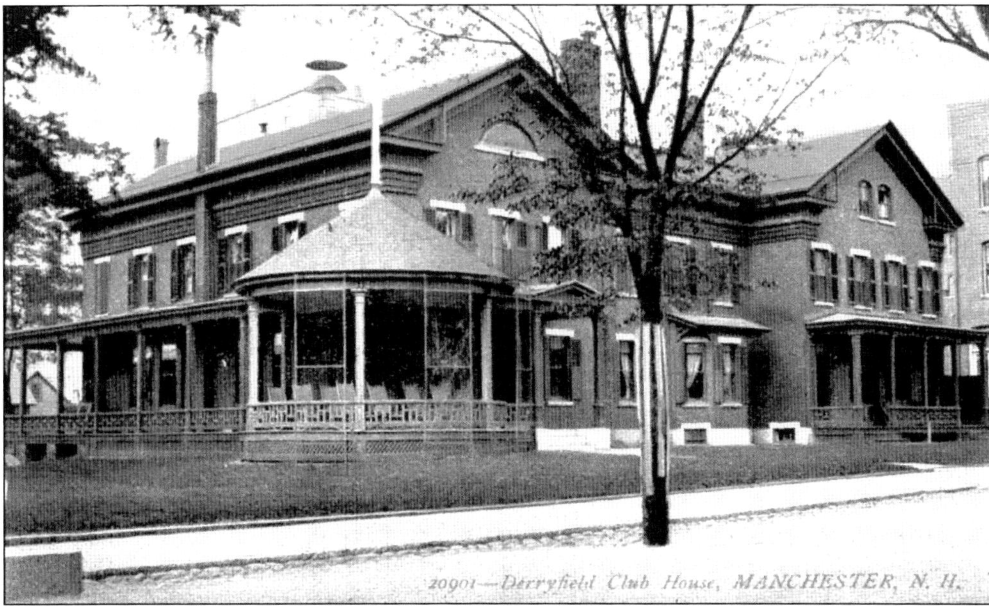

Behind the Kennard Block sat the Derryfield Club House, headquarters of a professional and businessmen's society founded in 1875. It suffered extensive damage during the fire of 1902. In 1905, the club hosted the members of the international delegation that came from Portsmouth after having signed the peace treaty ending the Russo-Japanese War. By 1950, the club house had ceded to the Merchants' Bank Building, which later gave way for Hampshire Plaza.

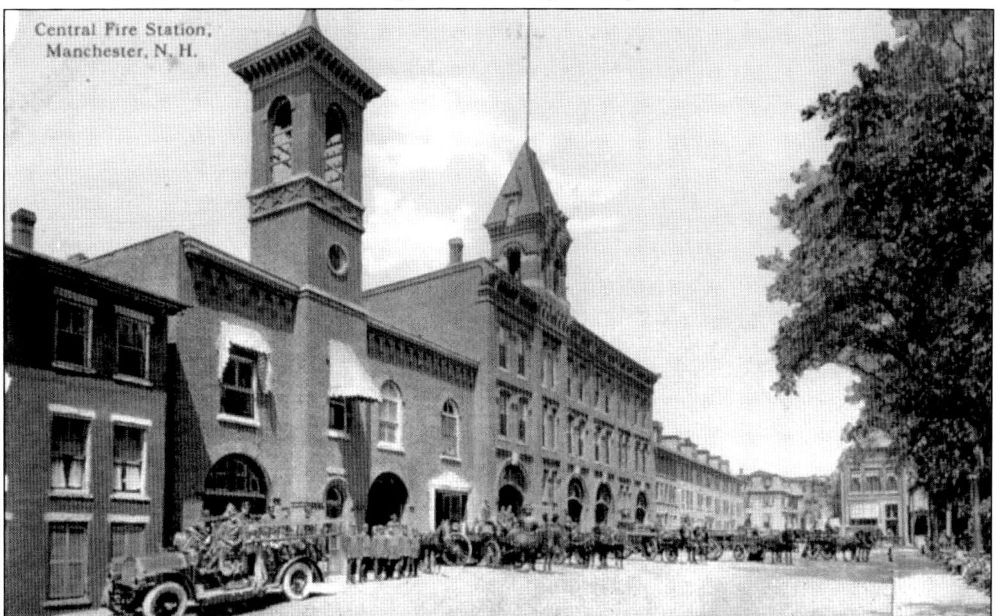

To better protect against fire, Manchester organized its fire department in 1839. The Merrimack No. 1 company bought a hand tub and built Manchester's first engine house on Vine Street. It later expanded to become Manchester's Central Fire Station. The opening in 1971 of a new Central Fire Station on Merrimack Street spelled the demise of the old station after more than 130 years of service.

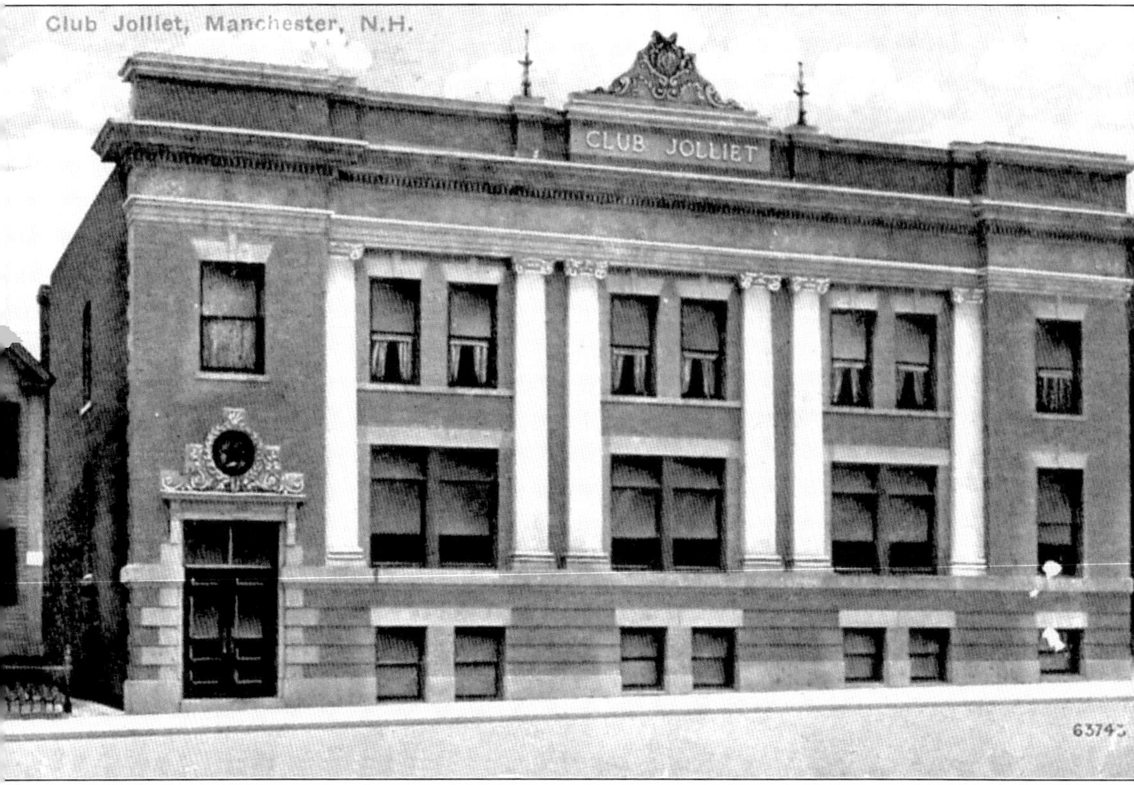

Built in 1910 by the Club Jolliet, a Franco-American professional and businessmen's society founded in 1884, the building at 52 Concord Street later housed the American Legion's Henry J. Sweeney Post and the People's Baptist Church. In 1929, the Association Canado-Américaine, now ACA Assurance, bought the building as its international headquarters and had the façade significantly remodeled by architect Jean-Noël Guertin. In 1990, the Centre Franco-Américain purchased the building and has continued sharing it with ACA. It includes a 30,000-volume library specializing in North American French culture, with rarities that attract scholars from throughout the world. It also contains a museum featuring the largest collection outside of Québec of works by Montréal sculptor Alfred Laliberté, as well as paintings by Marc Suzor-Côté and Lorenzo de Nevers, and sculptures by Manchester's own Lucien Gosselin. For many years, an ACA board member representing the area of Shawinigan, Québec, brought his young son with him to Manchester whenever he attended semiannual board meetings. The man's name was Willie Chrétien. His son, Jean, went on to become prime minister of Canada.

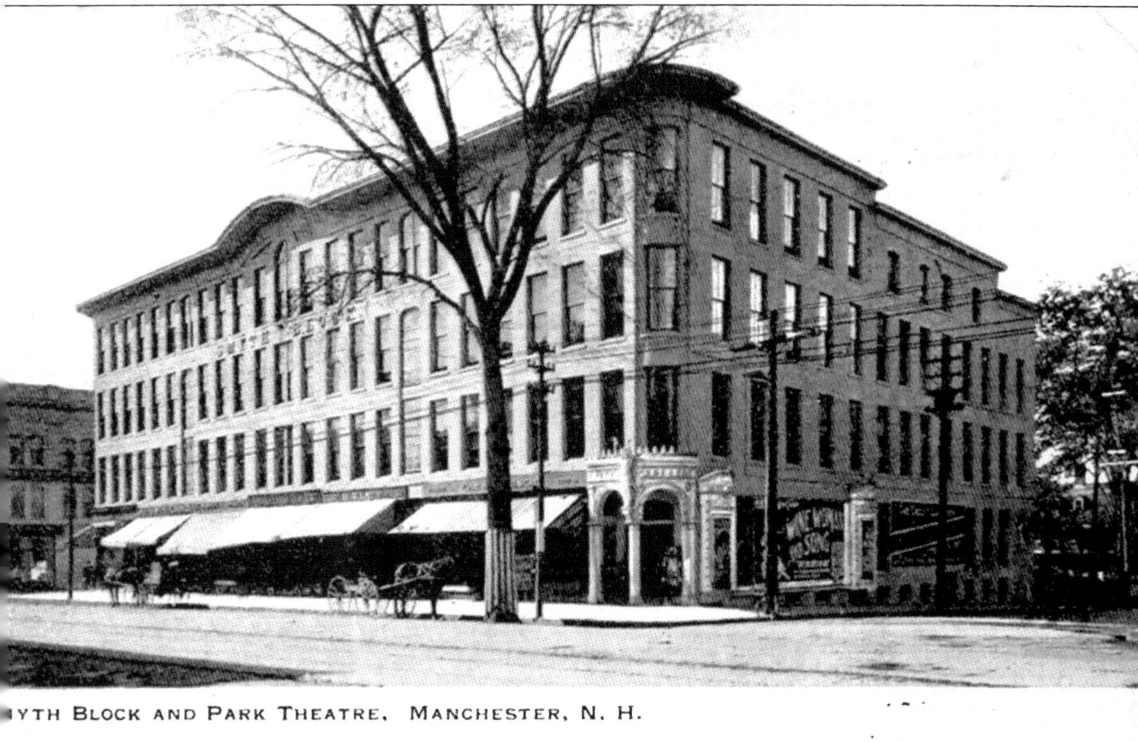

Built in 1854 by Mayor Frederick Smyth, Smyth's Block stood on Elm Street between Water and Spring Streets. Its many businesses included the Merrimack River Savings Bank and the First National Bank; Smyth held various managerial positions at both. Upstairs in Smyth's Hall on March 1, 1860, Smyth introduced an unpretentious speaker to an audience of 3,000 as "the next president of the United States." Abraham Lincoln blushed, but he soon realized that Smyth's seemingly outlandish prediction bore merit. In 1877, in the same room, Frederick Gower, Alexander Graham Bell's assistant, publicly demonstrated the telephone. It so impressed Amoskeag agent and former governor Ezekiel A. Straw that he had Manchester's first telephone line installed between his millyard office and the company's machine shop. Later, Smyth's Hall was renamed the Gorman and finally the Park Theatre, a showcase for plays, concerts, and lectures. The Great Depression saw its demise along with that of the Merrimack River Savings Bank. Smyth's Block housed stores and offices until its demolition in 1970 to make way for Hampshire Plaza.

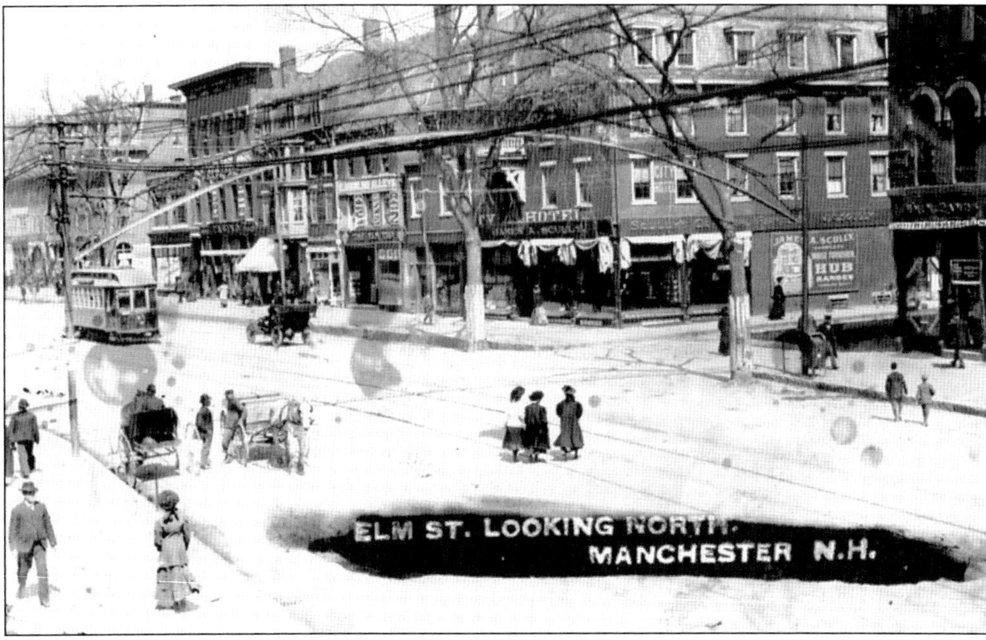

While in Manchester, Abraham Lincoln stayed at the City Hotel, later Foley's Hotel, seen here on the northeast corner of Elm and Lowell Streets. After his speech, he and Frederick Smyth came here and discussed politics late into the night. The following morning, Smyth returned to accompany Lincoln to the Amoskeag Millyard, where, according to one account, a shy young machinist, Edwin P. Richardson, humbly served as Honest Abe's tour guide.

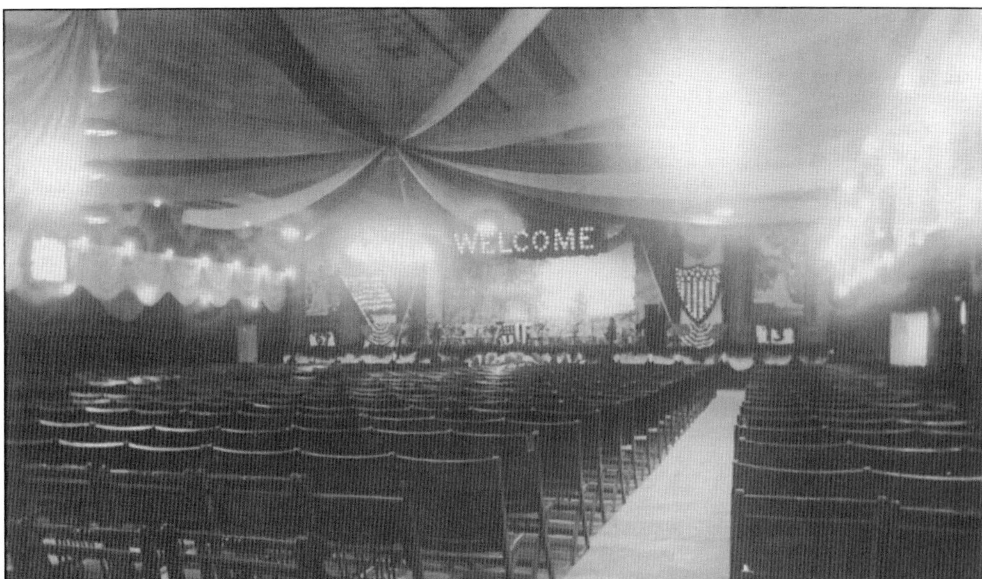

For several generations, Mechanics' Hall at 35 Lowell Street served as one of downtown's multipurpose centers, featuring bowling, billiards, films, dancing, and various types of public gatherings. Here, its auditorium is decorated for an event in 1913. Over time, it went by various names: Mechanics' Theatre, Academy Hall, Le Château, and the Ritz Ballroom. A major fire engulfing the buildings at 35–47 Lowell Street destroyed it on December 13, 1937.

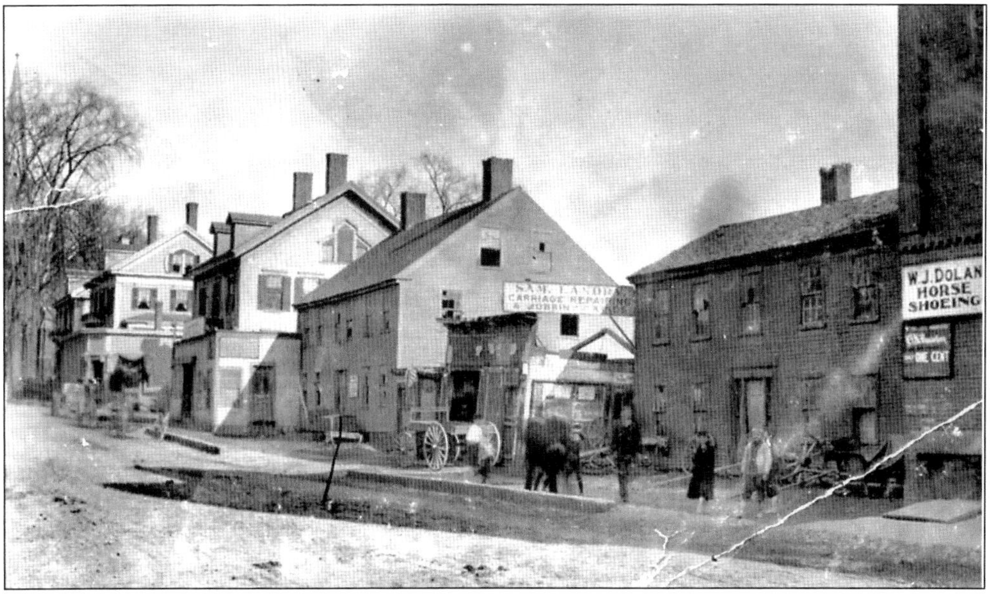

Seen here about 1910, the south side of Lowell Street near Birch Street (later Kosciuszko Street) had competing blacksmiths. Signs advertise William Dolan's horse shoeing, located at the rear at 53 Lowell Street, at the extreme right. Farther up the street, between dilapidated houses, Samuel Landry's carriage repairing is located at 65 Lowell Street, with his home, at 61 Lowell Street, hidden behind. About 1914, Adjutor Francoeur opened a lunch cart at 61 Lowell Street, which became David Lamontagne's Red Arrow Café about 1929. The rest is history.

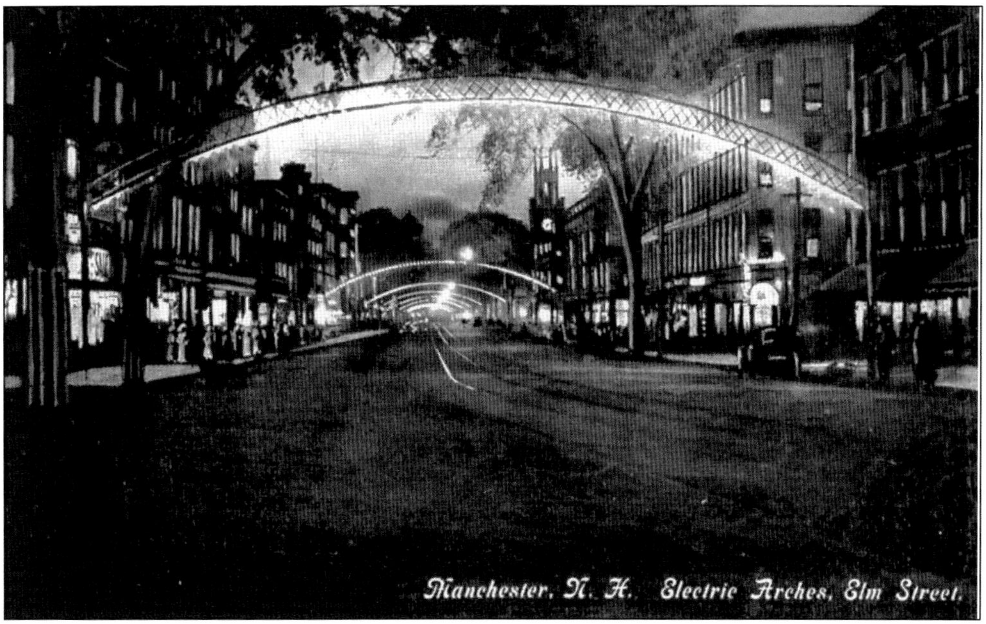

In 1908, Manchester was the first New England city to install a newly developed system of electric lighting, as seen here looking south on Elm Street near Lowell Street. It featured 10 arches between Bridge Street and Lake Avenue. Turned on for the first time amid much fanfare in December 1908, the arches were lit on Thursday and Saturday evenings, when stores remained open. In March 1919, the city removed the arches due to corrosion.

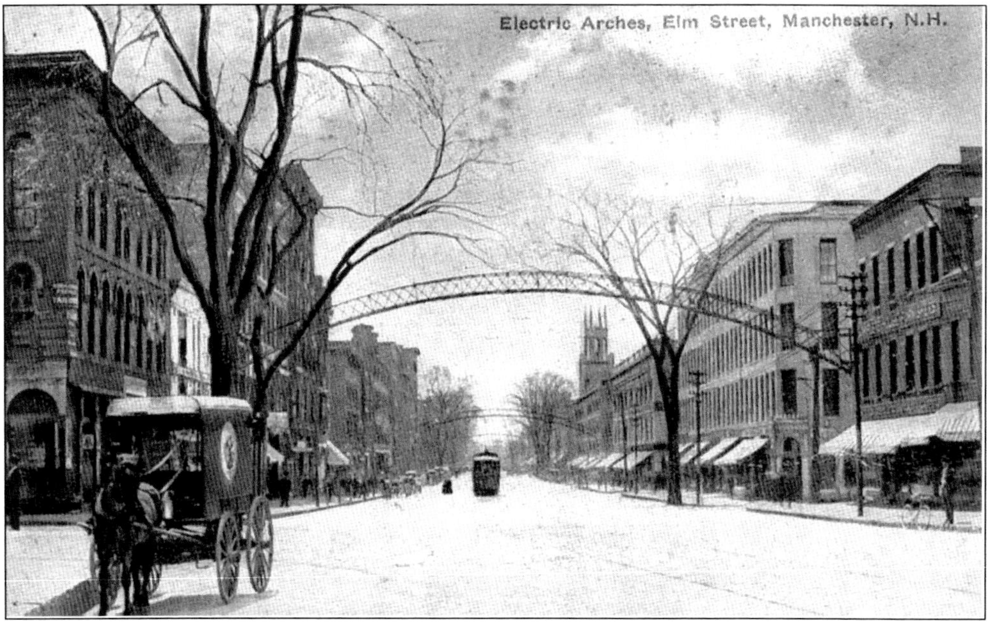

Still looking south on Elm Street, but from farther north, the thoroughfare's famous bend becomes noticeable. Several versions of why it exists have come down through history; the story most often told is attributed to Charles Stark, the general's great-grandson. Supposedly, Amoskeag refused to pay landowner James Wilkins's asking price for his property, which would have allowed Elm Street to go straight through. Consequently, the company avoided his property, thus creating the bend.

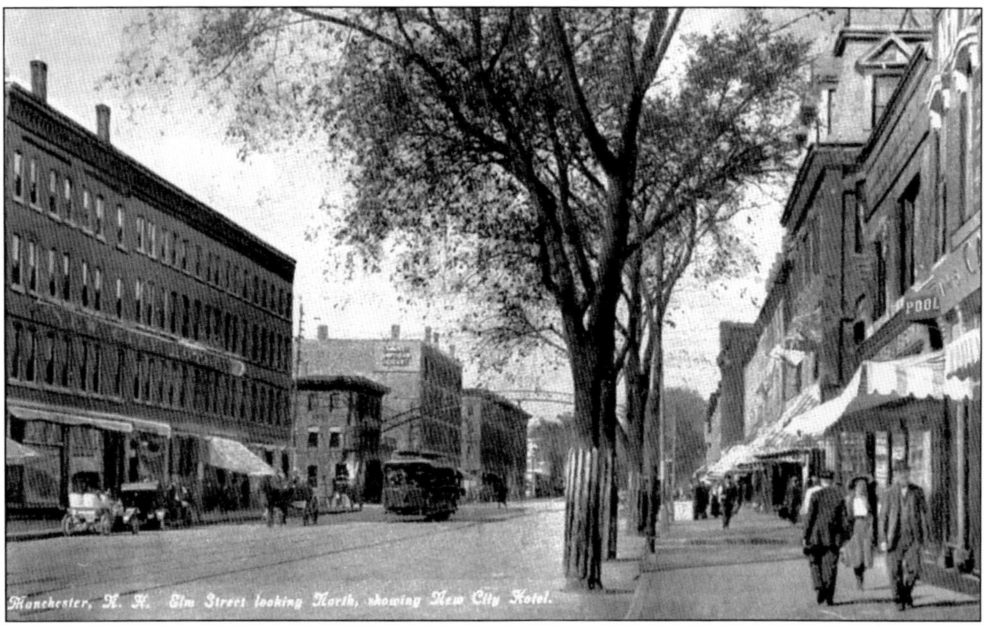

This *c.* 1910 view looks north toward the corner of Bridge and Elm Streets from near Lowell Street. All that remains today is the Chandler Block, barely discernible in the distant right background. All else, including Washington Street, gradually disappeared between the late 1970s and 1980s. The final stage of demolition occurred in 1989, when everything between West Bridge and Kidder Streets, seen here at the center left background, was razed. The area remained empty until 2004.

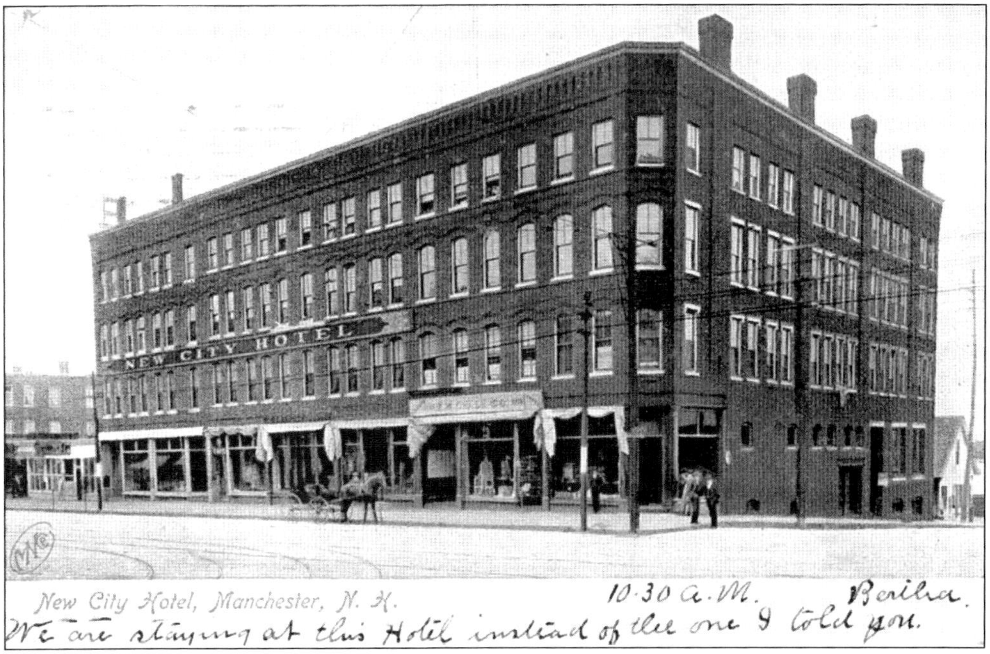

Located at the corner of Elm and West Bridge Streets, the Monadnock or "Upton's Block," another Butterfield design, was completed in 1892, just before its builder, N.H. Trust Company president Hiram D. Upton, had finished the Kennard Block. The New City Hotel and E. M. Chase Company were its two longest tenants. It was razed in 1987 in preparation for the new Bridge Street Bridge.

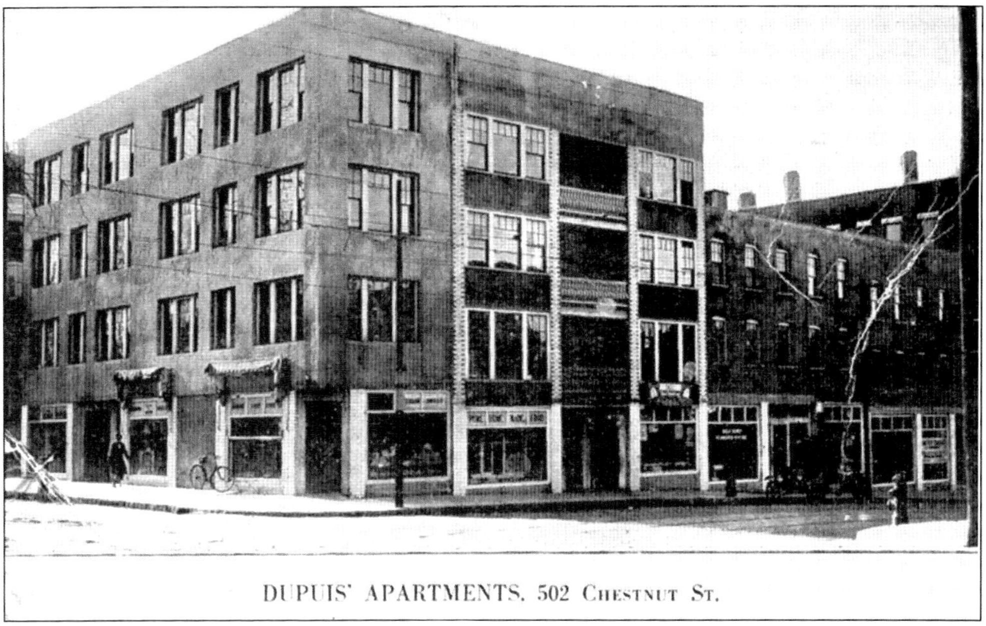

Nineteenth-century neighborhoods filled with elegant homes once lay within a block or two of Elm Street. However, by 1900, most of those homes had been demolished. Here, at the southwest corner of Bridge and Chestnut Streets, sat former governor Frederick Smyth's home for several decades beyond his 1872 move to the Willows. The Dupuis Apartments that replaced it gave way in 1960–1961 to the now-defunct McCown Motor Motel and its parking lot.

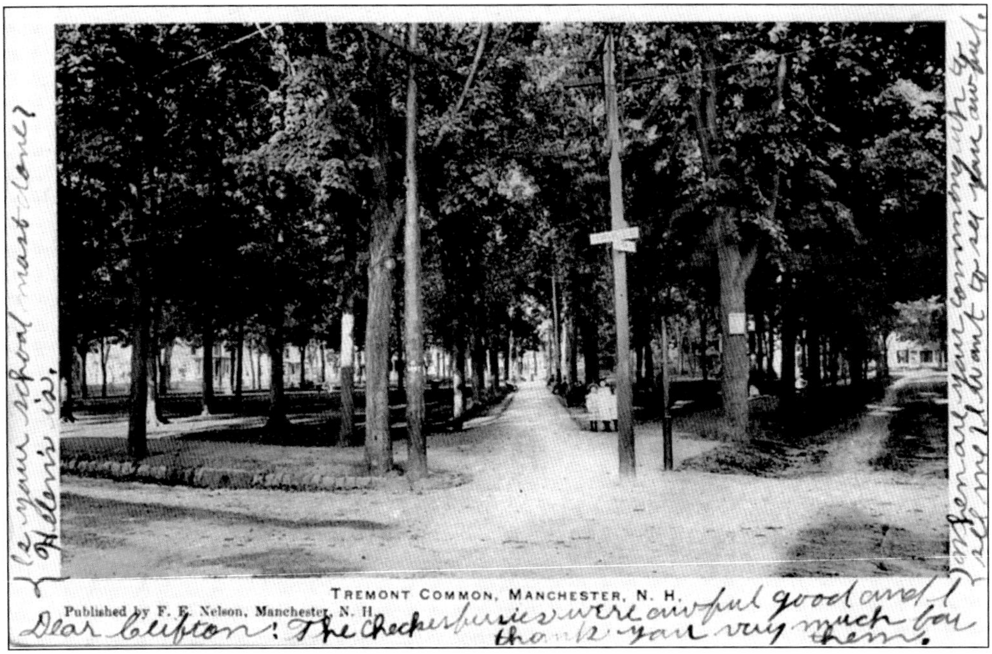

Deeded to Manchester by Amoskeag in 1848, Tremont Common, seen here from the corner of Pine and High Streets about 1905, was renamed Pulaski Park in 1933. The park recognizes Manchester's Polish American community by honoring Brig. Gen. Casimir Pulaski, Polish patriot and American Revolutionary War soldier. An equestrian statue of General Pulaski by Lucien Gosselin was dedicated on August 21, 1938. The immediate foreground later became a basketball court.

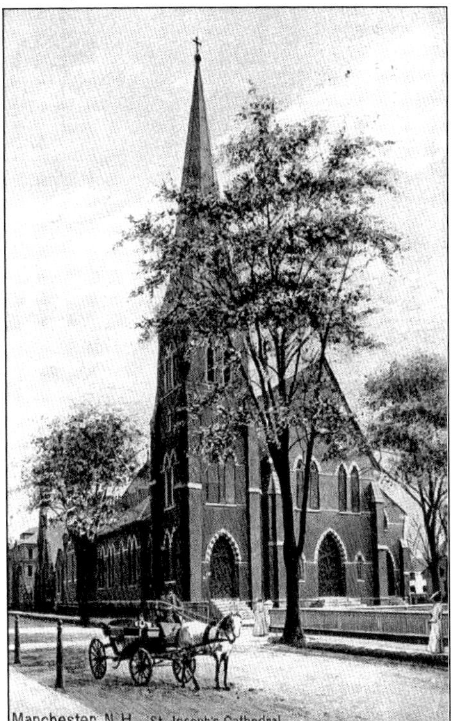

Founded in 1869 to accommodate Manchester's ever-increasing Irish American population, St. Joseph's, the city's second Roman Catholic parish, became the cathedral for the newly created Diocese of Manchester in 1884. Up to then, all of New Hampshire's parishes had belonged to the Diocese of Portland, Maine. Located at the southeast corner of Pine and Lowell Streets, it has undergone extensive interior renovations, while its exterior has changed but little.

Manchester's Great Fire of 1870 destroyed the First Baptist Church at the northwest corner of Manchester and Chestnut Streets. Members rebuilt on Union and Concord Streets in 1872. The 1938 hurricane destroyed its spire, seen here on this preprinted membership committee reminder. The reverse side reads, "Missed You Again, Last Sunday. You see we want you with us . . . Come along with us, next Sunday, wont you?"

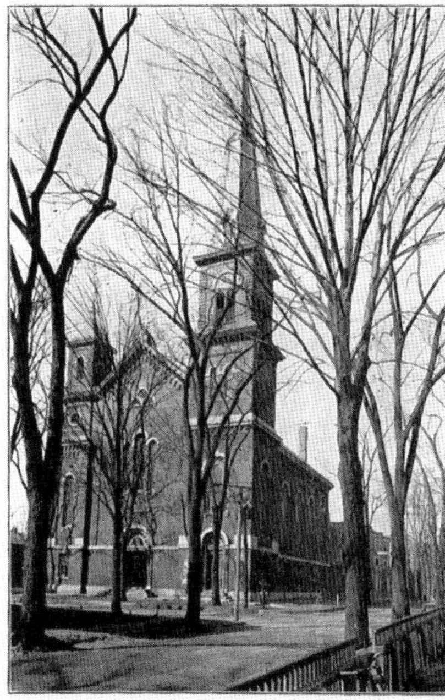

FIRST BAPTIST CHURCH

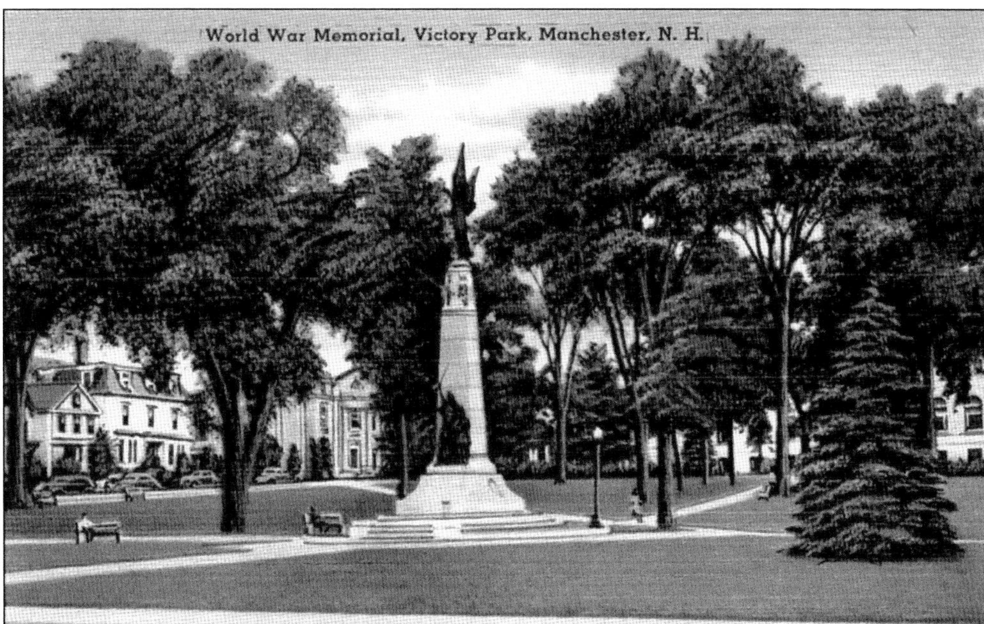

Laid out in 1839, Concord Square included a pond and was bounded by Concord, Vine, Amherst, and Pine Streets. Eventually, Chestnut Street intersected the square, and its western half later became a marketplace, a parking lot, and finally a parking garage. The eastern half became Victory Park, featuring sculptor Lucien Gosselin's 1929 World War I memorial. A memorial to René Gagnon, who raised the flag at Iwo Jima during World War II, was erected in 1995.

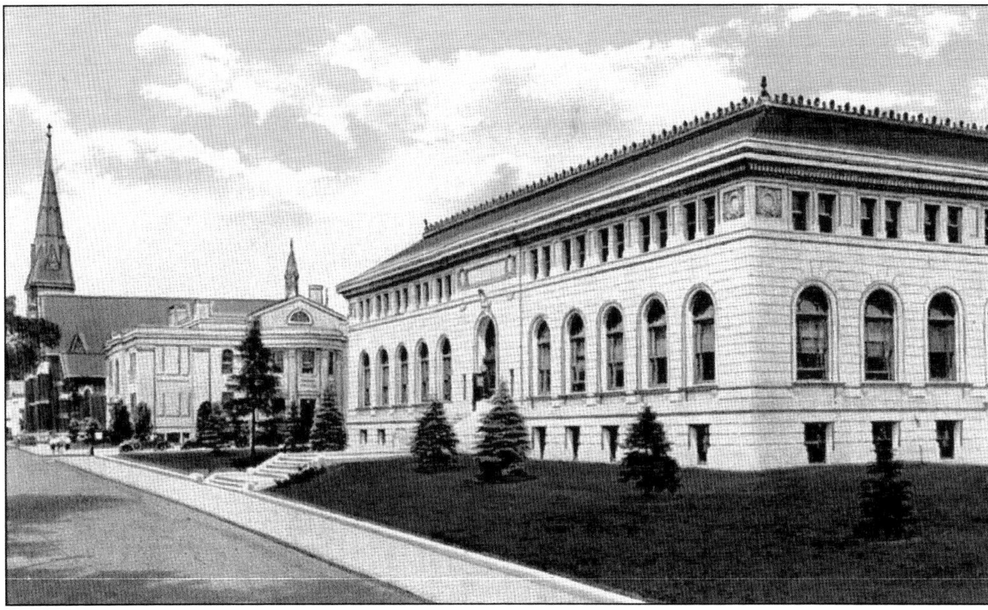

When the City Library on Franklin Street became inadequate, businessman and philanthropist Franklin Pierce "Frank P." Carpenter gave Manchester a new library in memory of his wife, Elenora Blood Carpenter, daughter of locomotive works agent Aretas Blood. Built in 1912–1914, the Carpenter Memorial Library is a chef-d'oeuvre of architects Edward L. Tilton of New York and Edgar A. P. Newcomb of Honolulu, designers of an identical library in Springfield, Massachusetts.

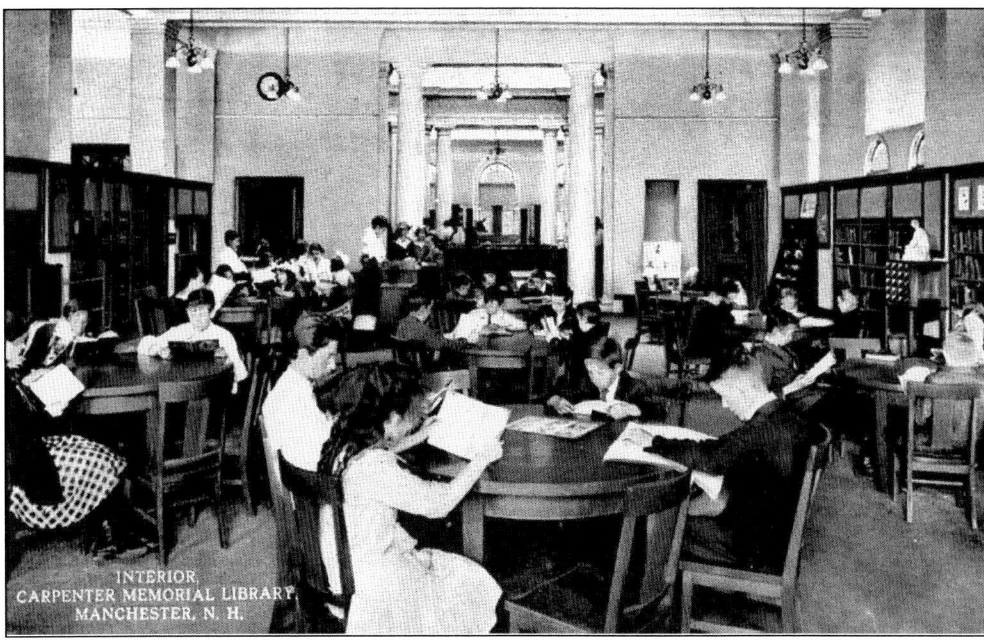

Made of white Vermont marble and also of New Hampshire granite from the same Concord quarry as the granite used in the Library of Congress, the new library was designed to hold up to 300,000 volumes. Besides its reading rooms, it features a grand staircase, a rotunda, and an auditorium. It housed the Manchester Historic Association's collection until 1931, when Carpenter gave that institution its own building, located diagonally across the street.

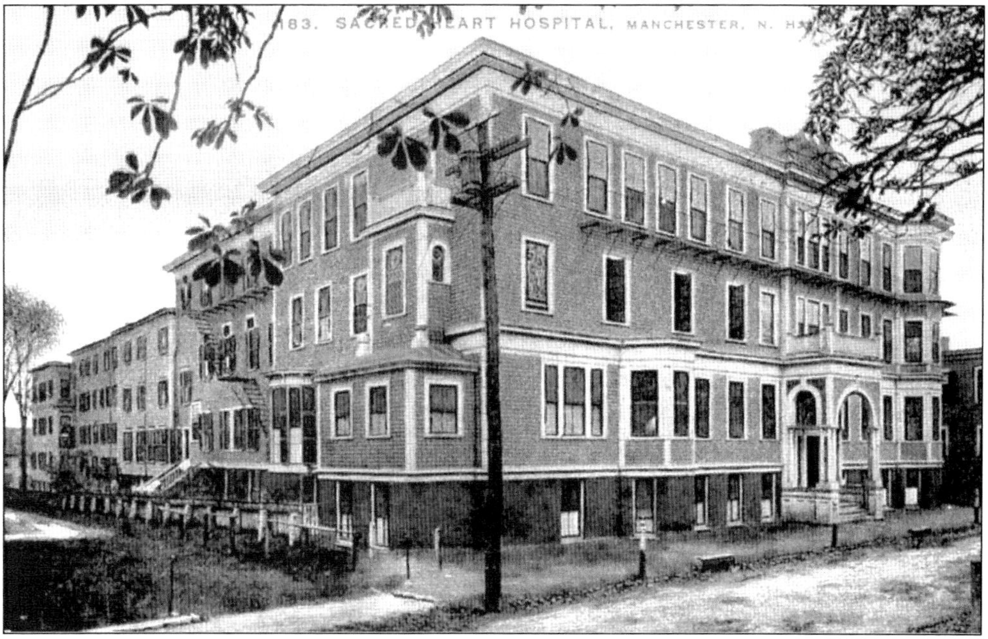

Opened in 1892 at 177 Amherst Street, the building that originally housed Sacred Heart Hospital was transported there from a lot adjoining St. Joseph's Cathedral. Its much larger yellow-brick Hanover Street extension was built in 1937. Sacred Heart Hospital became Catholic Medical Center East in 1974; it closed in 1979, the year in which the older structure was demolished. The extension subsequently became the Gov. Hugh J. Gallen Apartments.

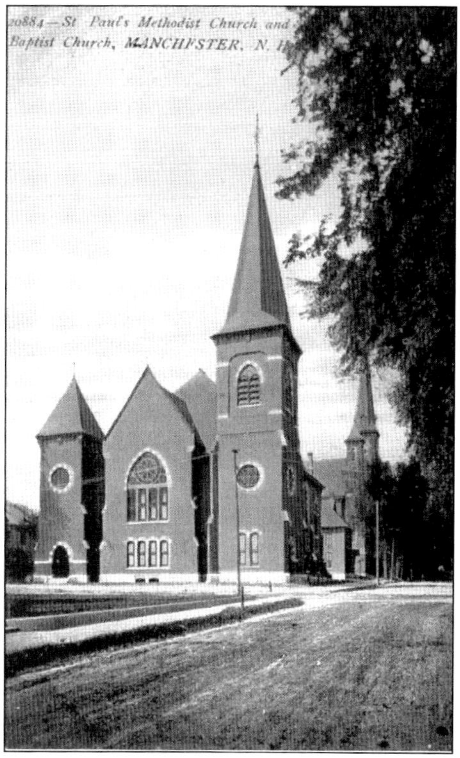

After the merger of several Methodist societies, St. Paul's Methodist Church, designed by William M. Butterfield, opened in 1882 at the northwest corner of Amherst and Union Streets. Its roots dated back to the Methodist-Episcopal Church built at Manchester Centre in 1829. In 1968, the congregation moved into its new building on Bruce Road, after which the old church was demolished. Today, the land serves as a parking lot.

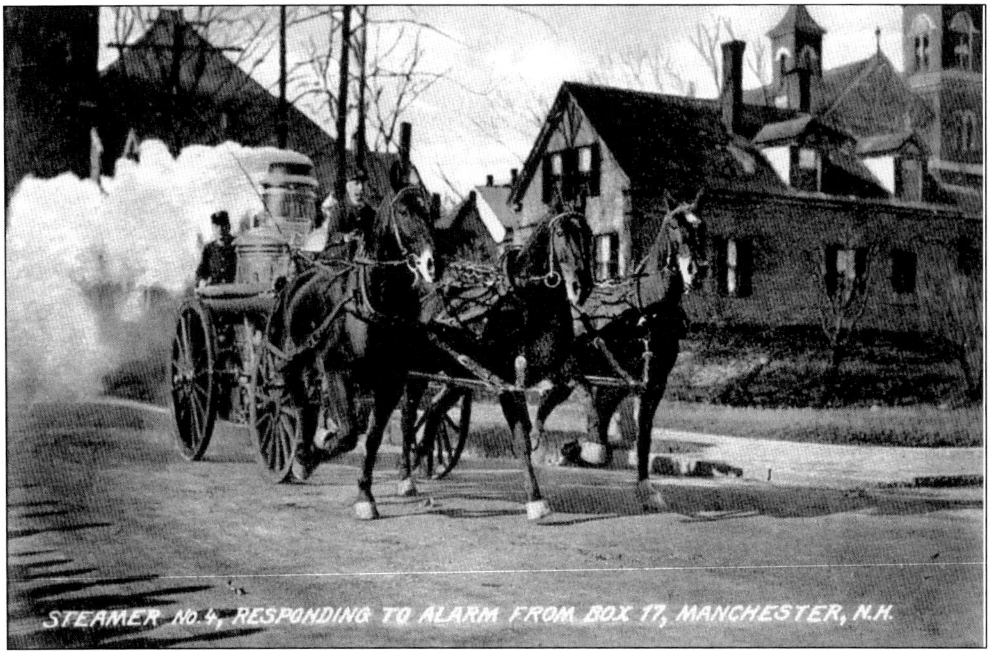

George Cann drives an Amoskeag steam fire engine along Amherst Street east of Union Street. These modern marvels were first perfected in 1859 in the Amoskeag Machine Shop by Nehemiah S. Bean, who had earlier created New England's original steam fire engine in Lawrence. The fire engines were shipped as far away as Europe, South America, and Asia, and proved outstanding at the Great Fires of Chicago (1871) and Boston (1872) as well as those following the San Francisco earthquake (1906).

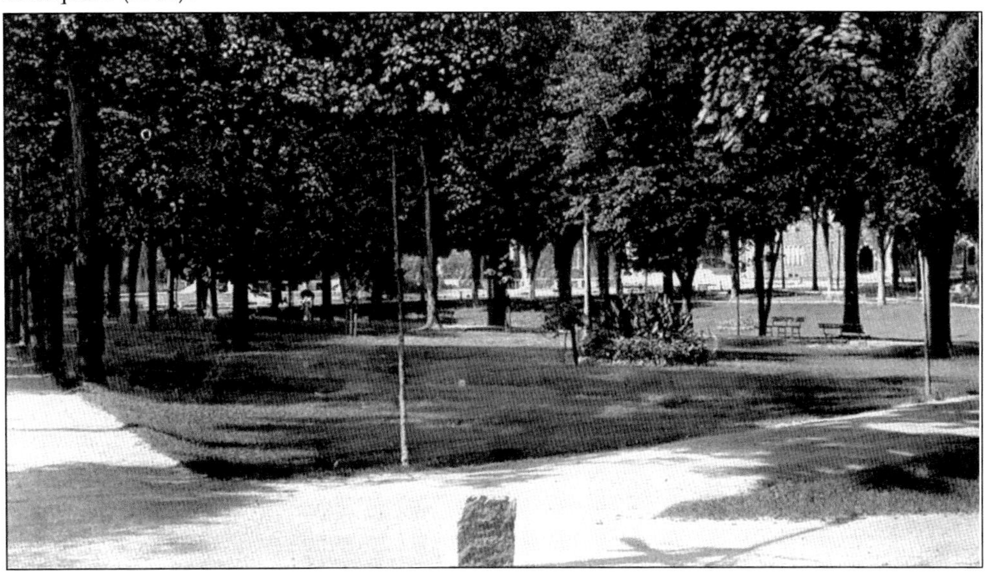

Laid out in 1852 and bordered by Hanover, Union, Amherst, and Beech Streets, Hanover Common once had a pond fed by Mile Brook, the source of other ponds in Concord and Merrimack Squares. Hanover Common features a monument honoring veterans of the Spanish-American War and another dedicated to Dr. Ben Richard Bronstein, the city's and state's first naval officer to die in World War II. The common was renamed Bronstein Park in his honor.

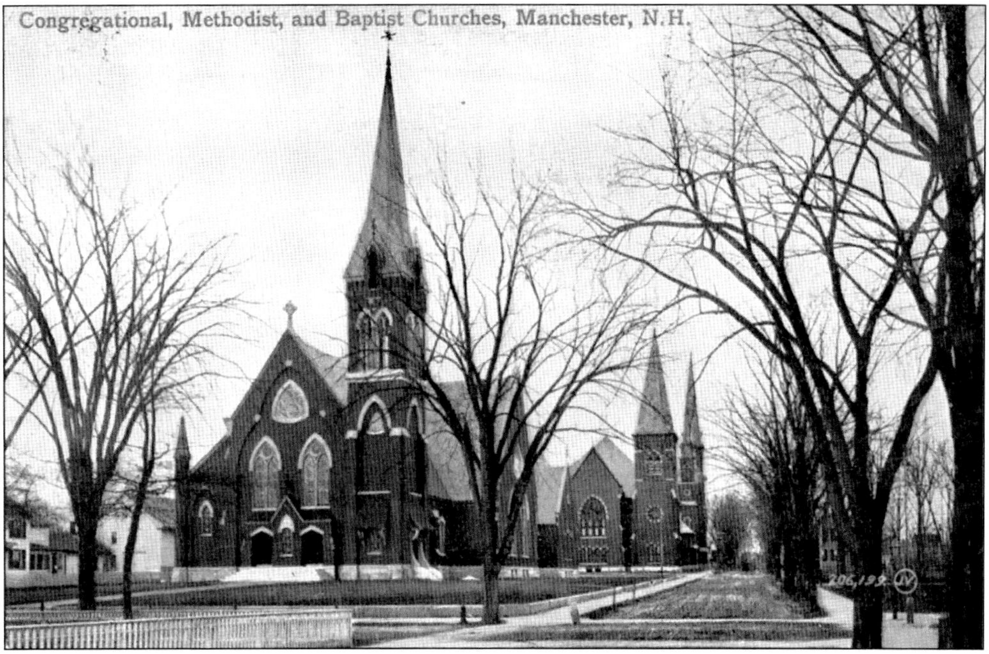

Manchester's reputation as home to many churches manifests itself rather well in this image, looking north on Union Street near the intersection of Hanover Street. Built in 1879, the present First Congregational Church was founded in 1828, with its roots traceable back to the first church in Derryfield Centre. Just beyond sit St. Paul's Methodist Church and the First Baptist Church.

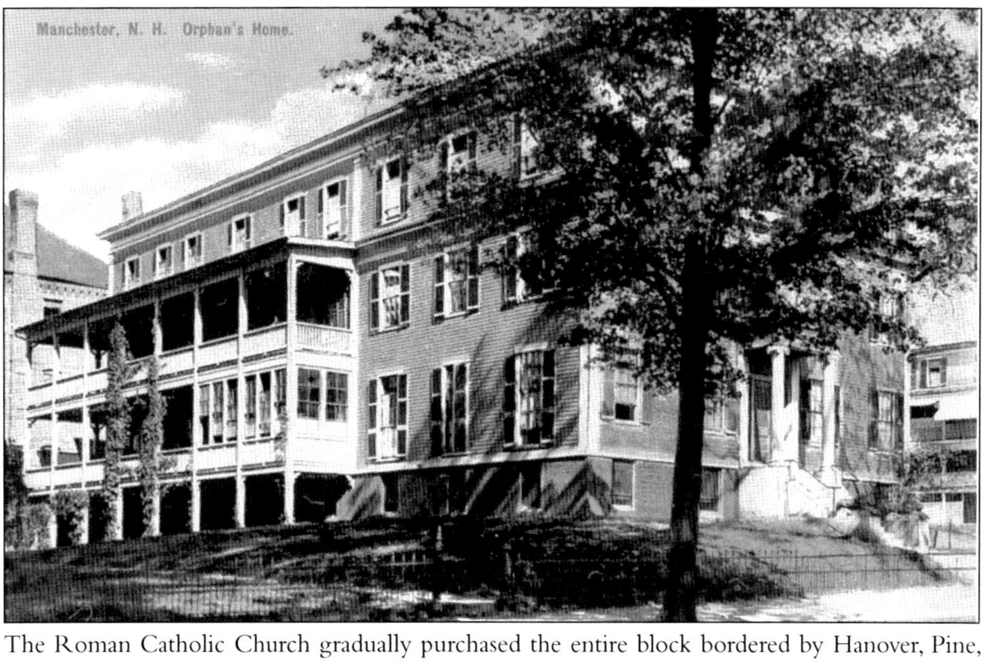

The Roman Catholic Church gradually purchased the entire block bordered by Hanover, Pine, Amherst, and Union Streets, with the exception of the First Congregational Church's lot. In 1874, St. Patrick's Orphanage opened at 184 Hanover Street. Eventually, its neighbors included St. Joseph's Orphanage for Boys (left), the Old Ladies' Home (right), the old and new Sacred Heart Hospital, and the Infant Asylum. Today, the few surviving buildings have other uses.

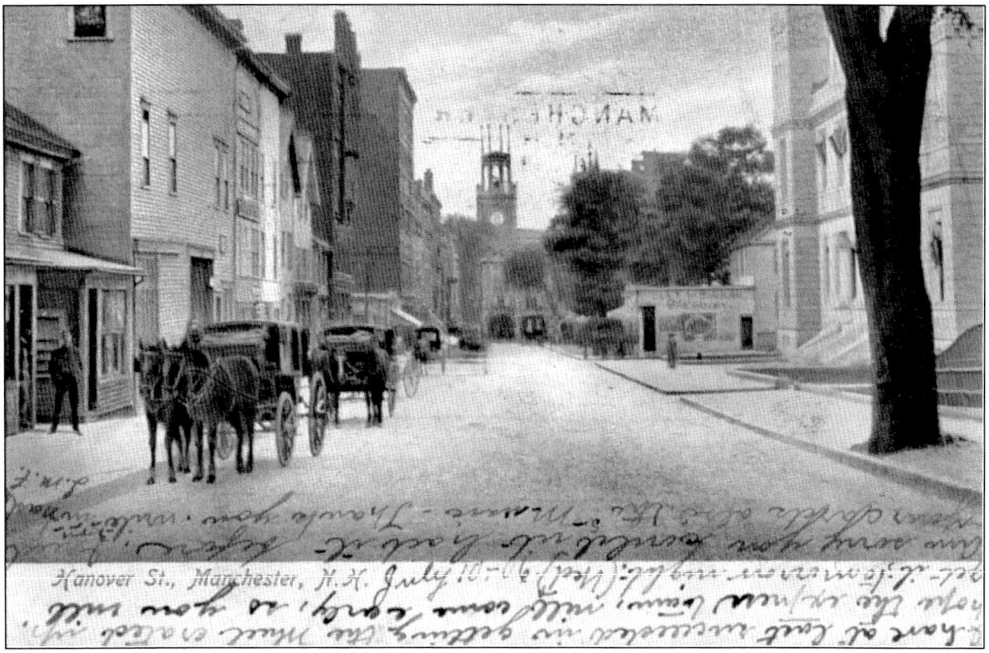

Here, looking west on Hanover Street from between Pine and Chestnut Streets about 1900, several wooden structures, mostly businesses mixed with a few residences, still line the south side. Elsewhere, brick or granite blocks, including the recently completed Post Office Building at right, reflect the downtown's expansion into what had been a residential neighborhood not long before. In 2005, the few remaining wooden buildings in this area are among downtown's oldest structures.

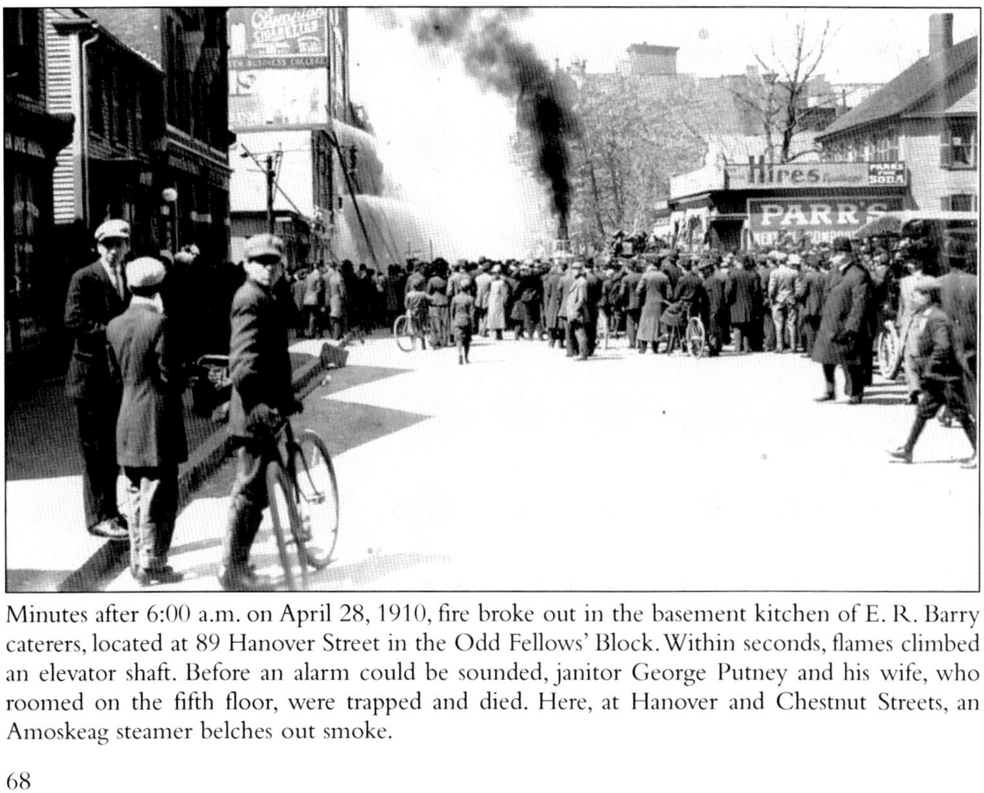

Minutes after 6:00 a.m. on April 28, 1910, fire broke out in the basement kitchen of E. R. Barry caterers, located at 89 Hanover Street in the Odd Fellows' Block. Within seconds, flames climbed an elevator shaft. Before an alarm could be sounded, janitor George Putney and his wife, who roomed on the fifth floor, were trapped and died. Here, at Hanover and Chestnut Streets, an Amoskeag steamer belches out smoke.

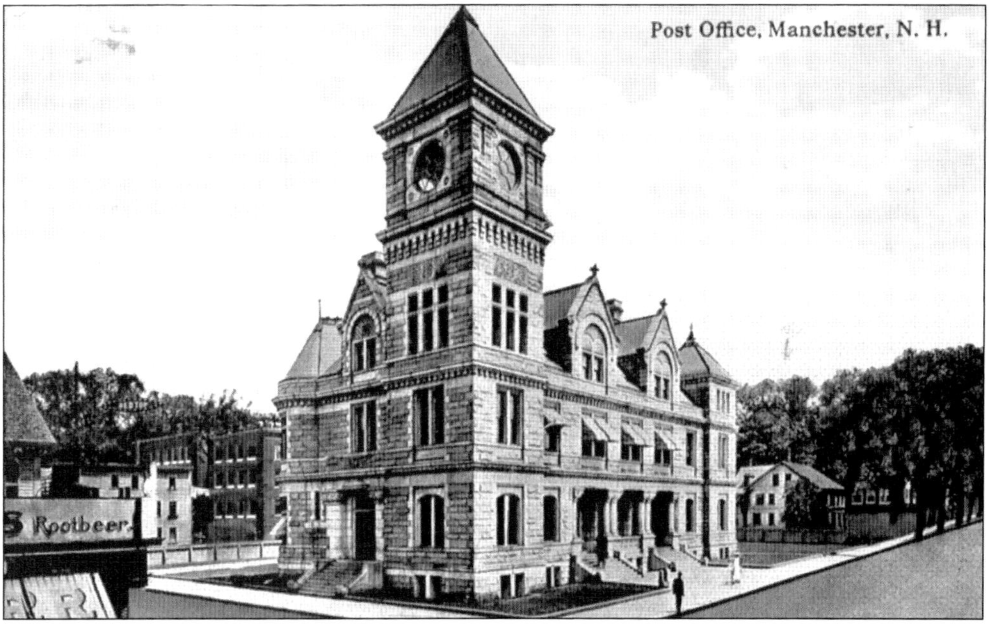

Between 1840 and 1891, the downtown post office was housed in eight successive locations, including City Hall, several stores, and a postmaster's residence. In 1886, work began on a more permanent home at the northeast corner of Hanover and Chestnut Streets. Underestimations of the cost delayed construction until 1891. Another post office, built on the same site, replaced this one in 1934. Today, downtown's post office is merely a substation in Hampshire Plaza.

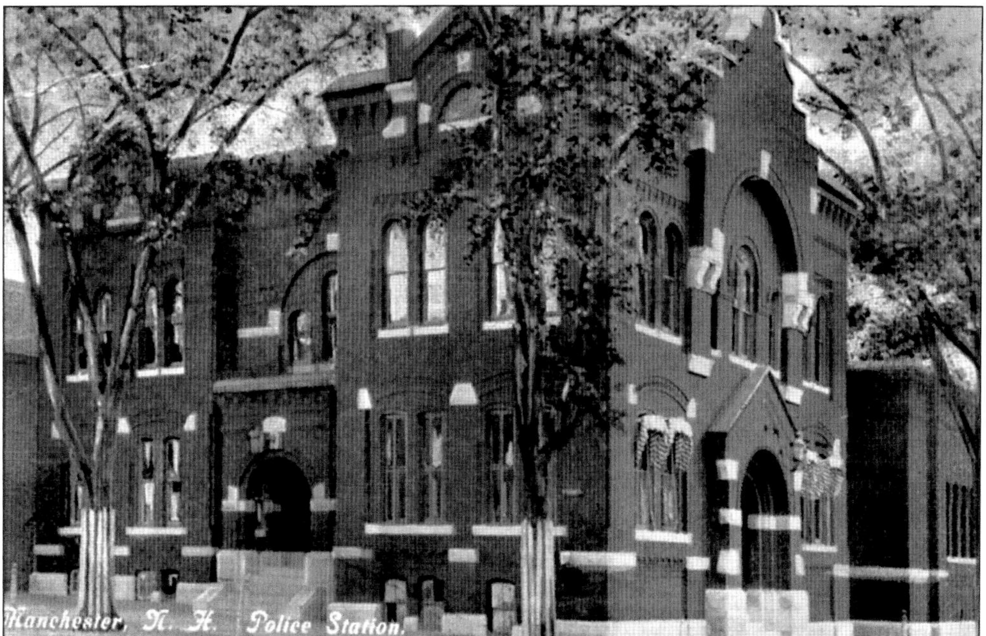

In 1881, when 21-year-old William M. Butterfield, a Maine native and budding architect, arrived in Manchester, his adopted city accorded him what he probably would have listed as his first important commission: the police station. Located at the southeast corner of Chestnut and Manchester Streets, it served the department's needs until 1977, when, deemed inadequate, it was demolished.

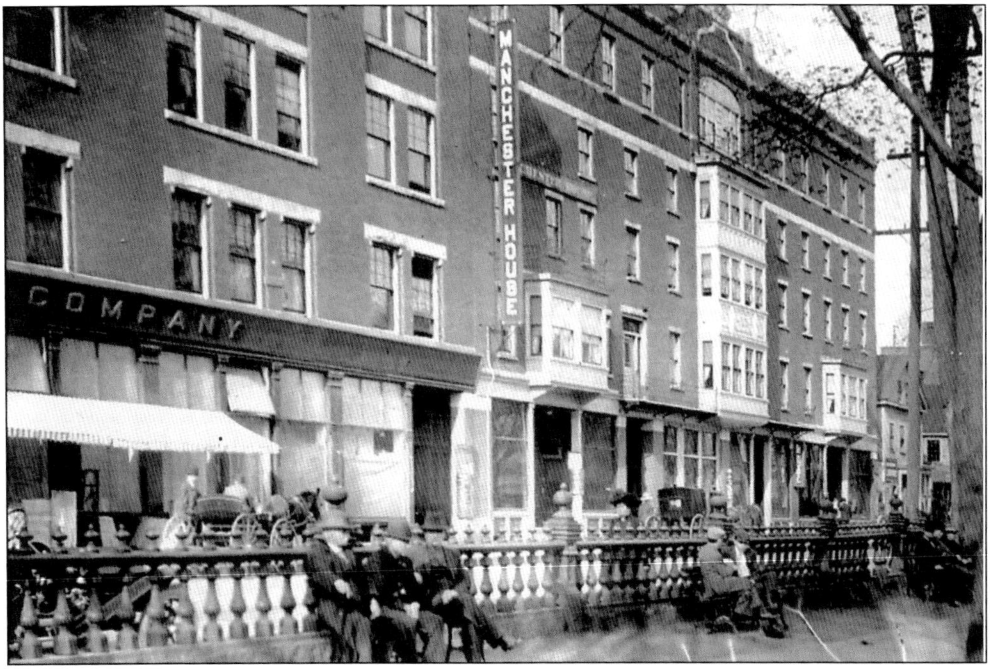

Built in 1839, the Manchester House, known as Shepherd's Tavern, sat at the northeast corner of Elm and Merrimack Streets. In 1887, crowds gazed in awe as the brick structure was raised and moved one lot east on Merrimack. After renovations, it became the New Manchester House; it was later known as the Rice Varick and, still later, as Warren's Hotel. Its upper floors burned in 1976.

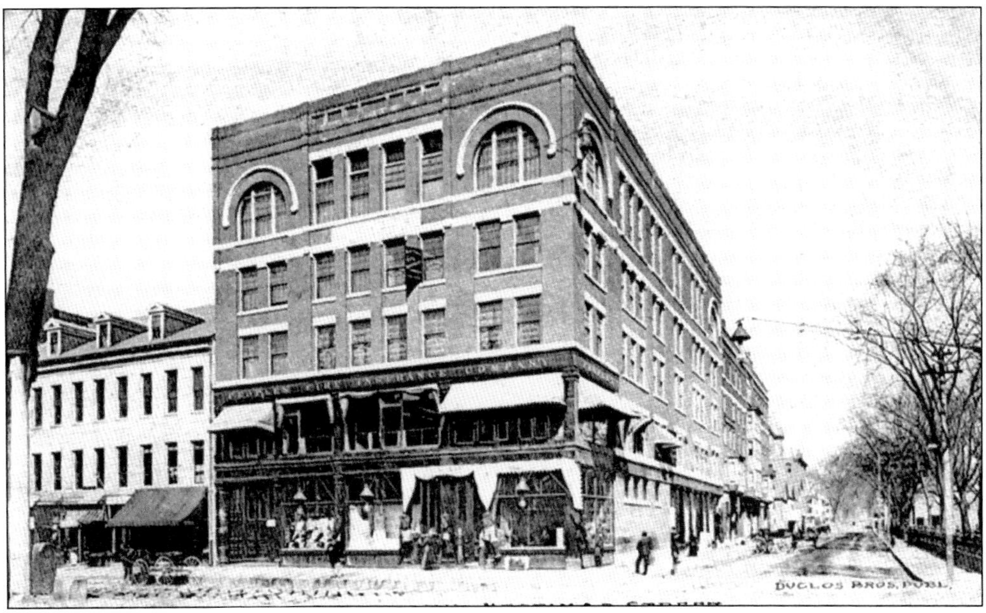

Moving the Manchester House freed up land that enabled J. H. Dearborn of Pembroke to build his Pembroke Block, which opened in 1891. One of its first tenants, the Weston & Hill Company (dry goods), later the James W. Hill Company, remained there until 1982. Hill's pneumatic tube system of sending and receiving payments fascinated Manchester's children. The Pembroke Block has undergone major renovations since a fire on July 13, 2002.

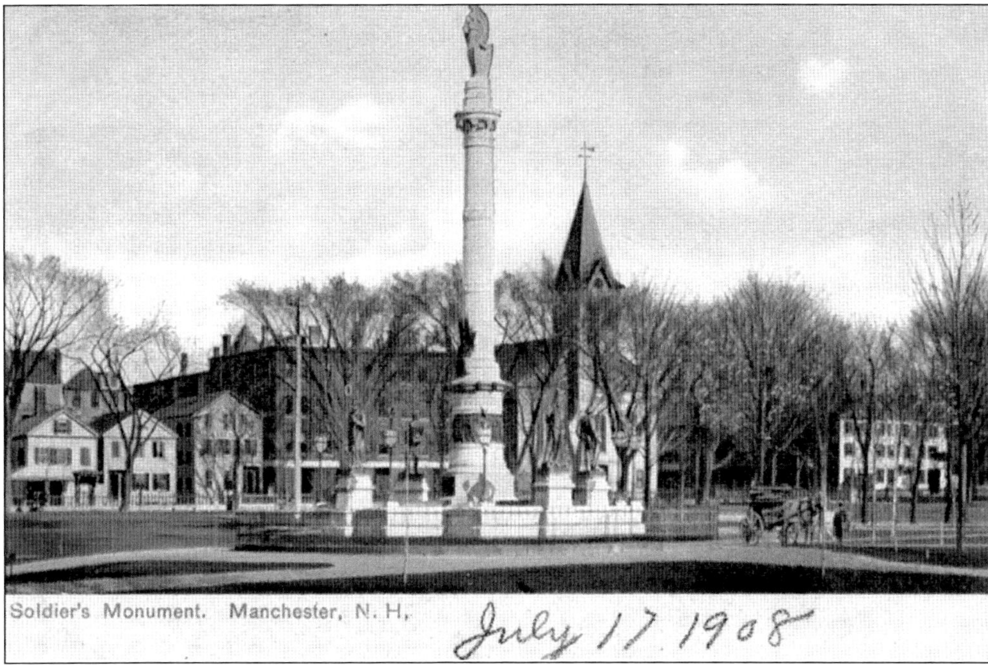

The largest of the original parks deeded to Manchester by the Amoskeag, Merrimack Square (later known as Monument Square, Merrimack Common, and now Veterans' Memorial Park), once had a pond filled not only with trout from its source, Mile Brook, but also with horned pout that drove the trout away. The park's centerpiece, seen here looking northeast toward Merrimack and Chestnut Streets, is a monument to the city's Civil War soldiers, erected in 1879.

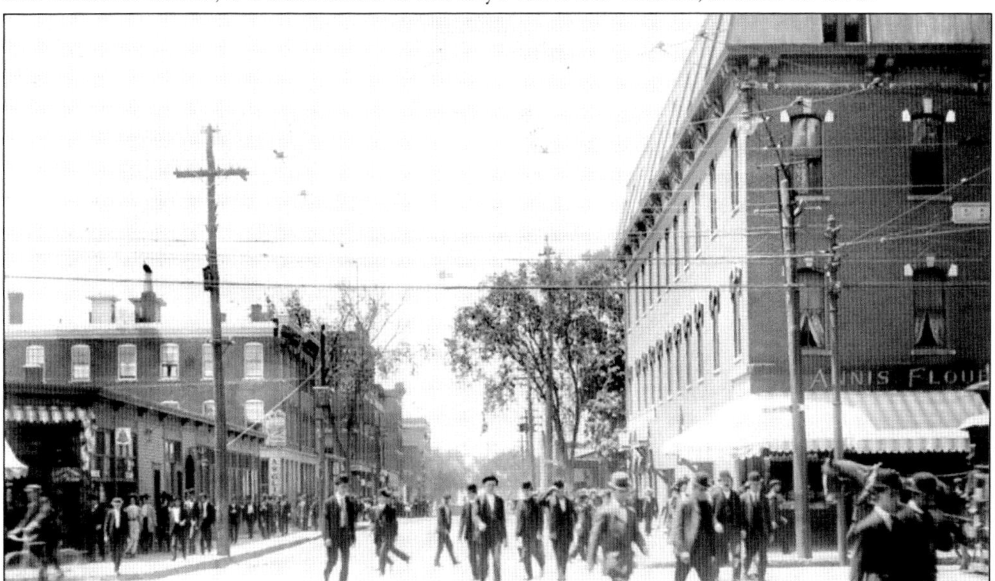

Judging by the shadows in this image, which looks down West Central Street from Elm Street, it is probably noontime in summer, as people head to lunch. At right is Prout's Block (1875), which was razed during 1982's major urban renewal project that removed West Central Street and created the Center of New Hampshire. The only survivor, seen in the distance, was the 7-20-4 Cigar building.

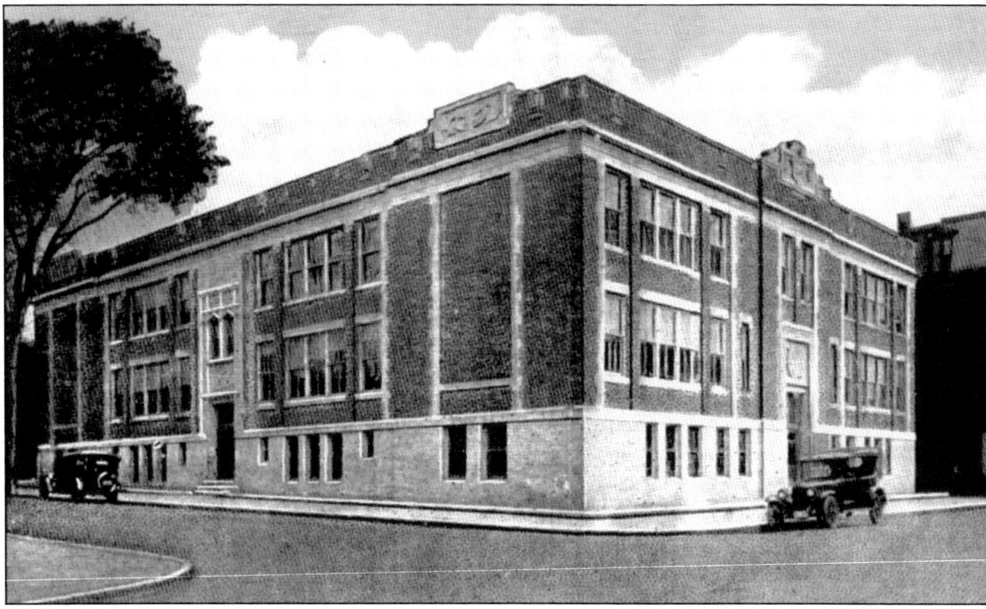

Completed in 1922, the newer Franklin Street School, located on Franklin and West Central Streets behind Prout's Block (at right), was considered modern and desirable in its day. After the Amoskeag company's closure, the school's enrollment steadily decreased as mill families living in nearby corporation housing moved away. Many viewed it as an excellent facility in the wrong location. Closed by 1974, it housed Manchester's Human Services Center until its demolition in 1982.

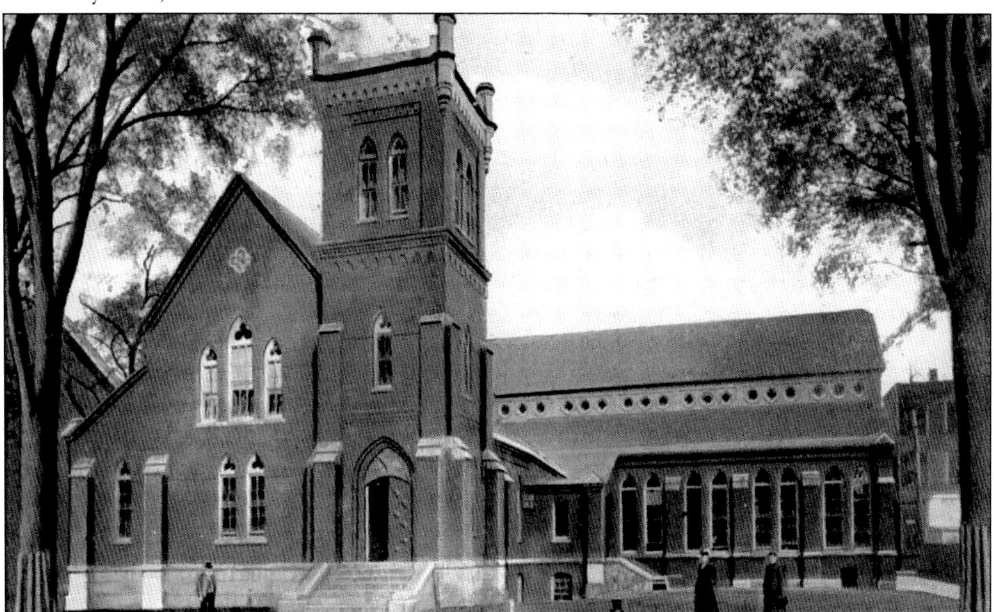

Manchester's City Library dates back to 1854, when the city purchased the collection of the 10-year-old Manchester Athenaeum and made it free to the public. After several moves, including one in 1856 after a fire destroyed much of its collection, the library occupied its own building, seen here on the east side of Franklin Street just south of Market Street, from 1871 until the opening of the Carpenter Memorial Library.

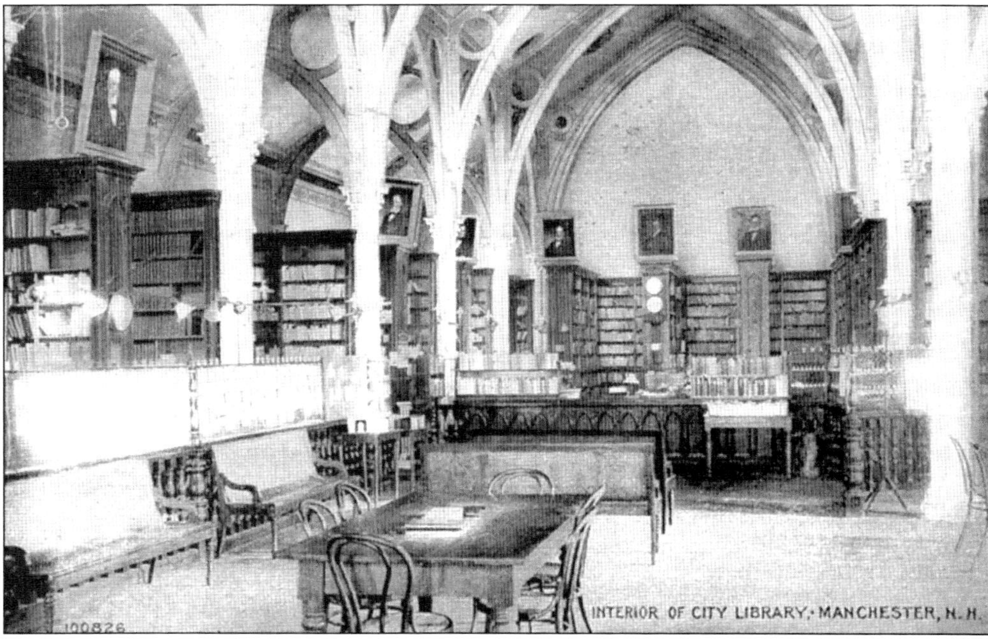

Both inside and out, the City Library's Gothic architecture created its rather churchlike ambiance. From the opening of the Carpenter Memorial Library until 1929, the old building served as headquarters for the Amoskeag Textile Club, part of the company's program of paternalism. Ironically, despite its ecclesiastical appearance, it was demolished and replaced in 1930–1931 by its neighbor, the Franklin Street Church, for its parish house.

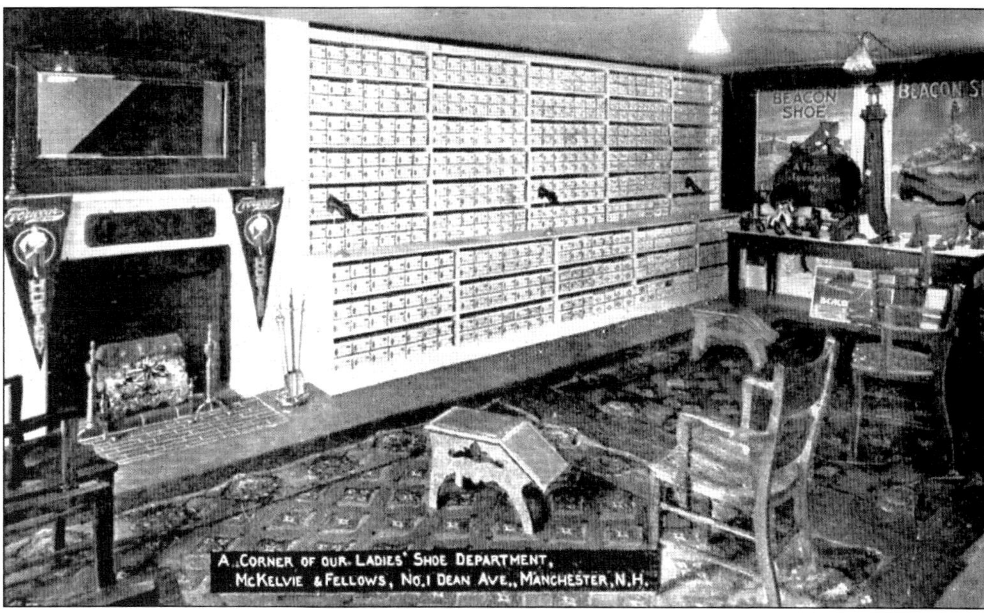

Today merely a narrow pedestrian shortcut from Elm to Franklin Street, Manchester's smallest street, Dean Avenue, better known as "Cat Alley," once had several residential and business addresses. For approximately 30 years beginning around 1908, John S. Fellows ran a shoe store at 1 Dean Avenue. For about the first 20 years, he was in partnership with Peter F. McKelvie, doing business as McKelvie & Fellows.

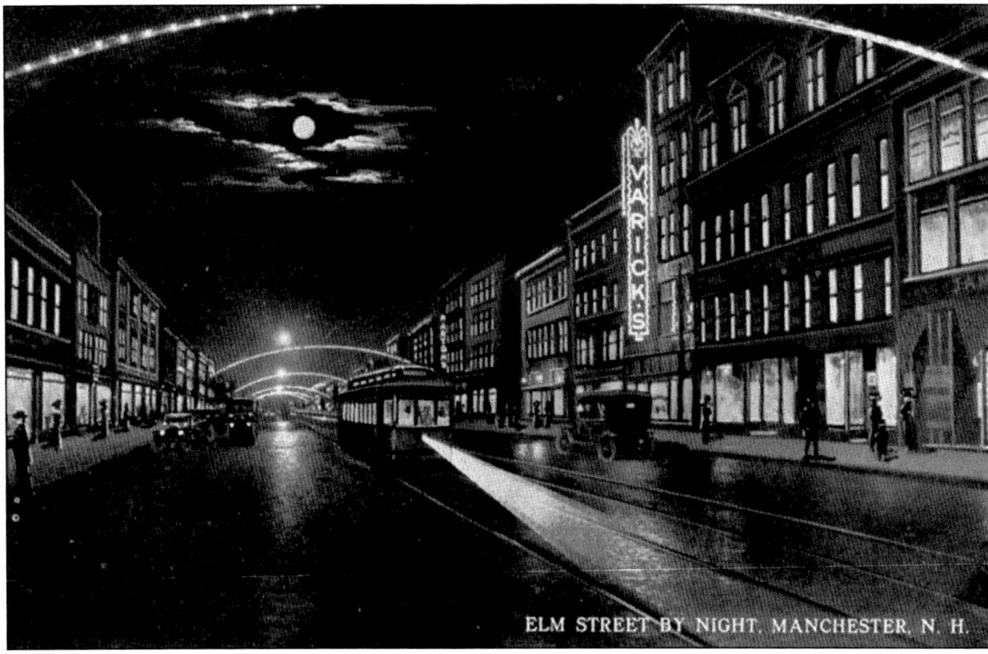

Long ago, lights from windows, storefronts, cars, and streetcars filled the downtown atmosphere, as seen in this view of Elm Street looking north between Merrimack and Manchester Streets about 1910. The lights were especially bright on Thursdays, payday in the Amoskeag mills and elsewhere, which brought numerous shoppers to the mostly locally owned businesses, such as Varick's department store, seen at the right. For effect, someone inserted a moon in the northern sky on this postcard, an astronomical impossibility here.

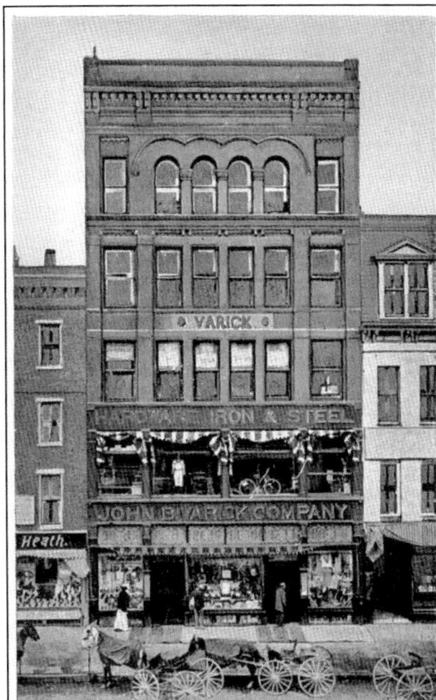

John B. Varick Co, Varick Building, Manchester N. H.

Since 1851, the name Varick has been a permanent fixture on the east side of Elm Street between Merrimack and Manchester Streets. The John B. Varick Company, seen here about 1905, survived three fires that destroyed its buildings, most recently on June 24, 1914. More than 55 years after the company's closing, the name remains on the present building's façade. Ulric Bourgeois founded Varick's photography department, which published dozens of postcards.

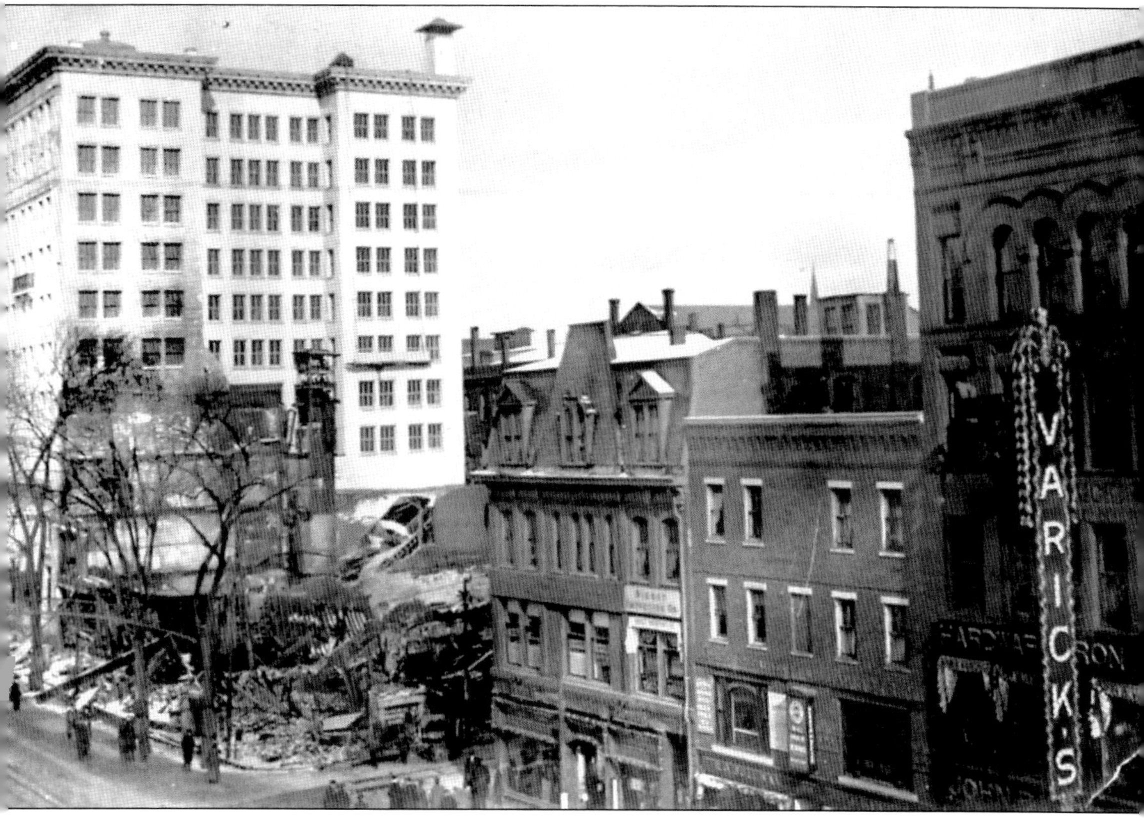

Built after its predecessor burned in 1855, the Merchants' Exchange Building, located on the northeast corner of Elm and Manchester Streets, was one of downtown's largest blocks. On January 29, 1914, not quite five months before fire would destroy its neighbor, the Varick Building (seen here at the extreme right), the Merchants' Exchange met the same fate. It is seen in ruins at the left. Beyond, in the distance, stands the nearly completed Amoskeag Bank Building. In addition to offices and apartments, the Merchants' Exchange housed several businesses, most prominently the Merchants' National Bank and the Hillsborough County Savings Bank, the Barton Company department store, and L. M. Folsom's dry and fancy goods store. Within hours of the fire, the same-day edition of the Manchester *Mirror & American* carried an advertisement advising Merchants' Bank customers that they were welcome to conduct their regular banking business uninterruptedly, as the Mechanics' Savings Bank in the new Kennard Block had offered space for such a purpose. Meanwhile, both Barton's and Folsom's quickly found a unique solution to keep customers satisfied.

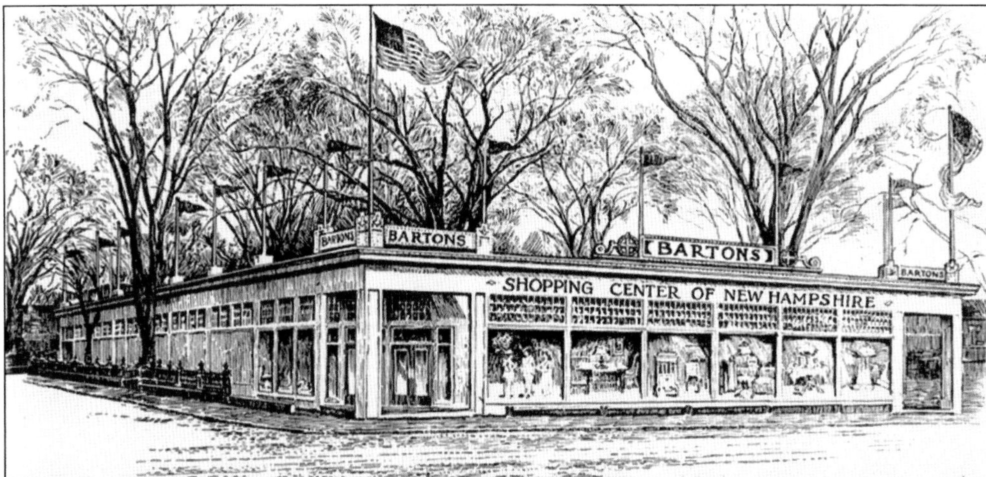

THE BARTON COMPANY'S TEMPORARY STORE, erected on Merrimack Common, Manchester, in 13 working days, beginning February 7, 1914. Size of building, 220x96 feet. Number of men engaged, 200. Number of electric lights, 1,977. Number of trees enclosed, 10. Lumber used, 500,000 square feet. Glass and sash, 4,200 square feet. Hardwood flooring, 30,000 square feet. Number of sprinkler heads, 260. Square feet of wall boards, 50,000. Radiation, 5,000 feet. Paint used, 500 gallons.

Founded in 1850 by Otis Barton, who, having died one year before the 1914 conflagration, was spared having to see a lifetime of labor in ashes, the Barton Company wasted no time in reopening. In a mere 10 working days, beginning February 7, 1914, Barton's had a crew of 200 men construct a specially designed one-story temporary store at the southeast corner of Elm and Merrimack Streets on Merrimack Common.

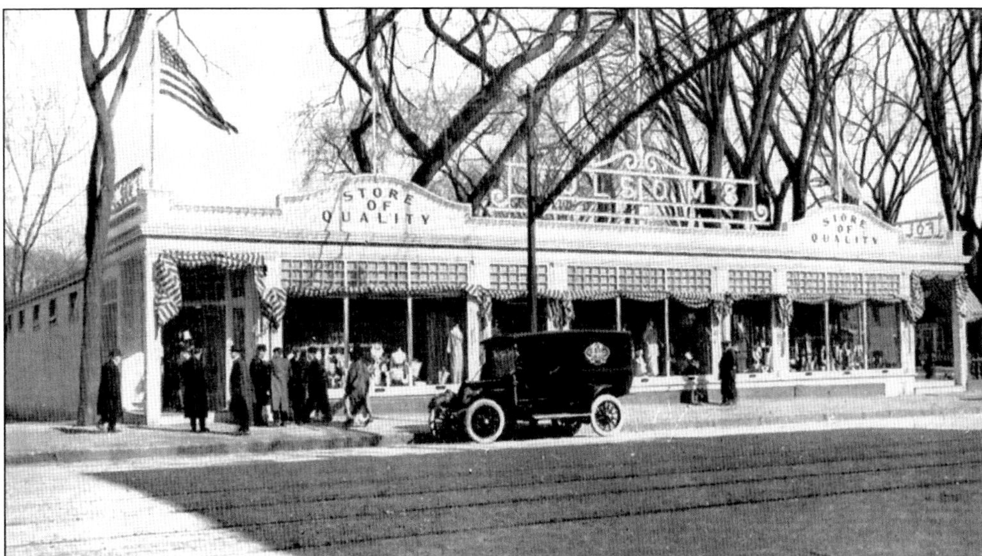

L. M. Folsom's Store, Merrimack Common, Manchester, N. H.

Meanwhile, Leslie M. Folsom had his own temporary store erected in a design similar to that of Barton's, located just to the south of it on Merrimack Common, adjacent to Pleasant Street. Perhaps the most fascinating aspect of these construction projects, besides their speed, was that both structures went up in spite of the many trees on the common. The trees were actually enclosed within them and protruded from their roofs.

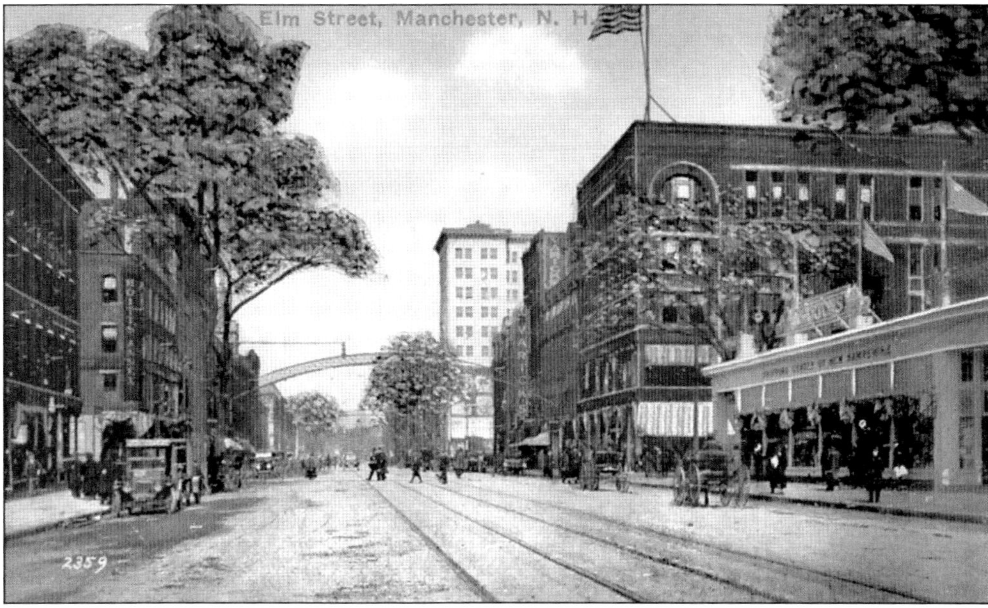

Considering its temporary status, Barton's appears quite permanent on Merrimack Common, seen here looking north on Elm Street sometime between the Merchants' Exchange and Varick fires. In fact, the store's location defied the agreement made with Amoskeag when it deeded land for city parks in the 19th century, which stipulated that no roads or buildings ever be constructed within the parks' bounds. After Amoskeag's demise, permanent structures were allowed to exist.

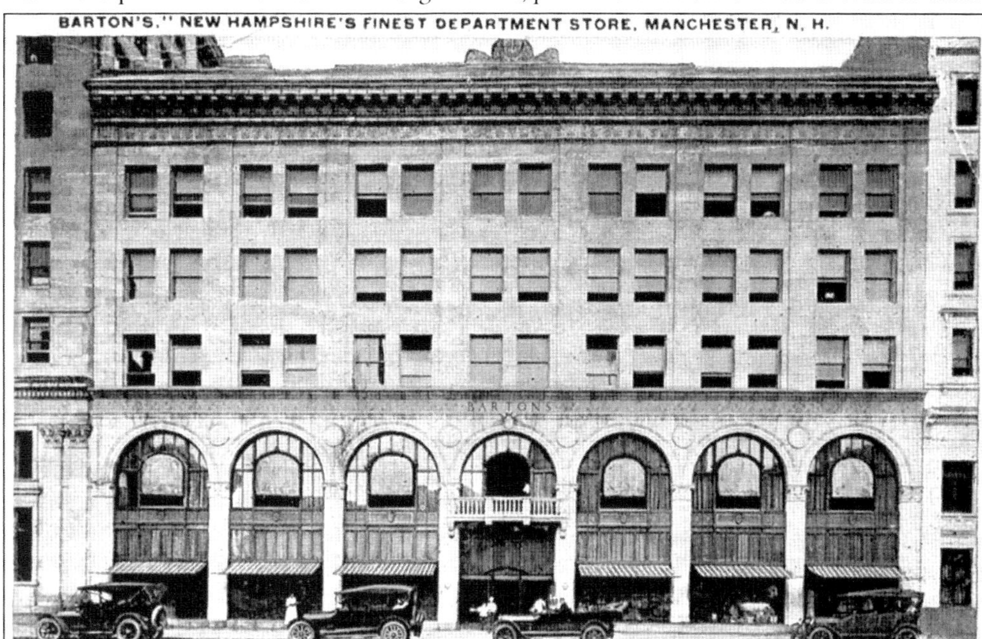

By 1916, Folsom's had moved in across Elm Street, while Barton's returned to its original site in a new structure that, along with the new Merchants' Bank Building, complemented the architecture of their neighbor to the north, the Amoskeag Bank Building. Leavitt's Department Store later replaced Barton's. Both Leavitt's and the former Merchants' Bank were demolished in 1979–1980.

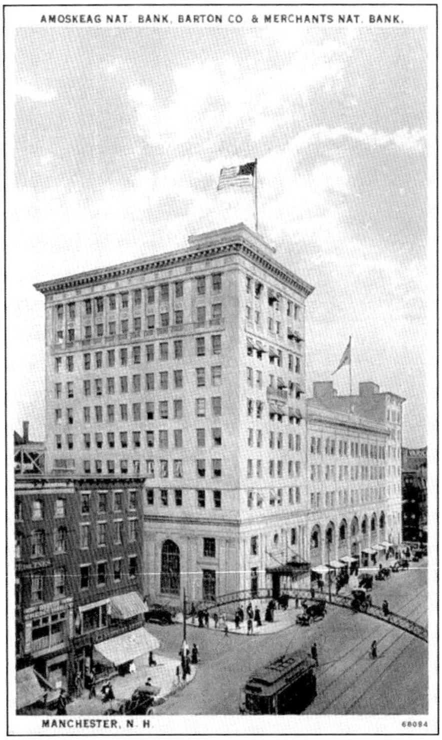

Between 1912 and 1914, Manchester residents witnessed the construction of what was, up to then, downtown's tallest, most modern, and, fortunately, most fireproof structure, the 10-story Amoskeag Bank Building, located at the southeast corner of Elm and Hanover Streets. Its construction was nearly completed when it suffered minimal damage during the Merchants' Exchange fire. The Amoskeag Bank opened in April 1914. By 1916, the entire block had been rebuilt.

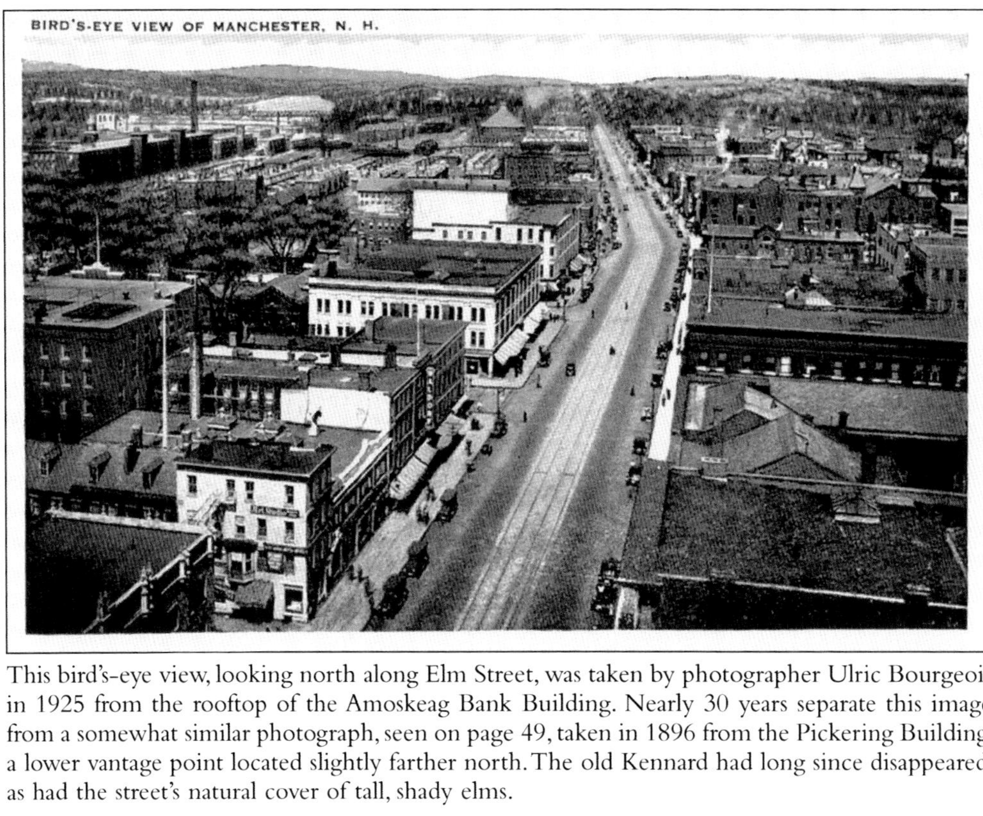

This bird's-eye view, looking north along Elm Street, was taken by photographer Ulric Bourgeois in 1925 from the rooftop of the Amoskeag Bank Building. Nearly 30 years separate this image from a somewhat similar photograph, seen on page 49, taken in 1896 from the Pickering Building, a lower vantage point located slightly farther north. The old Kennard had long since disappeared, as had the street's natural cover of tall, shady elms.

Four

Exploring the East Side

Early on, besides settlements at Derryfield Centre and Amoskeag Falls, the East Side remained largely forest or farmland. Subsequently, mixed residential and business clusters, named either for settlers or contemporary residents, began dotting the landscape: Janesville, Towlesville, Hallsville, Bakersville, Youngsville, and Goffe's Falls. Still, forest and farmland lay between villages, which were connected by roads. Streets that today run diagonally are usually remnants of those roads that were done away with by Amoskeag's 1838 street grid and by later developments.

By the 1840s, residential areas arose near downtown, with the wealthy living within the bounds of Bridge, Chestnut, Hanover, and Union Streets. Eventually, as downtown expanded and the neighborhoods became more middle class and working class, wealthier residents built new homes farther north.

During Amoskeag's early years, its much-desired corporation housing was open only to U.S. natives and to British-born workers at the management and skilled labor levels, thus causing unskilled immigrants to seek alternative housing. Consequently, ethnic neighborhoods formed, at first just east of Union Station, where immigrants arrived, and later out toward the east, southeast, and southern areas, which have since become largely middle-class neighborhoods. The area bounded by Hanover, Chestnut, Auburn, and Maple Streets has often been the first stop for many immigrants, beginning in the 1840s and continuing today, and has therefore remained consistently ethnic. Its population has included Irish, Québécois, Eastern Europeans, Middle Easterners, Latinos, Africans, and Asians. It continues to be a neighborhood rich with the smells of ethnic foods and the sounds of various languages and music.

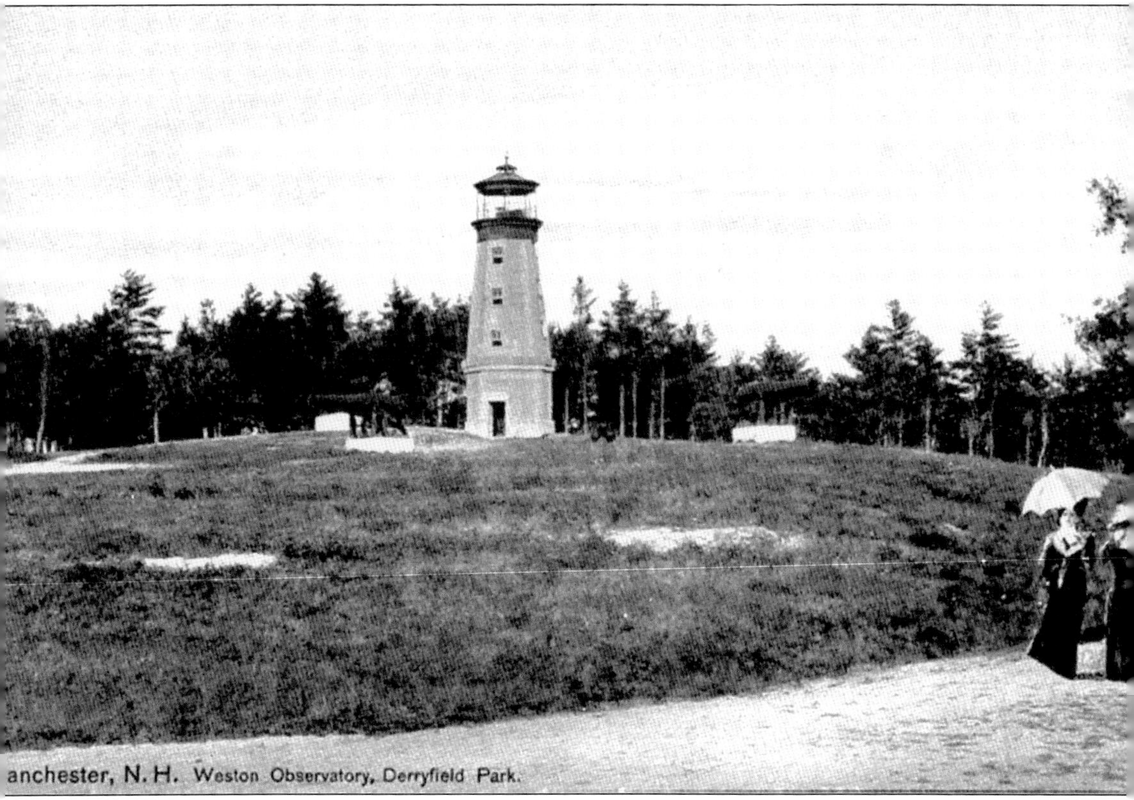

Former mayor and New Hampshire governor James A. Weston, who died in 1895, bequeathed $5,000 to his hometown for the construction of an observatory. It was to be built "for the advancement of science, for educational purposes, and for the use, enjoyment, benefit, and mental improvement of the inhabitants of Manchester." From its opening in 1897 until World War II, Weston Observatory offered visitors atop Oak Hill in Derryfield Park a splendid view of Manchester and other parts of New Hampshire. Later deemed unsafe, it remained closed and continued to deteriorate. From 1968 to 1977, the Weston Observatory Restoration Committee, a citizens' group led by local carpenters' union official and New Hampshire state senator Louis-Israël Martel, raised funds from private individuals, businesses, and organizations in order to rehabilitate the historic structure. Various labor unions and businesses donated work hours and materials to the project. On September 11, 1977, the City of Manchester retook possession of Weston Observatory and rededicated it, naming a new street leading to it Louis-Israël Martel Drive. It has since reopened intermittently.

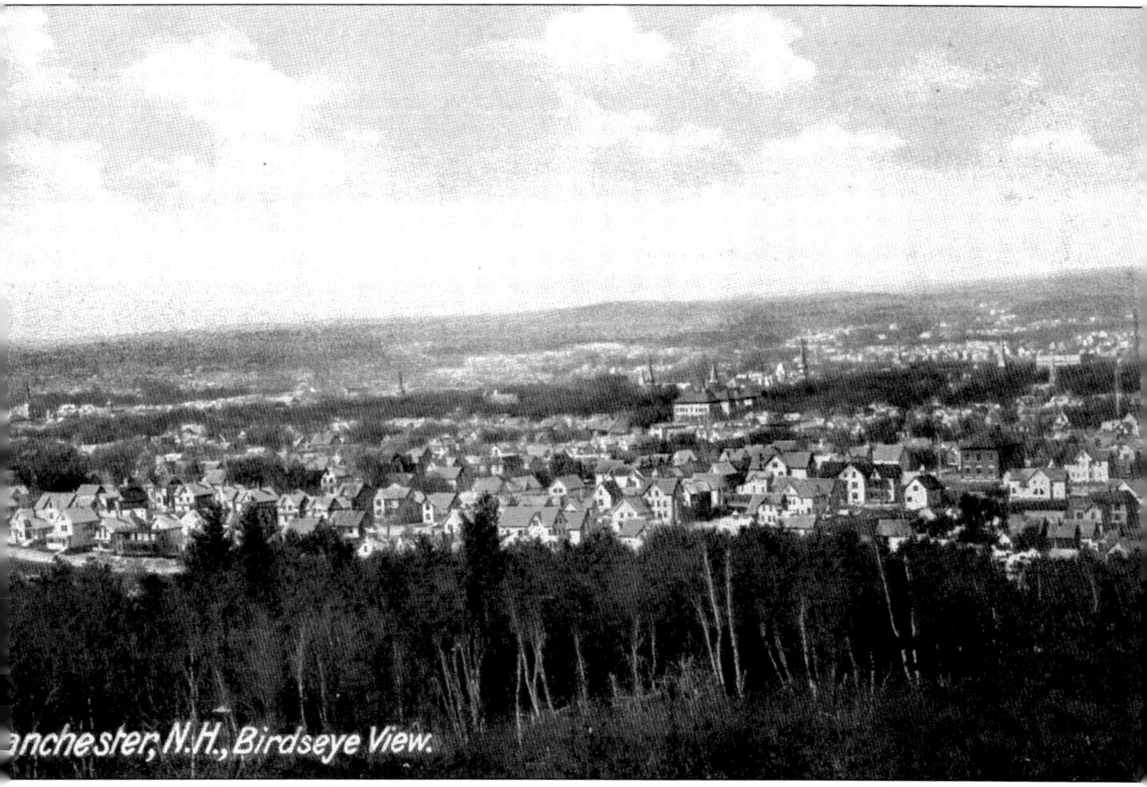

The opening of Weston Observatory in 1897 gave average Manchesterites a bird's-eye view of their city as they had never before experienced. Using a photographer's loupe, readers can best appreciate what photographer John G. Ellinwood saw. Some of the structures still exist today, while others have long since disappeared from the city's skyline. Among the church steeples are, from left to right, those of St. Augustin's, St. Anne's, Merrimack Street Baptist, First Congregational, First Unitarian, First Baptist, St. Joseph's Cathedral, and Grace Episcopal. Also visible are St. Agnes Boys' School, Central High School's Classical Building, the Post Office Building, the Pearl Street School, the old Kennard, the Amoskeag's great West Side boiler house chimney, and the Ash Street School. Despite its listing on the National Register of Historic Places, Weston Observatory has, in recent years, fallen back into disrepair and is currently the object of a new restoration effort. Should this latest project be successful, it will eventually allow today's residents to see how much their city has changed since 1897 or even since 1977.

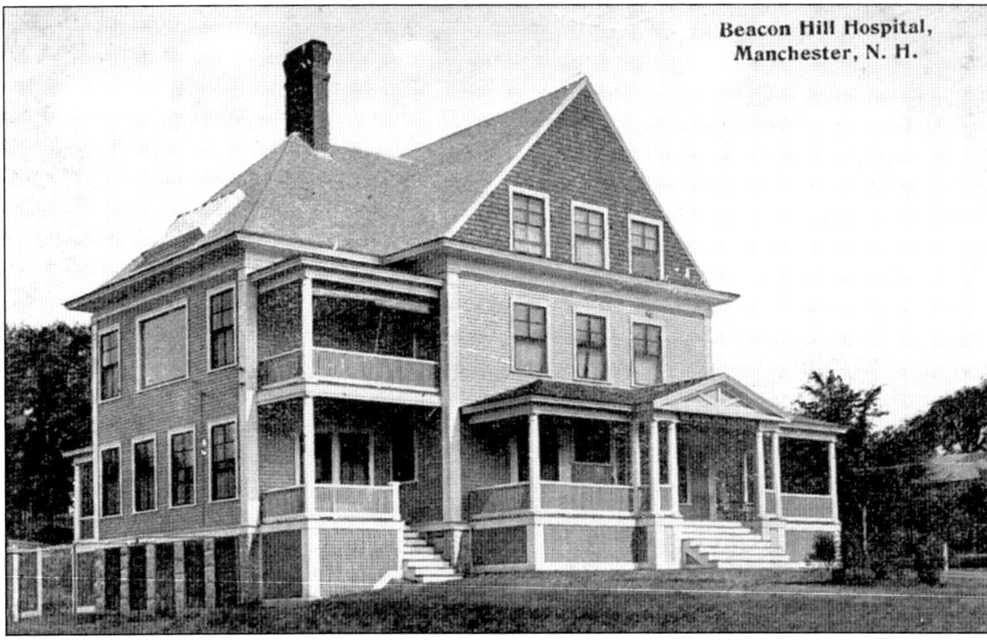

From the late 19th century to the mid-20th century, besides its larger hospitals, Manchester had several smaller, privately owned neighborhood hospitals and clinics of various sorts. Located near the northeast corner of East High and Belmont Streets, the Beacon Hill Hospital was one such facility, which operated for nearly 20 years beginning about 1908. Since its closing, the building has undergone significant exterior changes, and it now serves as a residence.

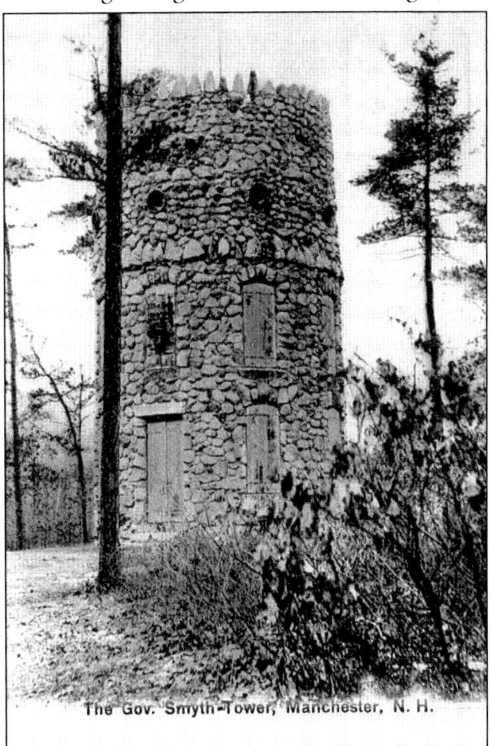

In 1888, former governor Frederick Smyth erected Smyth Tower on his land near the top of Smyth Road. Renovated in 1938–1939 by the Works Progress Administration and donated to the city by Smyth's widow, Marion, it became an amateur radio station. After World War II, Smyth's estate donated the land to the U.S. government for the Veterans' Hospital. The Smyth Tower has been listed on the National Register of Historic Places since 1978.

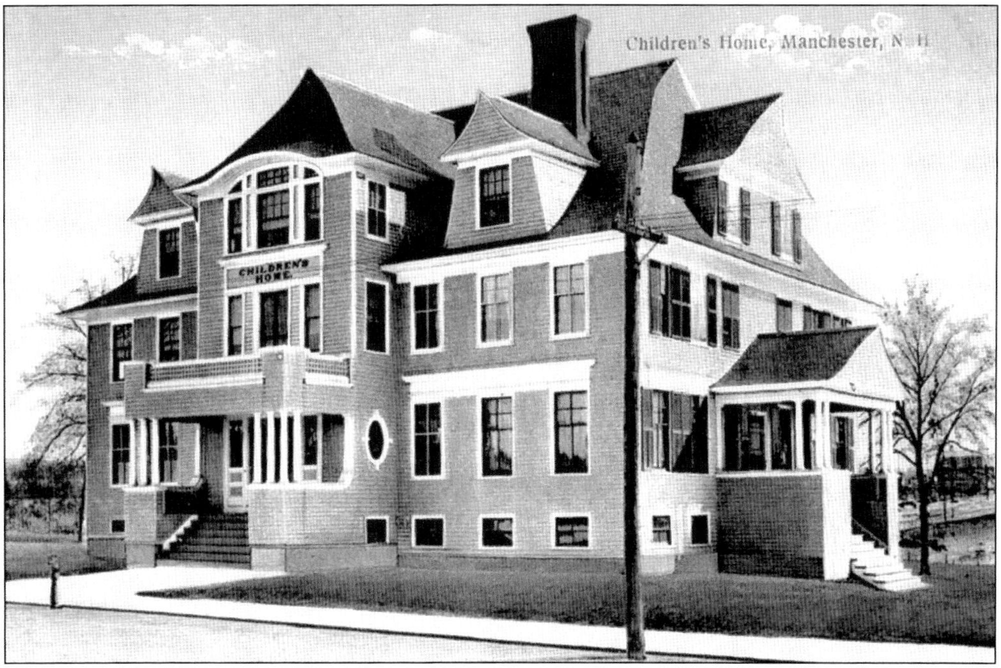

Established in 1884 "for indigent and neglected Protestant children," the Manchester Children's Home found a permanent location at 135 Webster Street in 1894. Partially demolished and rebuilt in the mid-1970s, it is now called Webster House, a temporary home for children who cannot live with their parents. In a Thanksgiving 1914 postcard greeting to her cousin, a Manchester woman wrote, "We might be thankful when so many are homeless."

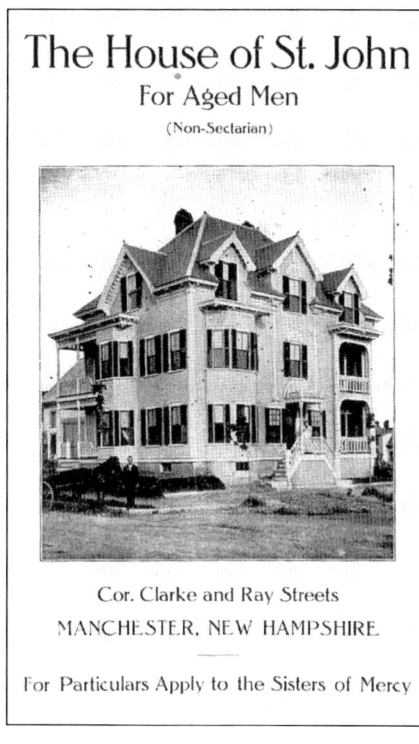

For roughly 45 years beginning in 1909, the Sisters of Mercy operated the House of St. John for Aged Men at 151 Ray Street. Proof of its non-sectarian policy of admittance, as herein advertised, was its harboring of Charlie Lambert, the Hermit of Mosquito Pond, during his last two years of life. Although he escaped to his beloved woods twice, the nuns succeeded in converting him to Roman Catholicism.

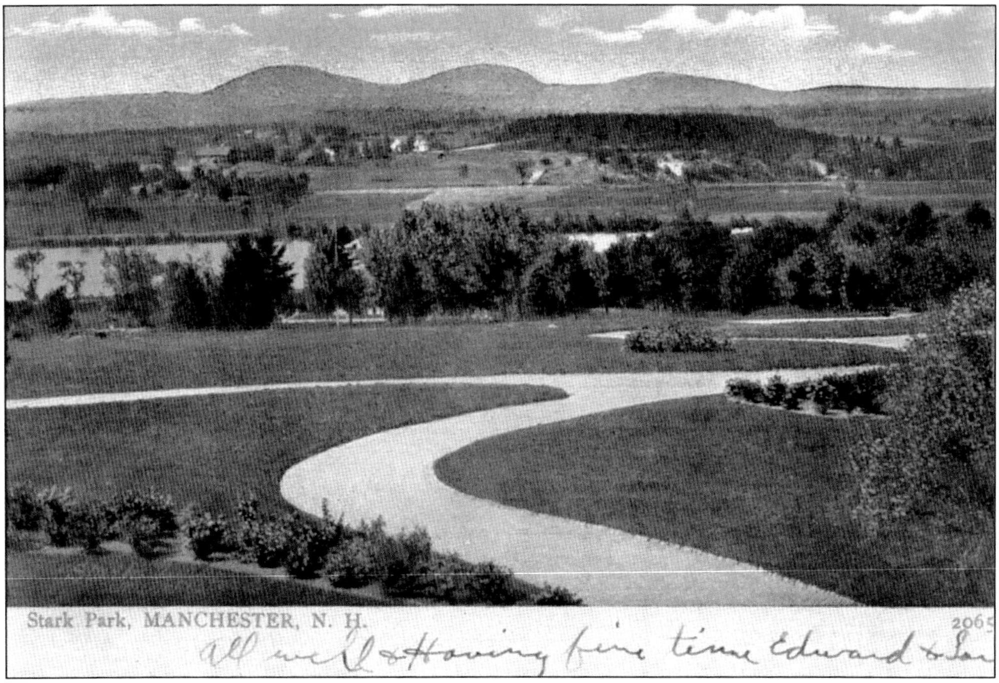

For more than a century, Manchester residents have enjoyed strolling, riding, and picnicking in Stark Park. Located along River Road on land that originally belonged to Archibald Stark's 800-acre farm, it not only contains the family cemetery but also an equestrian statue of Gen. John Stark by Richard Recchia, erected in 1948. Today, trees block the view looking west toward the Merrimack River and Uncanoonuc Mountains, seen here about 1895.

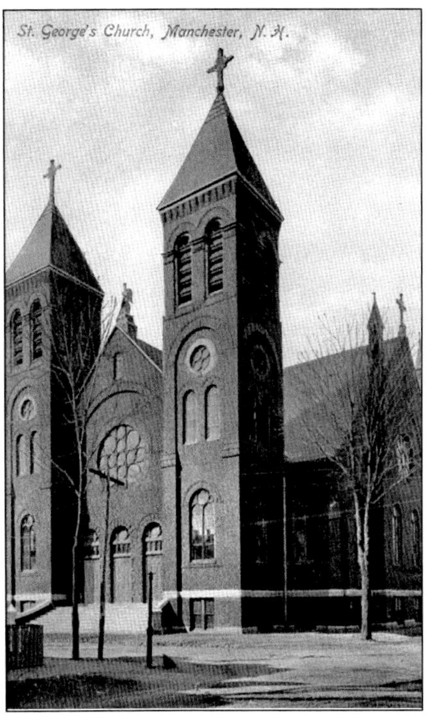

Located at the southwest corner of Pine and Orange Streets, l'Église Saint-Georges, or St. George Church, was completed in 1893, three years after the founding of the parish, which served French-speaking Roman Catholics living north of Hanover Street. The original church burned during the night of December 20–21, 1952. The parish closed on November 23, 2002, its newer church having recently become home to the Diocesan Museum.

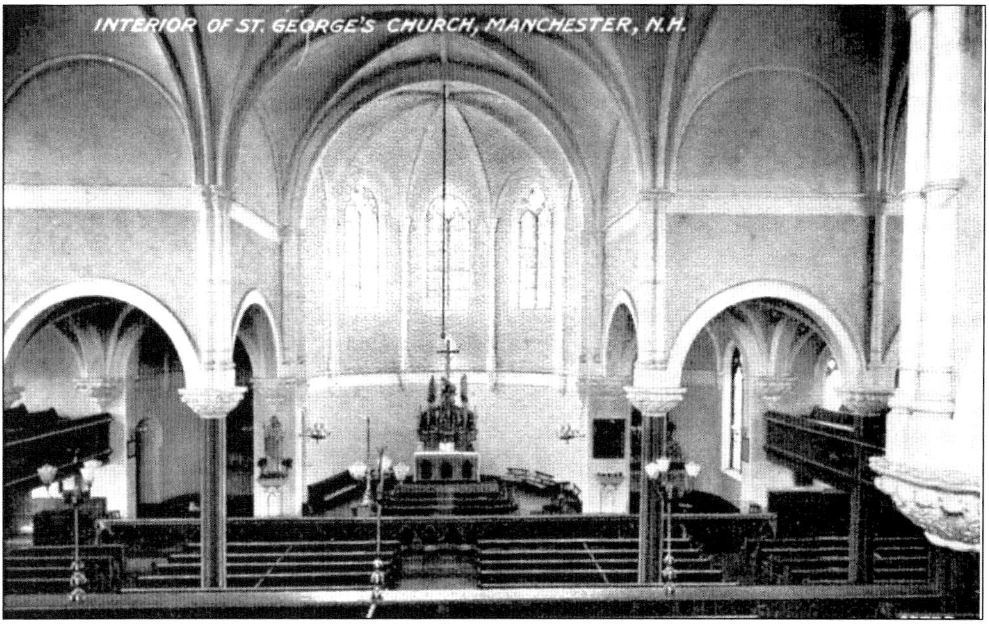

Literary connections abound in old St. George. The church was the location of the christening of a famous Manchester-born Montréal poet, Robert Choquette, on April 23, 1905; the wedding of Alfred DeRepentigny and Laurette Royer by Rev. Joseph Ernest Vaccarest on May 12, 1924; the christening of their daughter, Marie Grace, on September 10, 1924; and Grace's wedding to George Metalious on February 27, 1943. Reverend Vaccarest was the uncle of Ernest Hebert, author of *The Dogs of March* and other novels.

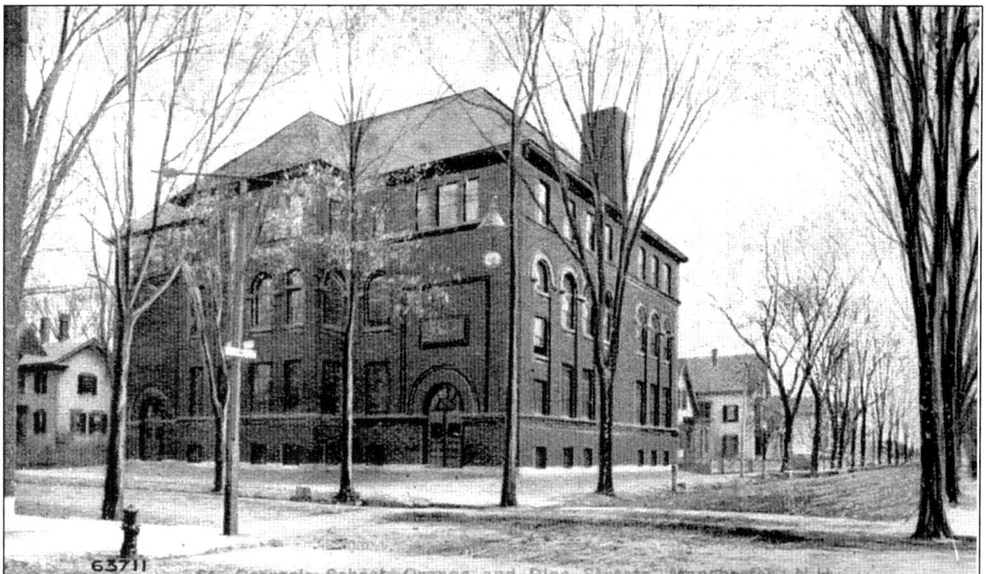

L'École Saint-Georges (1898–1970) typified the New England Franco-American bilingual parochial school system, wherein students arrived in first grade already fluent in French and English. The English half of the school day consisted of subject matter required by the state, while the French half involved reading, grammar, and the most sacred subject, *le catéchisme*. Having been adapted into the École Saint-Georges Apartments, the building is on the National Register of Historic Places.

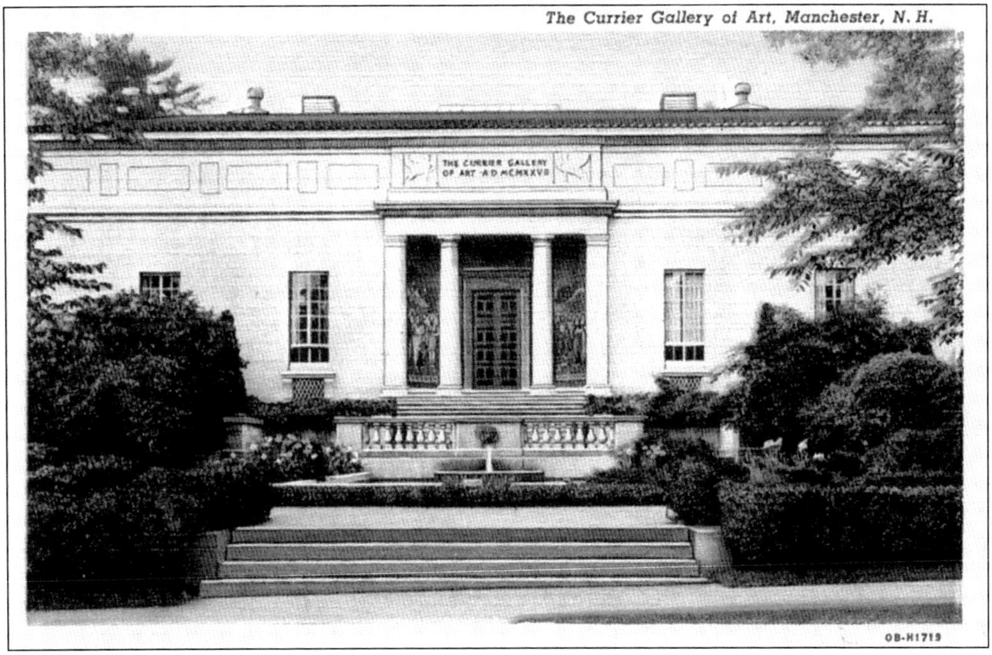

Opened in 1929 on the former estate of Gov. Moody Currier, the Currier Gallery of Art (now the Currier Museum of Art) is among the finest institutions of its type. It features the best works of artists both locally and internationally renowned, including the Zimmerman House, one of two Manchester homes designed by Frank Lloyd Wright. Both the Currier's original building and the Zimmerman House are on the National Register of Historic Places.

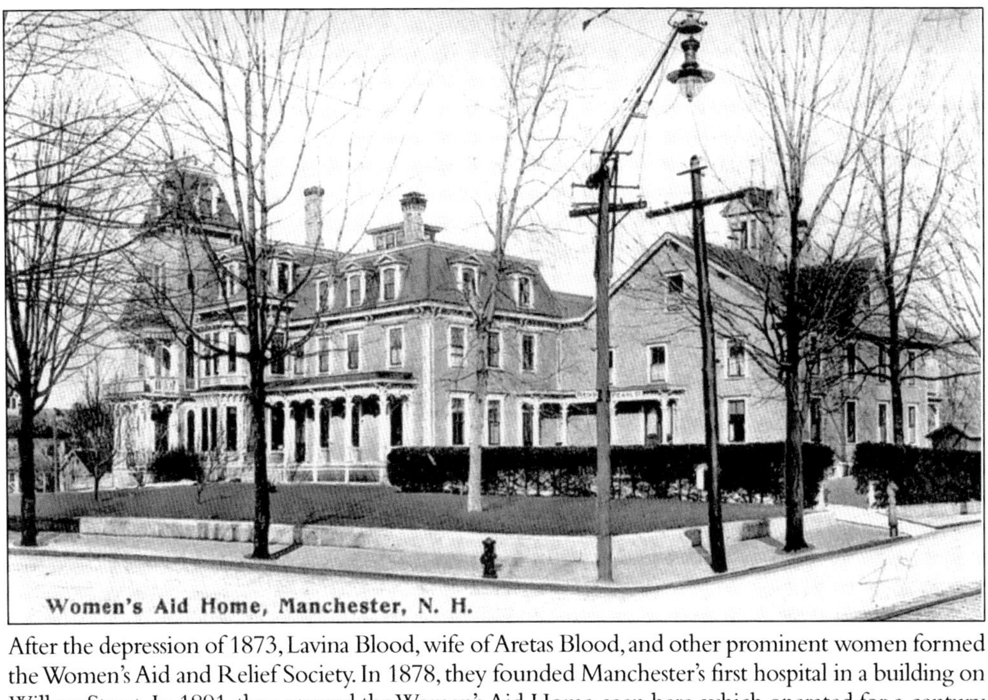

After the depression of 1873, Lavina Blood, wife of Aretas Blood, and other prominent women formed the Women's Aid and Relief Society. In 1878, they founded Manchester's first hospital in a building on Willow Street. In 1891, they opened the Women's Aid Home, seen here, which operated for a century at 180 Pearl Street. A newer building, now the Currier Art Center, replaced it in 1951.

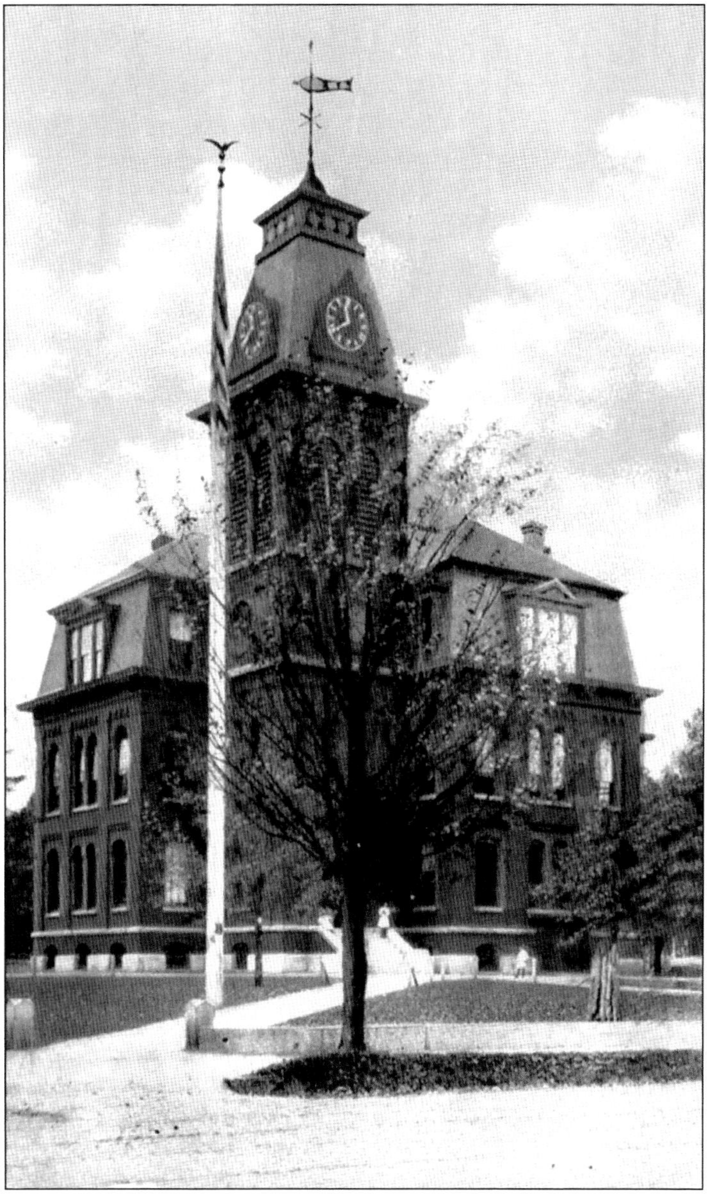

Completed in 1874 according to plans by architect George W. Stevens, the Ash Street School was reputedly the first in the country built on a cruciform design. It featured classrooms with windows on three sides, electric bells, and the only clock tower of its size in New Hampshire with a gravity escapement and compensating pendulum. In 1876, these characteristics earned it an award as a model school building at the U.S. Centennial Exposition in Philadelphia. Several generations of Manchester children studied within its walls, including a girl named Grace DeRepentigny, who wrote her first stories there for English class. She grew up to become Grace Metalious, author of four novels, including the best-selling novel of its time, *Peyton Place*, which was published in 1956 and has sold 10 million copies. Her autobiographical novel, *No Adam in Eden* (1963), prominently features "the corner of Bridge and Ash Streets," site of the Ash Street School. Listed on the National Register of Historic Places since the mid-1970s, the school now serves as the administration building for the Manchester School Department.

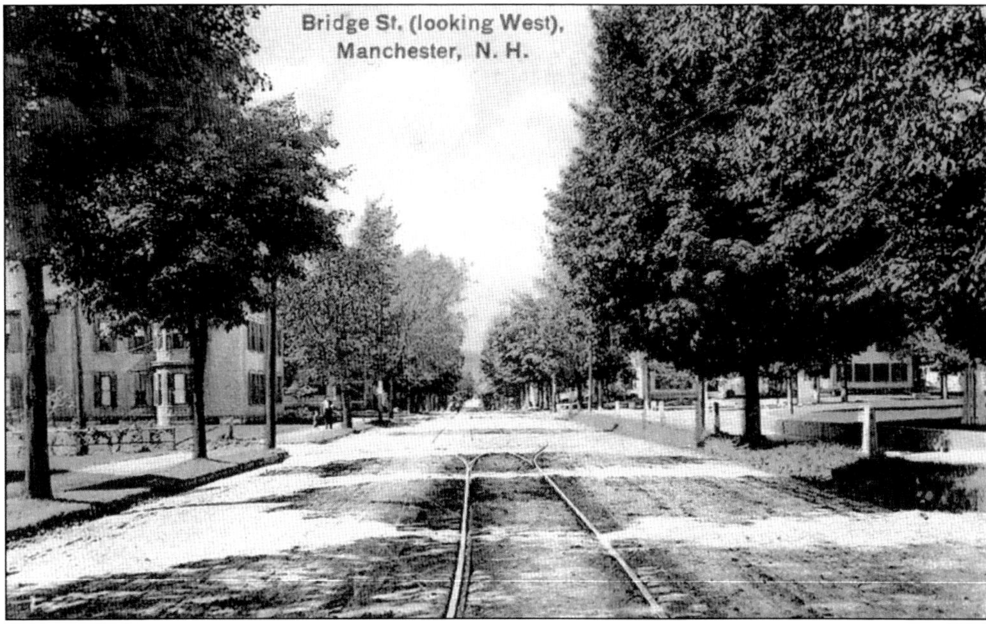

Stepping away from the grounds of the Ash Street School to stand in the middle of Bridge Street, seen here looking west toward Ash Street from the intersection of Maple Street, was a much safer experience about 1910 than it would be in today's heavy traffic. Nonetheless, the presence of trolley car tracks shows that Bridge Street has served as one of the city's primary avenues for many decades.

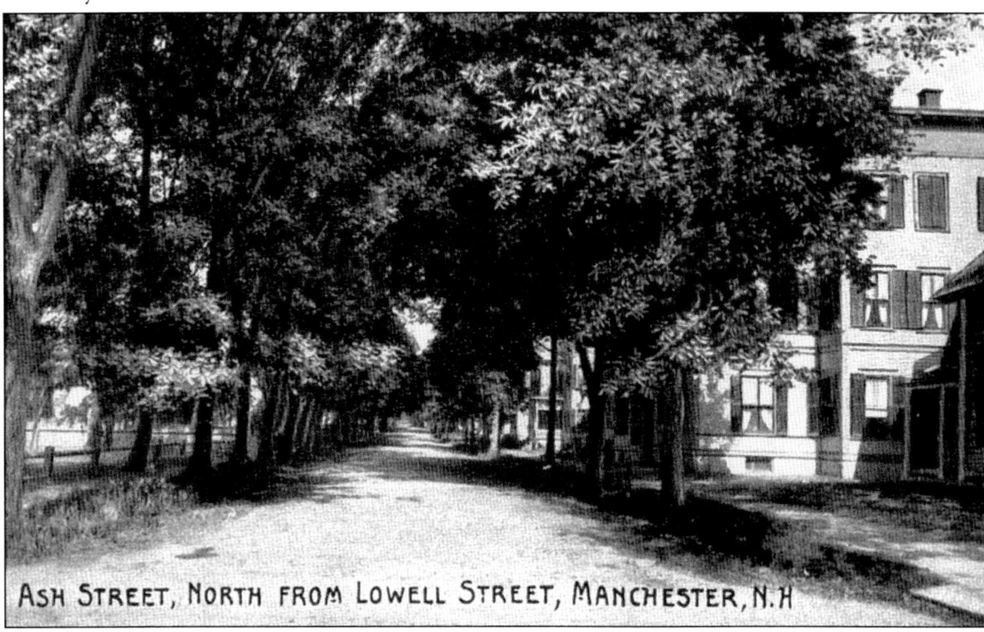

Ash Street, seen here looking north from the intersection of Lowell Street in 1910, remains a quiet side street today, except for brief periods when students from nearby Central High School arrive and leave. In her first-floor apartment in the large house at right, 51 Ash Street, Georgianna DeRepentigny McConnell hosted the wedding reception for her niece, Grace DeRepentigny, and George Metalious on February 27, 1943.

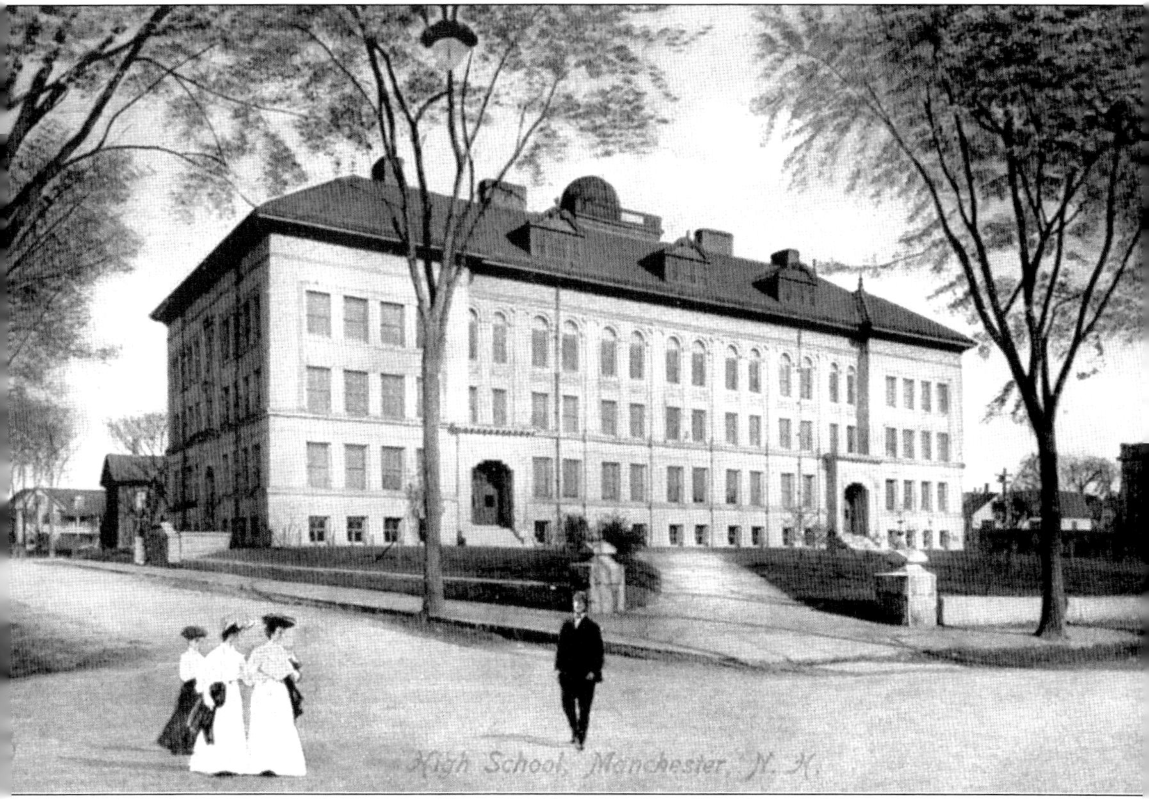

Known simply as "the High School" from its birth at the northeast corner of Lowell and Chestnut Streets in 1846 through its first 80 years, Manchester Central High School moved into a red-brick edifice on Beech Street north of Concord Street in 1867. In 1896, architect William M. Butterfield drew plans for a larger yellow-brick high school immediately to the north, and the old school was demolished to make room for the new building's front lawn. The façade of the new structure, which is called the Classical Building, bears the names of some of the world's greatest minds. Other individuals with familiar names, including Revlon cosmetics cofounders Joseph and Charles Revson, *Peyton Place* author Grace Metalious, and, more recently, actor-comedian Adam Sandler, once walked the halls of Central High. It is where Metalious, signing "Grace de Repentigny," published her first short story, "The Fuller Brush Man," in the *Oracle*, Central's literary magazine, in November 1942. Undoubtedly, the Central alumnus who drew the most inspiration from the school's ambiance was Bob Montana, class of 1940-A, who immortalized his alma mater as the fictional Riverdale High in his comic strip, *Archie*.

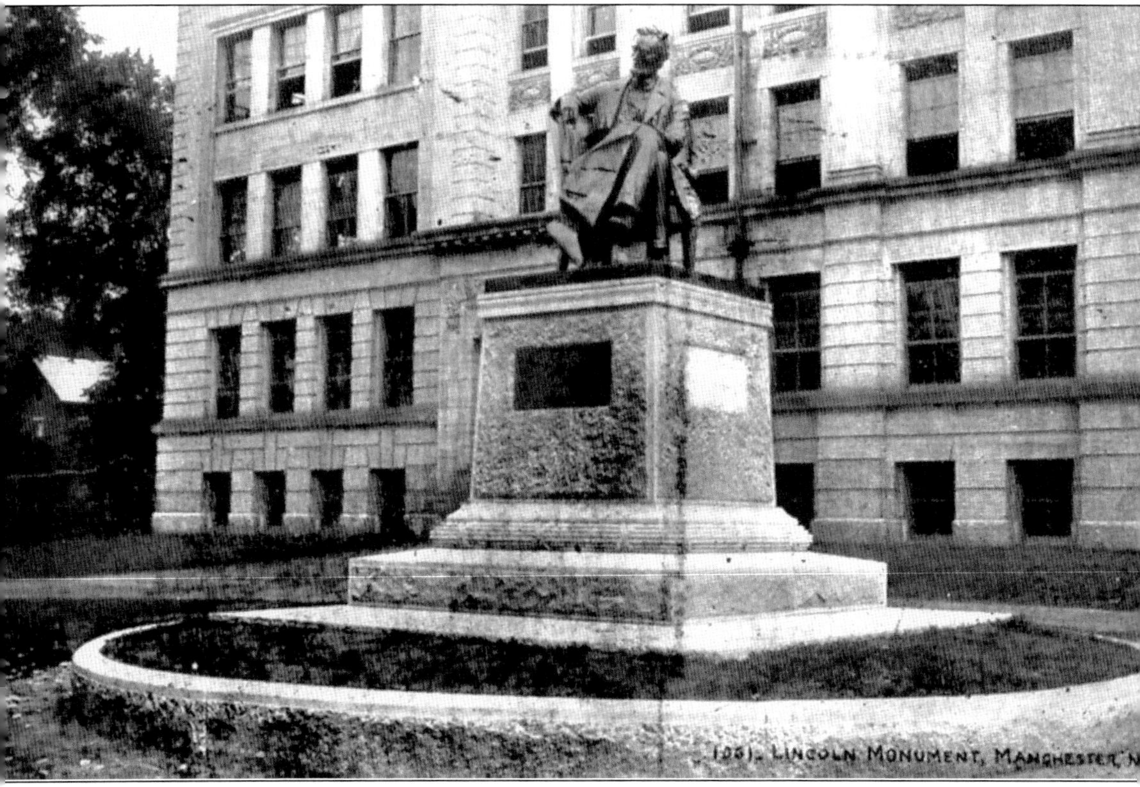

The career of sculptor John Rogers took root during his years as a draftsman in the Amoskeag Machine Shop, 1851–1857. While rooming with the family of his friend and coworker, Edwin P. Richardson, in their Middle Street Amoskeag corporation tenement, Rogers used clay from the banks of the Merrimack River at Hooksett to mold his earliest sculptures. He later won national recognition for his "Rogers' Groups" of table-size sculptures depicting everyday American life. In 1895, he presented the city of Manchester with a large plaster statue of a seated Abraham Lincoln. For many years, it remained in the old City Library on Franklin Street. After Rogers died in 1904, his friend Richardson, Lincoln's guide during his visit of the Amoskeag Millyard in 1860, inspired his companions at the GAR Louis Bell Post to have Lincoln's statue cast in bronze and placed on the grounds at Central High. The statue was dedicated on Memorial Day 1910. In 2004, new construction at Central included relocating Lincoln's statue on the renovated plaza. He now looks to the west rather than the south.

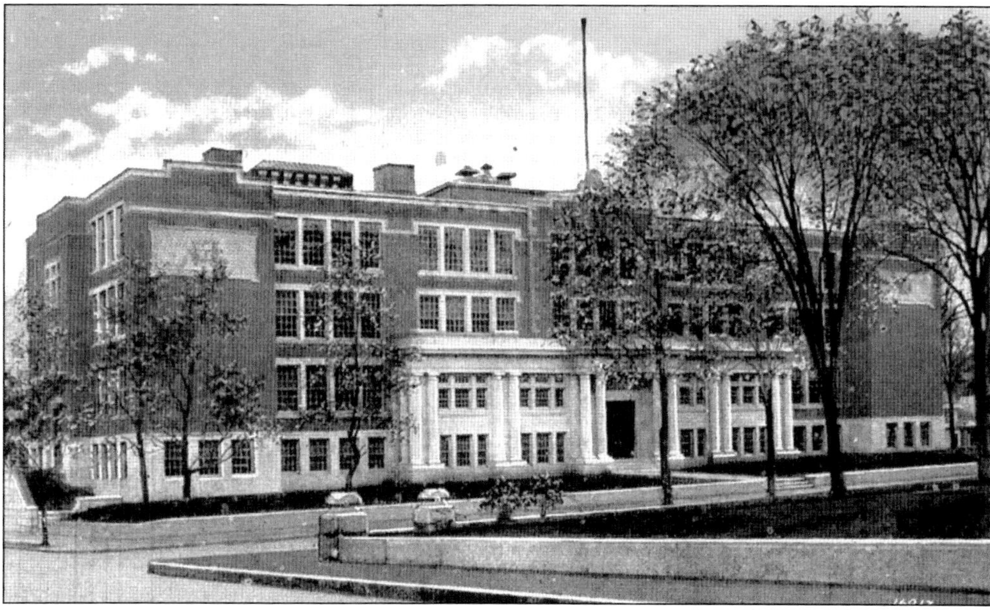

When it opened in September 1922, the Practical Arts School added another chapter to the long history of Manchester Central High School. Other than classrooms, it houses the Practical Arts Auditorium, where students and the general public have for decades enjoyed musical and theatrical performances of every type. Until recently, a tunnel connected this building to the Classical Building.

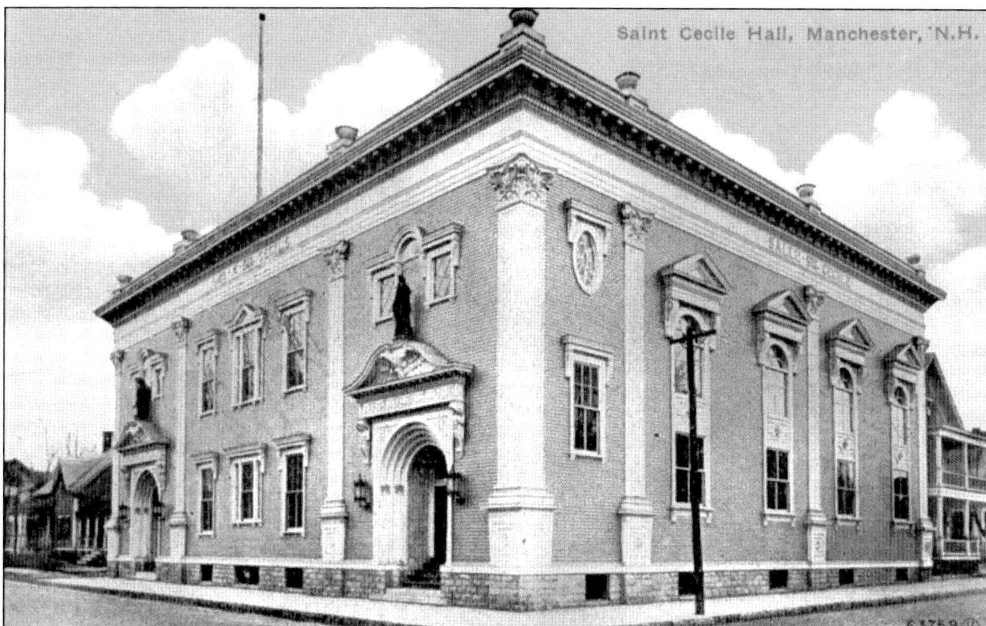

Saint Cecile Hall, Manchester, N.H.

Opened in 1911, Salle Sainte-Cécile, or St. Cecilia's Hall, was named for the patron saint of musicians. It attracted not only parishioners of St. Augustin, to whom it belonged, but also Manchester's entire Franco-American community. Here, audiences enjoyed French-language concerts, operas, plays, and other artistic representations. Stripped of its ornate architectural features in the 1960s, it now houses the Police Department Athletic League and Cops 'N' Kids Together.

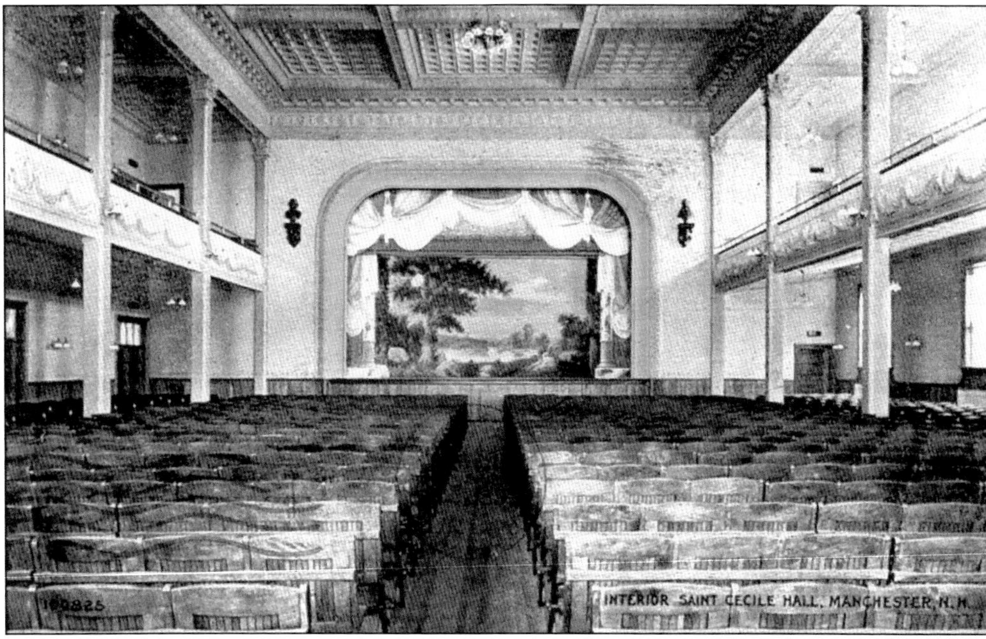

Salle Sainte-Cécile served as one of several venues for the annual Festival de la Bonne Chanson (Festival of the Good Song), a competition featuring choral groups representing each of the city's eight Franco-American parochial schools and others from surrounding towns. Many adults, now middle-aged or older, recall having had to sing in French before an audience filled with relatives, nuns, priests, and the general public.

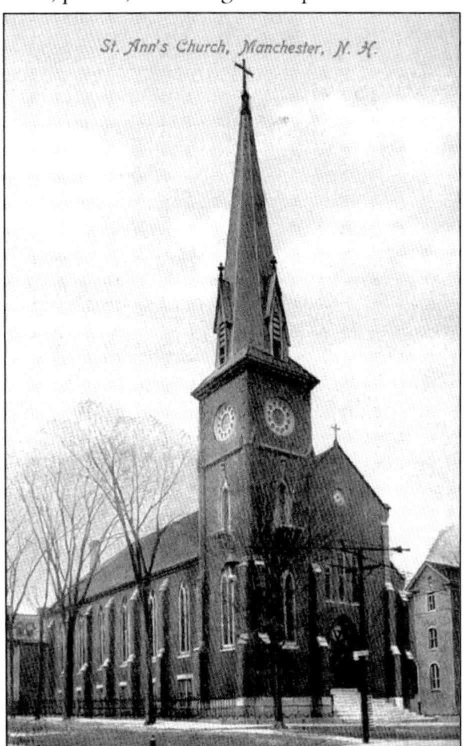

When the first St. Anne's Church, built in 1849–1850, became unsafe, the present structure, seen here at the southeast corner of Merrimack and Union Streets, replaced it in 1852. As Manchester's first Roman Catholic parish, it fell victim to the anti-Catholic Know-Nothing Movement. After a firemen's muster on July 4, 1854, rioters vandalized the church and nearly set it afire. Closed since 2003 due to needed repairs, its fate remains uncertain.

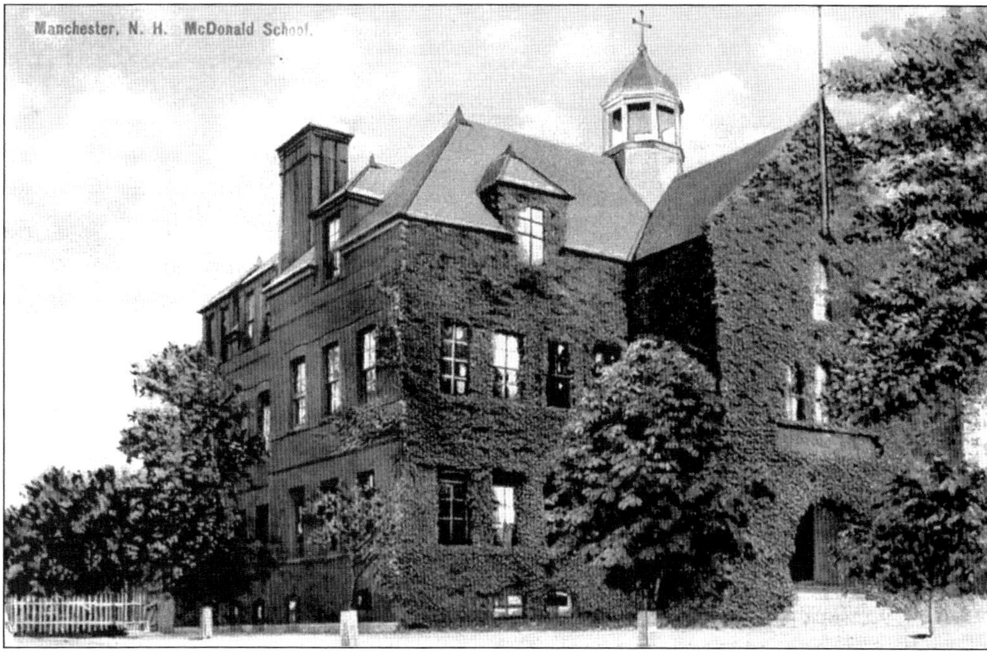

Opened in 1893 and named for St. Anne's founding pastor, Rev. William McDonald, the McDonald School stood on the southeast corner of Union and Laurel Streets. Originally a girls' school, it became coed when the boys' school, St. Agnes, on Cedar and Union Streets, was sold to the founders of the nearby Assumption of the Virgin Mary Greek Orthodox parish about 1941. The McDonald School burned on March 26, 1970.

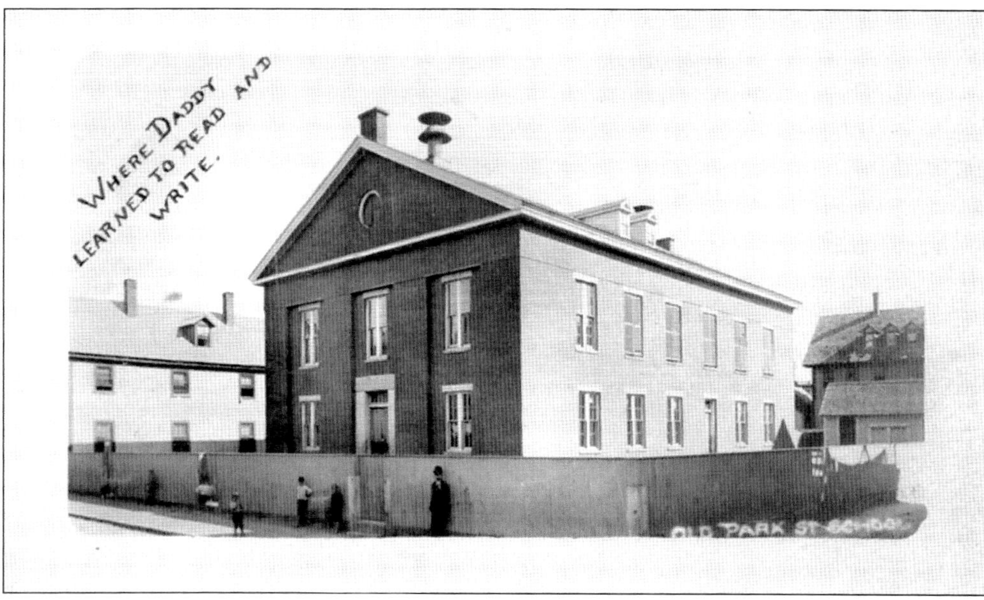

The Park Street School stood near Elm Street, on the present site of the Verizon Arena. Park Street was renamed Lake Avenue about 1886. In 1861, constitutional considerations notwithstanding, city officials gave exclusive use of the school to St. Anne's parish for a boys' school. From 1863 to 1868, taxpayers financed the salaries of principal Thomas Corcoran and the teachers, among them several Sisters of Mercy. Vacated in 1893, the school was demolished shortly thereafter.

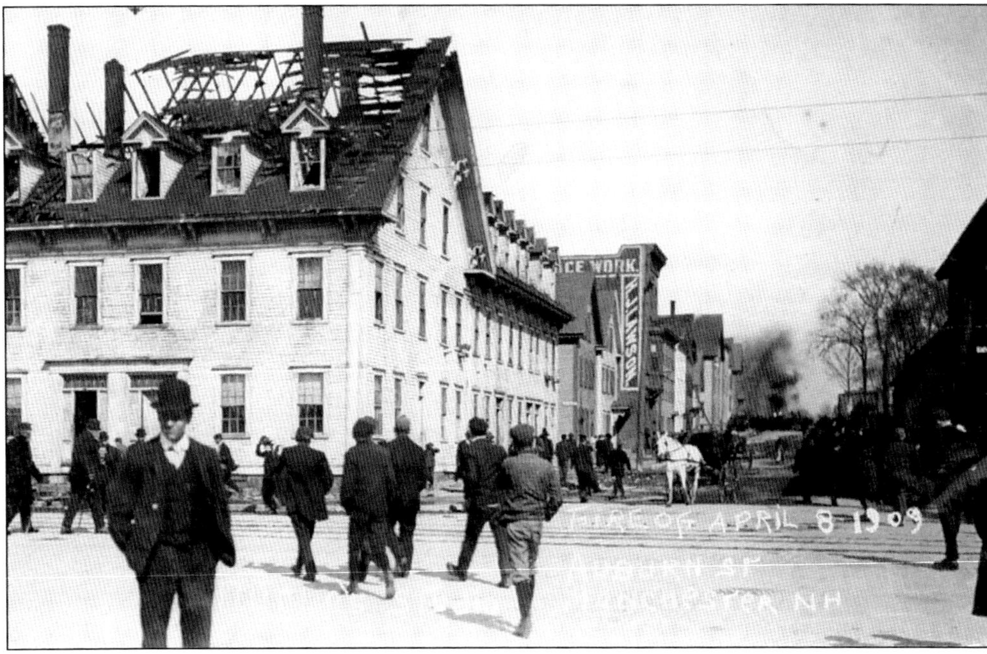

One of the city's biggest conflagrations occurred on April 8, 1909. Allegedly caused by a defective chimney, the fire broke out in the Auburn Block, seen here at the northeast corner of Elm and Auburn Streets. Fanned by strong winds and fed mostly by wooden structures, the flames spread and soon involved some 30 buildings within the area bounded by Elm, Auburn, Beech, and Cedar Streets.

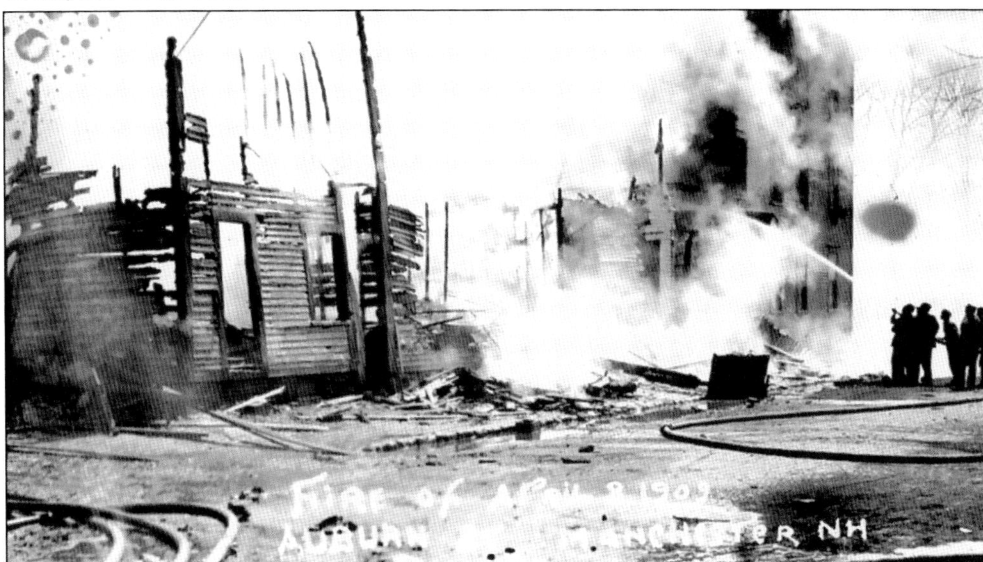

Although the *Manchester Union* reported that no one perished in the fire, hundreds lost their homes. As the flames spread, residents carried their belongings to Valley Cemetery or to Park Square, now Kalivas Park, to avoid pilferers who had struck elsewhere. Despite the disastrous ambiance, the *Union* wrote humorously of "strong rugged men carrying out things of little value," such as a toy piano and a parrot that kept repeating "Hello Bill" to its carrier.

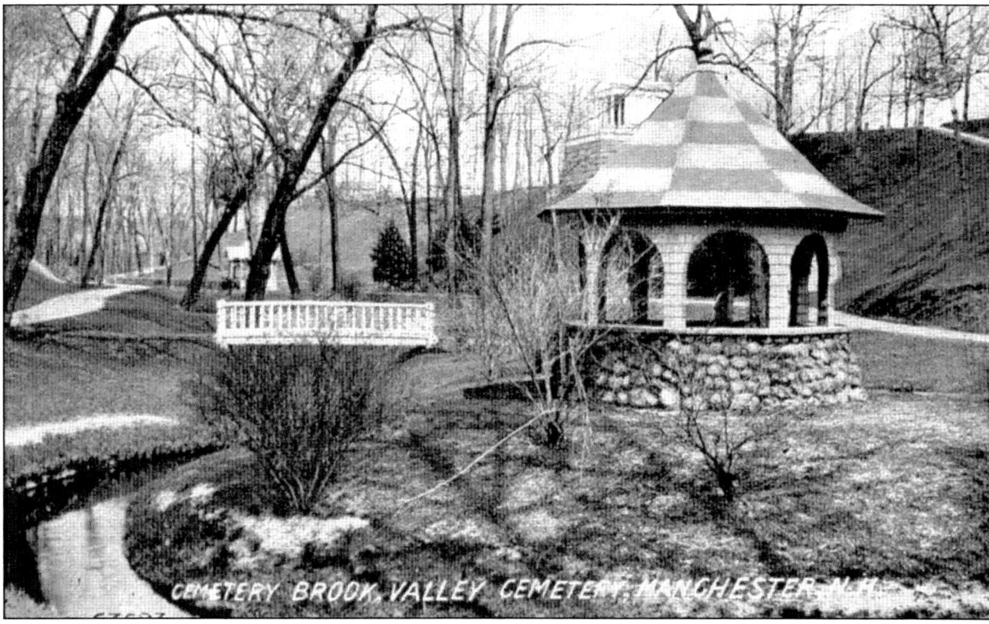

Although Manchester had several small graveyards, some dating from Colonial Derryfield, by 1841, recognizing the need for a larger burial ground, the Amoskeag offered 20 acres of woodland for Valley Cemetery. Inspired by such garden cemeteries as Mount Auburn in Cambridge and Père Lachaise in Paris, Valley Cemetery retains its Victorian ambiance, where visitors rambling along footpaths past age-old gravestones and mausolea seem to leave the 21st century for the 19th.

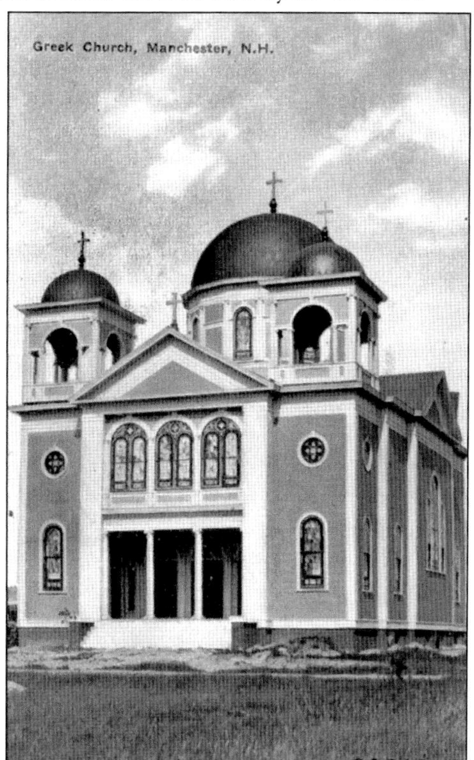

Having held services in various locations since the mid-1890s, Manchester's Greek American community welcomed its own house of worship, St. George Hellenic Orthodox Church, built "literally with the sweat of those first immigrants" in 1906–1907. Located at 97 Pine Street, it served until the opening in 1966 of a new St. George Greek Orthodox Church on Hanover and Kenney Streets, which became a cathedral in 1970. The old church was subsequently demolished.

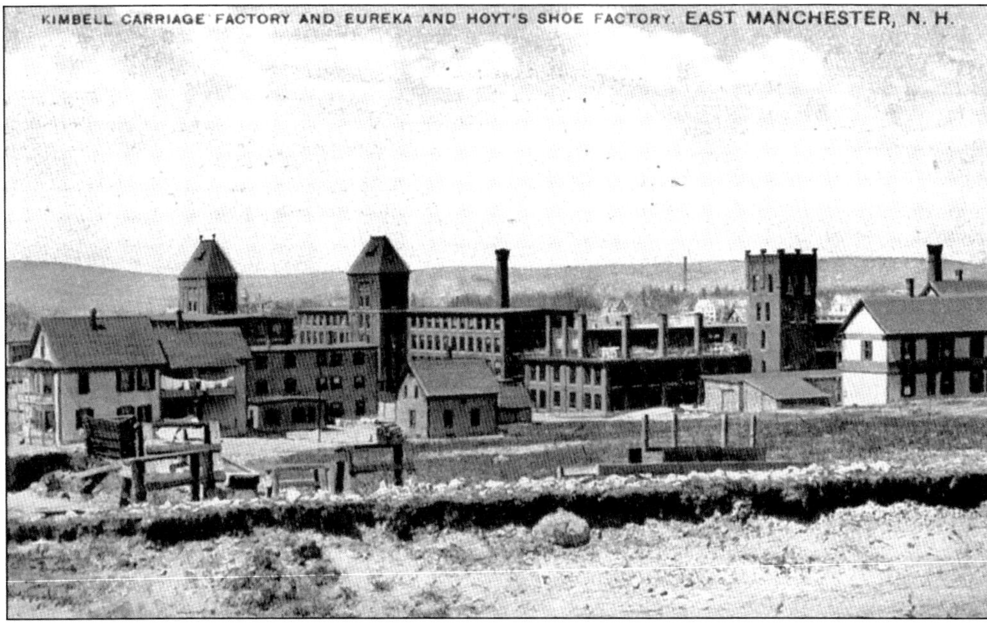

If textiles dominated other industries along the Merrimack River, shoes reigned in East Manchester's factory district. Although small-scale shoe manufacturing began in Manchester as early as the 1840s, the larger industrialized plants did not come into being until the 1880s and well into the 20th century. Seen here, looking northwest from Wilson and Somerville Streets, are the F. M. Hoyt Shoe Company, W. H. McElwain's Eureka Shoe Factory, and the Kimball Carriage Factory.

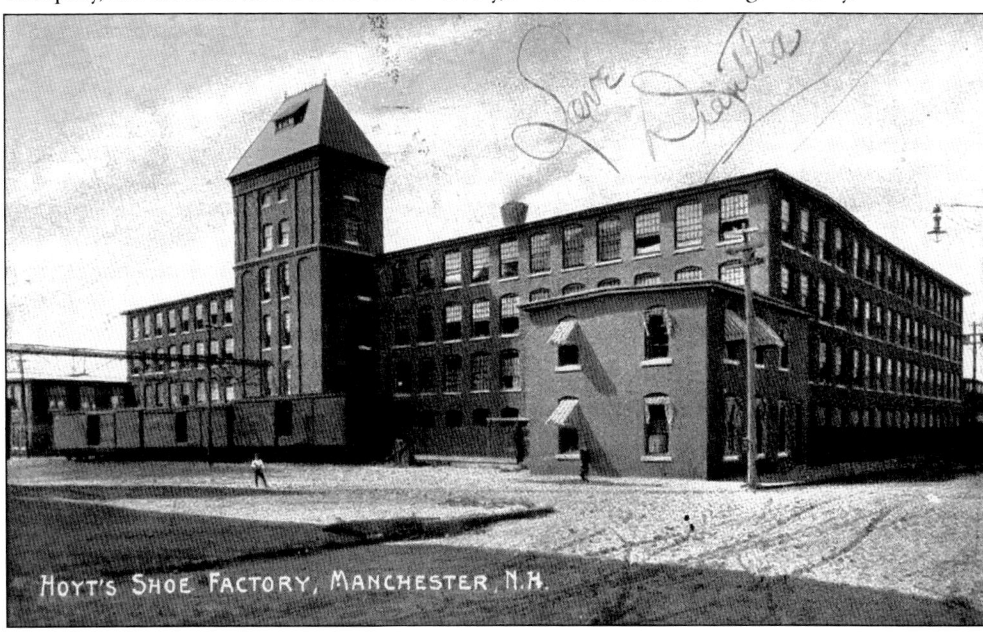

Francis M. Hoyt opened his F. M. Hoyt Shoe Company in 1892. It was constructed by the Queen City Land and Building Association, whose treasurer was Alonzo Elliott, a name connected with many such projects. The Hoyt was but one of several factories that sat on or near one of Manchester's best-known industrial intersections, Lincoln and Silver Streets. Today, the old factory has a renewed purpose as Twin Towers.

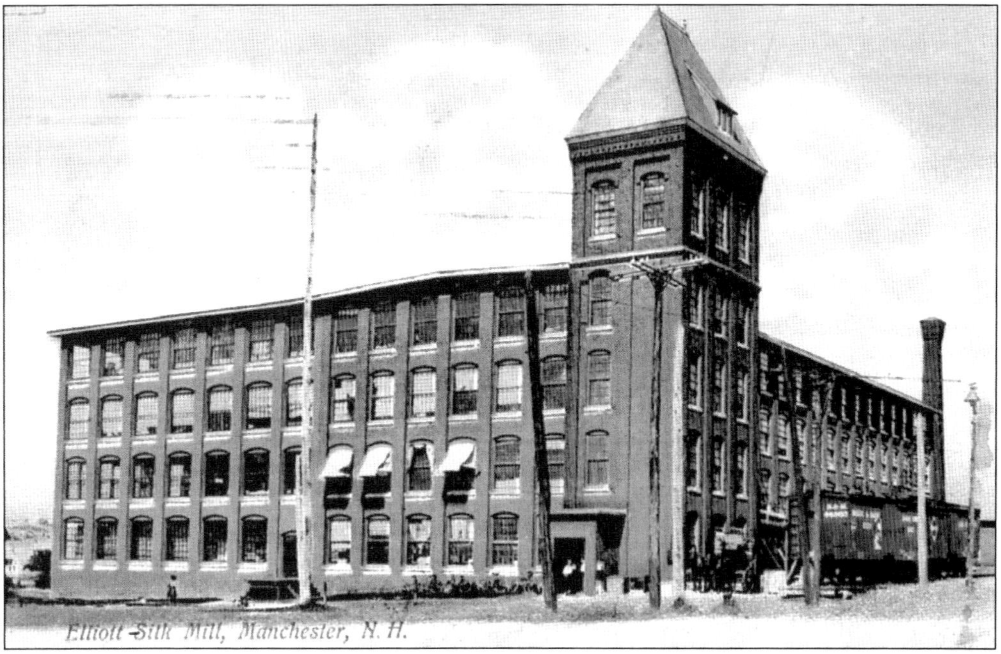

Incorporated in 1892 and named for its treasurer, Alonzo Elliott, the Elliott Manufacturing Company made underwear in its mill located at the northeast corner of Wilson and Valley Streets. Toward the end of World War II, it became the Wilson Brothers Elliott Manufacturing Division. It closed by 1947. From 1949 to 1998, the S. A. Felton Brush Company occupied the building, after which it was demolished to make room for a Walgreen's pharmacy.

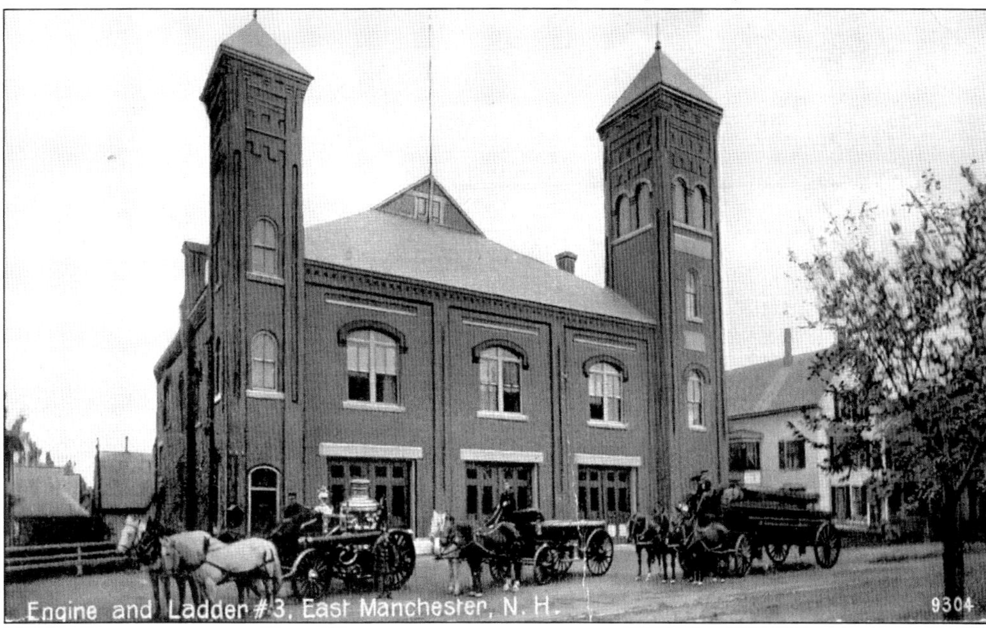

On February 8, 1888, having acquired a steam fire engine from Manchester Locomotive Works, members of Merrimack Hose Company No. 4 reorganized as Merrimack Steam Fire Engine Company No. 3 and moved into new quarters at 421 Lake Avenue. The station served until 1979, after which it sat vacant. On February 8, 2002, its 114th birthday, the station was destroyed by fire.

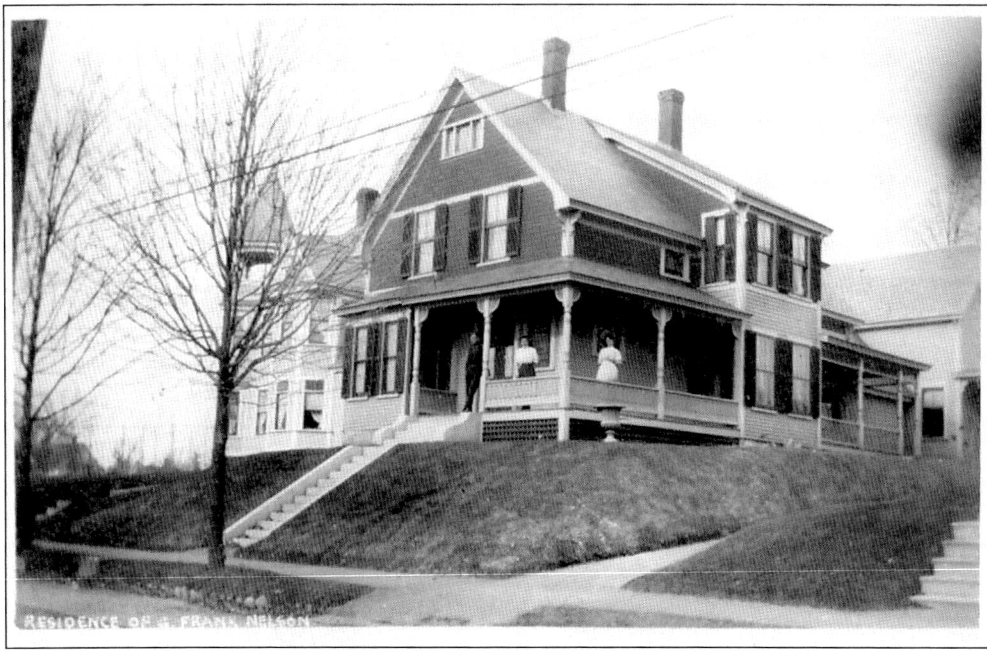

Here again is an example of private citizens having their own photographs printed as postcards. As the identification in the lower left-hand corner indicates, this was the residence of G. Frank Nelson at 516 Lake Avenue. He is listed in the Manchester city directory as a fireman and as a watchman for the post office. In 1910, his wife, Nellie, wrote a message inquiring about an aunt.

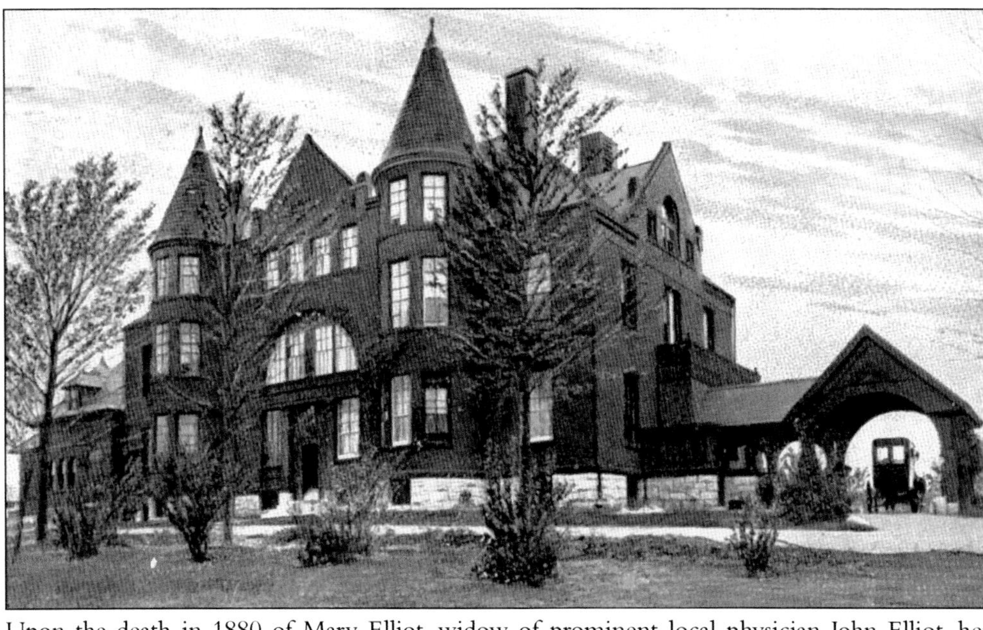

Upon the death in 1880 of Mary Elliot, widow of prominent local physician John Elliot, her will called for the establishment and maintenance of what today constitutes Manchester's oldest medical facility, Elliot Hospital. Incorporated in 1881 and constructed in 1888 on 27 hilltop acres in East Manchester, Elliot Hospital has developed into one of New Hampshire's best-equipped and most highly regarded hospitals. The original building survived until 1975.

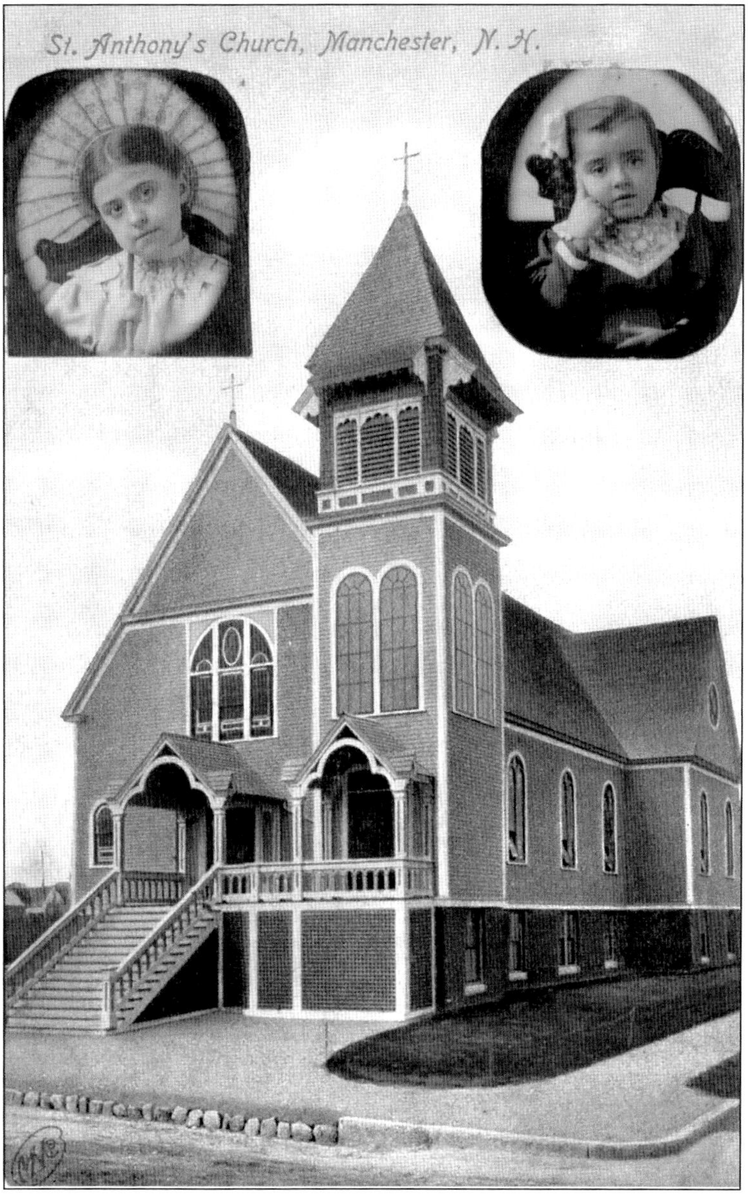

Founded in 1899 to serve East Manchester's ethnically mixed shoe-shop and factory district, Paroisse Saint-Antoine de Padoue, or St. Anthony Parish, took on a Franco-American identity in 1911 with the establishment of the nearby English-language parish of Our Lady of Perpetual Help. Originally built in 1900 on the west side of Belmont Street between Valley and Hayward, the church had neither a steeple nor a basement. In 1903, it was picked up and transported to a higher foundation at the southwest corner of Belmont and Silver Streets, where renovations included the addition of a steeple. With a larger church in use since 1955, the old wooden structure met its demise in 1967. Today, after the closing or merger of several of Manchester's eight Franco-American parishes, St. Anthony's offers the city's only Mass held totally in French. Here, a Manchester mother carefully glued tiny photographs of her daughters before sending this postcard to a relative in Worcester, Massachusetts, with a message in French: "Deign to accept the kisses of your little cousins."

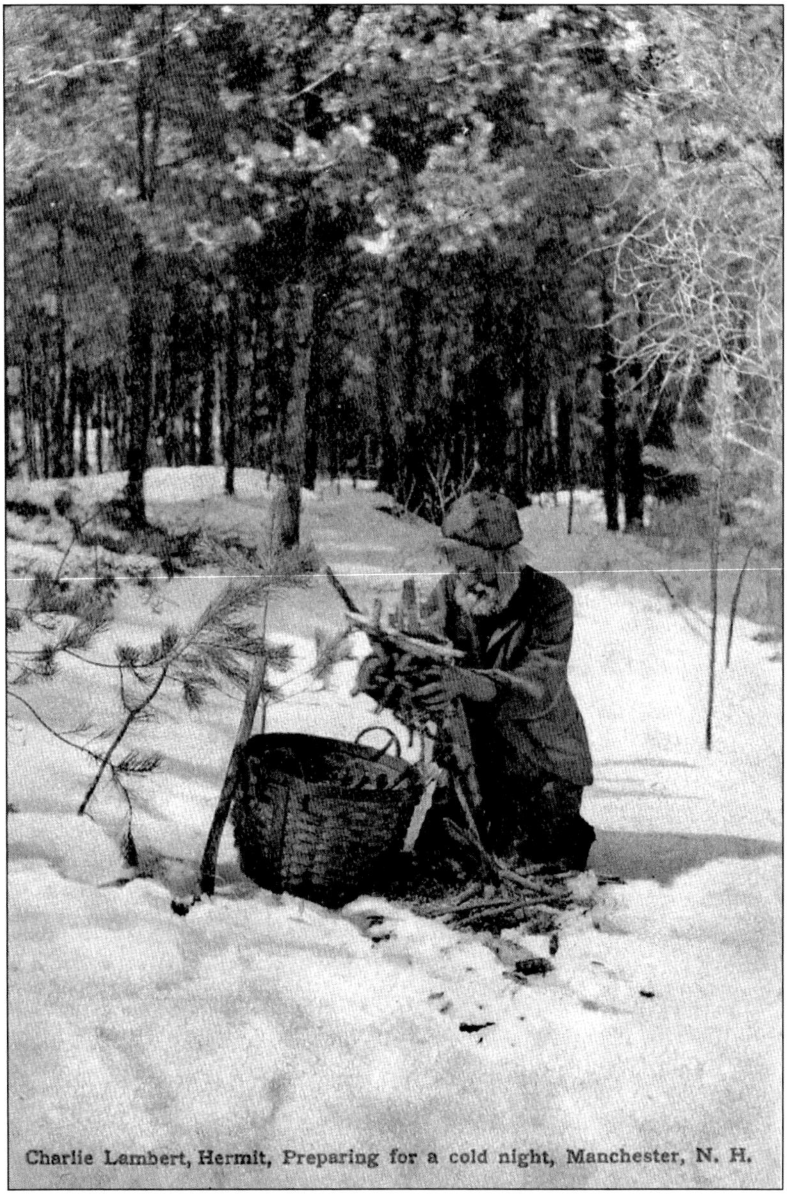

Charlie Lambert, Hermit, Preparing for a cold night, Manchester, N. H.

Born in Lincolnshire County, England, in 1823, Charlie Lambert studied animal husbandry and botany, especially the medicinal properties of herbs and roots. Having traveled around Europe, he came to the United States in the early 1840s. He visited several states before settling in Manchester. Shortly thereafter, the distraught victim of unrequited love, he acquired 40 acres of woods and farmland near Mosquito Pond, now Crystal Lake. He retreated onto that land, where he built his cabin without utilities and lived life à la Thoreau for approximately 70 years. He raised sheep, farmed, and sold herbs to a local apothecary, but he lived an otherwise self-sufficient, solitary life, reading, writing poetry, and collecting Native American artifacts from his land. Photographer Ulric Bourgeois befriended him about 1900 and documented every aspect of his daily life. Appearing on postcards, ironically, Charlie became the "famous" Hermit of Mosquito Pond, as a 1909 message mailed to Boston attests: "Visited the hermit today." Forced out of the woods for health reasons at age 89, he died at age 91 in 1914.

Five

Discovering the West Side

Despite the West Side's historical and cultural wealth, its proud residents must often defend it against a general lack of knowledge or interest, coupled with an attitude of superiority, on the part of outsiders. Curiously, as if it were a city apart, some New Hampshire maps have "West Manchester" and even "Pinardville" plotted as locations distinct from Manchester. Perhaps all of this is rooted in the fact that, until 1853, the West Side was, indeed, a separate entity.

Previously, with Manchester's boundary line drawn down the middle of the Merrimack, the thriving early residential and business areas of Piscataquog and Amoskeag Villages belonged to Bedford and Goffstown, respectively. Both had post offices well before Manchester did: Piscataquog's opened in 1816, Amoskeag's in 1828. The latter village boasted its popular Amoskeag Tavern, where the Marquis de Lafayette and Andrew Jackson, among others, were honored guests. Beginning in the 1860s, German immigrants contributed significantly to Piscataquog Village's socioeconomic and religious climate.

Meanwhile, a vast area of fields and woodlands in the central part of the West Side, previously the 1,100-acre farm of Gen. John Stark's aide-de-camp, Robert McGregor, remained mostly undeveloped until the city built the third McGregor Bridge in 1881. Before long, McGregorville filled up with residences and businesses, largely but not exclusively populated by Québécois immigrants and their Franco-American descendants. Farther west, Pinardville eventually completed the picture.

Today, after urban renewal, assimilation, and parish closings, longtime West Siders cling preciously to whatever traditional ambiance survives in their midst.

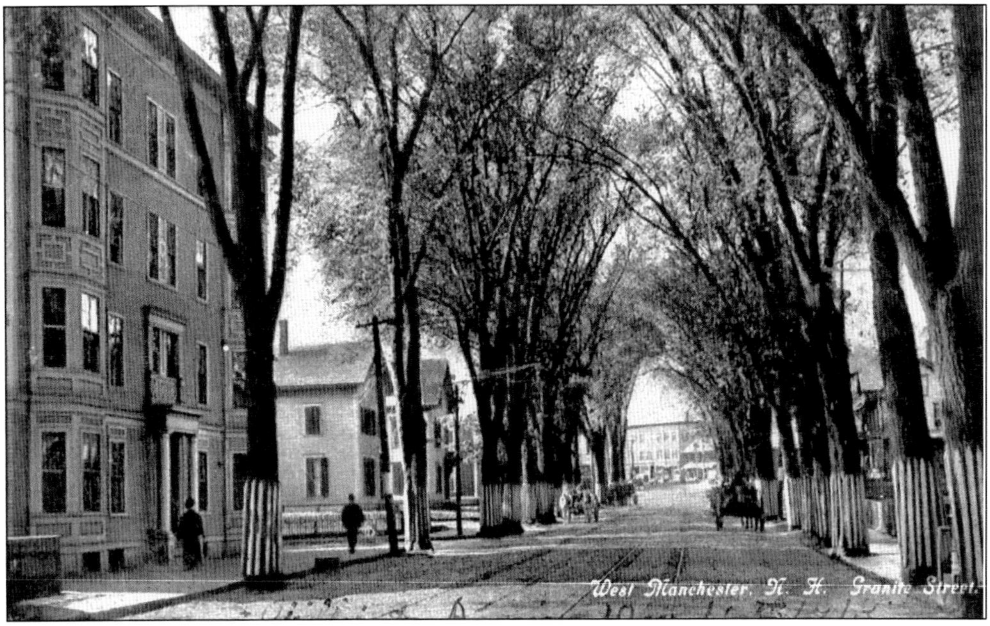

Toward the end of the 19th century, the view looking west on Granite Street between Turner and Second Streets gave the impression of a quiet, residential neighborhood. In fact, just up ahead, Clapp's Corner bustled with activity. It was home to John L. Niven's men's clothing, Caldwell Sisters' dry goods, Clapp's groceries, Hotel Merrimack, Henri Hébert's barbershop, Horatio Fradd & Company groceries, and Wing Lee's laundry, to name a few.

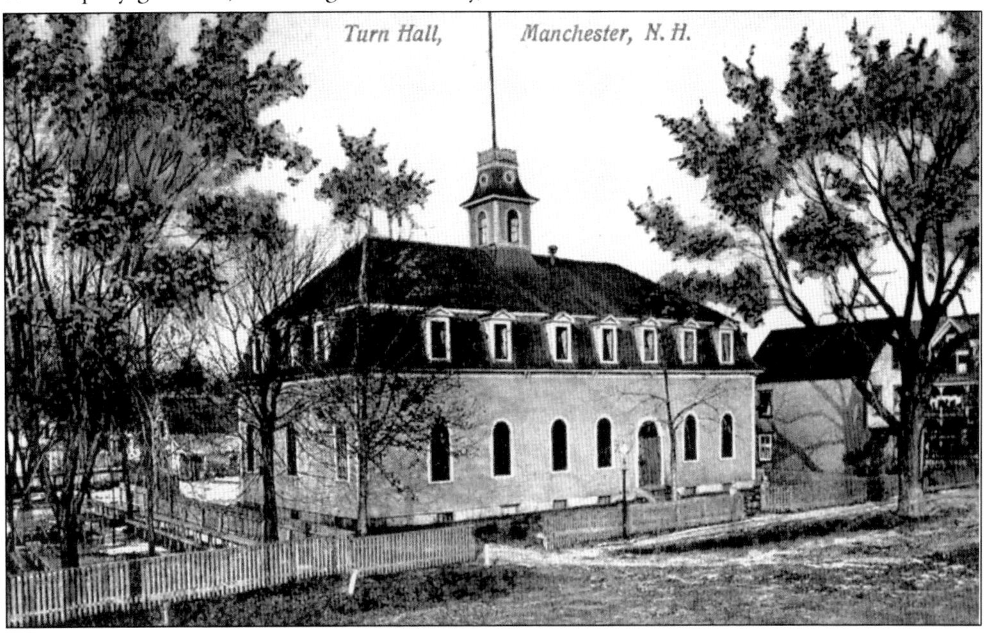

In 1870, Manchester's German community founded Turnverein, a gymnastic society, and immediately began to build a Turnhalle, or gymnasium, in the evenings after work. Located at 265 Turner Street, the Turnhalle housed the Turnschule, or gymnastic school, which fostered the development of both body and mind. The Turnhalle also served as an all-purpose activity center for the community. A fire in 1936 destroyed the original Turnhalle, and its replacement burned in 1984.

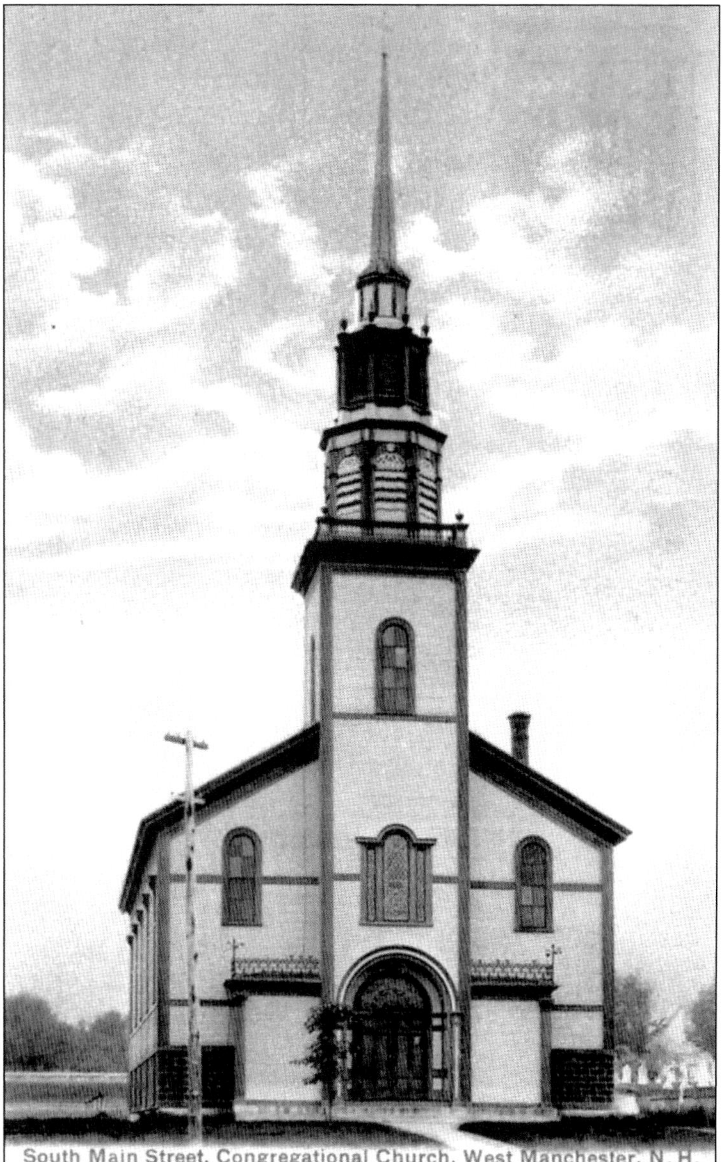

In 1820, weary of crossing the Merrimack to attend the only available religious services in the area at Manchester Centre, residents of Piscataquog Village built a meetinghouse adjacent to the Piscataquog Village Cemetery. The heirs of the recently deceased village merchant William Parker, who had donated land for the cemetery six years earlier, financed the project. The meetinghouse served various religious societies over the decades and underwent many renovations and additions. For a time in the 1840s, it served as the Piscataquog Village Academy. In 1883, with the help of Franklin Street Church members, the meetinghouse became the South Main Street Union Congregational Church, seen here near the intersection of South Main and Milford Streets. Destroyed by fire on November 7, 1916, it was replaced in 1917 by the larger, more modern red-brick structure known today as the South Main Street Church. The current church features an exterior remnant of the old church: its weather vane, which, during the fire, fell from the steeple and landed in the cemetery with its arrowhead lodged 22 inches into the ground.

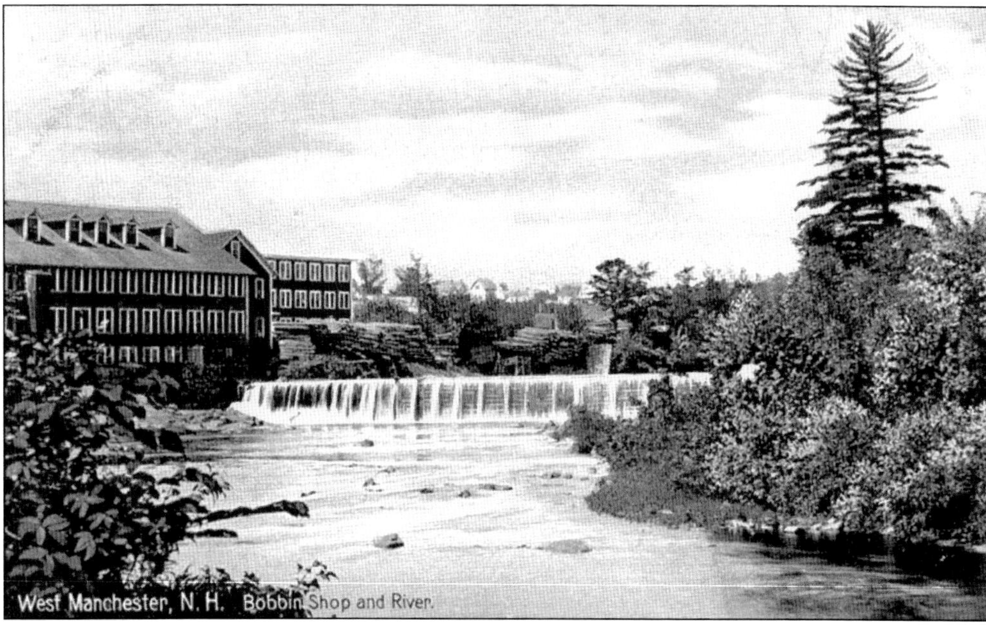

The Piscataquog River below Varney Street from Bowman to Riddle Streets once had its own miniature millyard. Beginning about 1878, the James Baldwin Company operated both a feed enterprise in the former Watts & Holmes gristmill and, more importantly, a bobbin and shuttle factory that in 1901 became the U.S. Bobbin & Shuttle Company. After the 1936 flood, other businesses occupied the complex. Today, only its power distribution center remains, housing GAM Electronics.

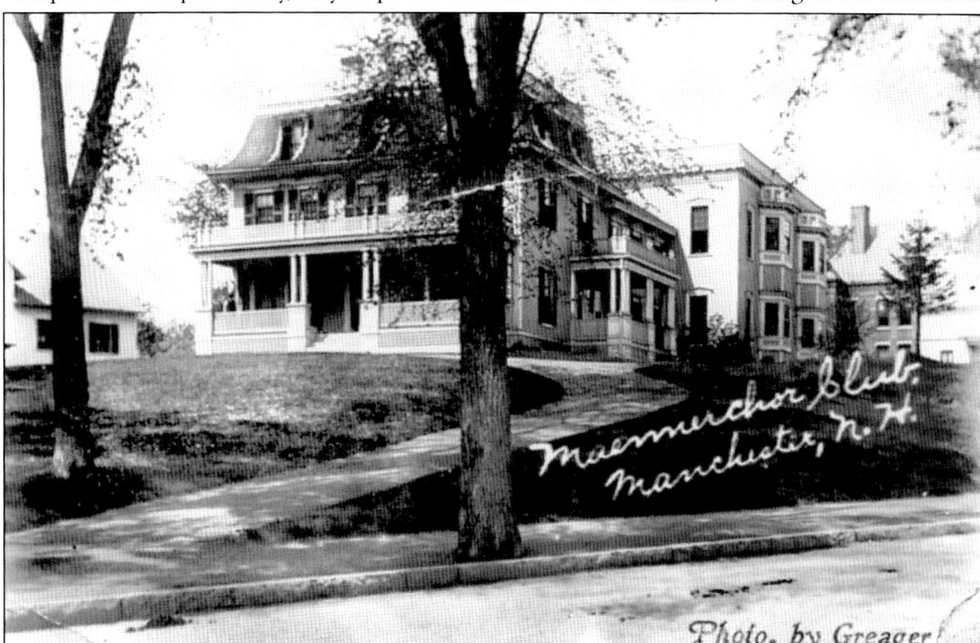

The Victorian mansion remembered as the Sacré-Coeur Parish rectory, near the southwest corner of South Main and Varney Streets, was once home to grocer Ira Barr's family. About 1904, it became the headquarters of Männerchor, a renowned 500-member German men's choral society. Sacré-Coeur Parish acquired the building in 1920 and sold it and other nearby property in the mid-1990s.

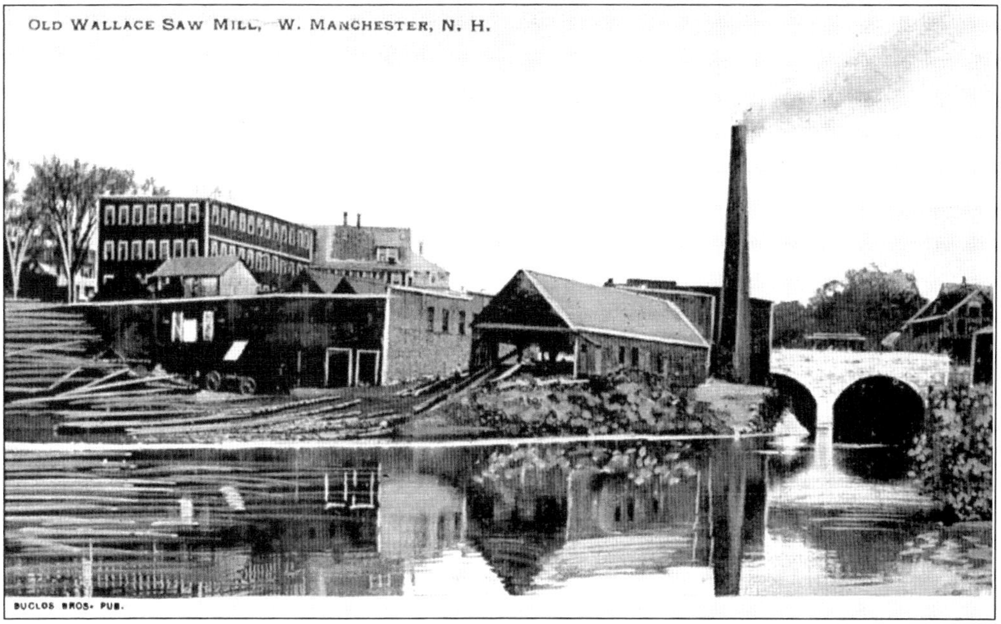

The site of Col. Andrew C. Wallace's sawmill (1853–1899) and the West Side Lumber Company (1899–1982) along the Piscataquog River's south bank near Log Street has long had a connection with wood. During the Colonial era, teams of oxen hauled timber from points northwest via Mast Road. Here, logs destined for the British Royal Navy's masts were deposited into the Piscataquog and floated down the Merrimack River to Newburyport.

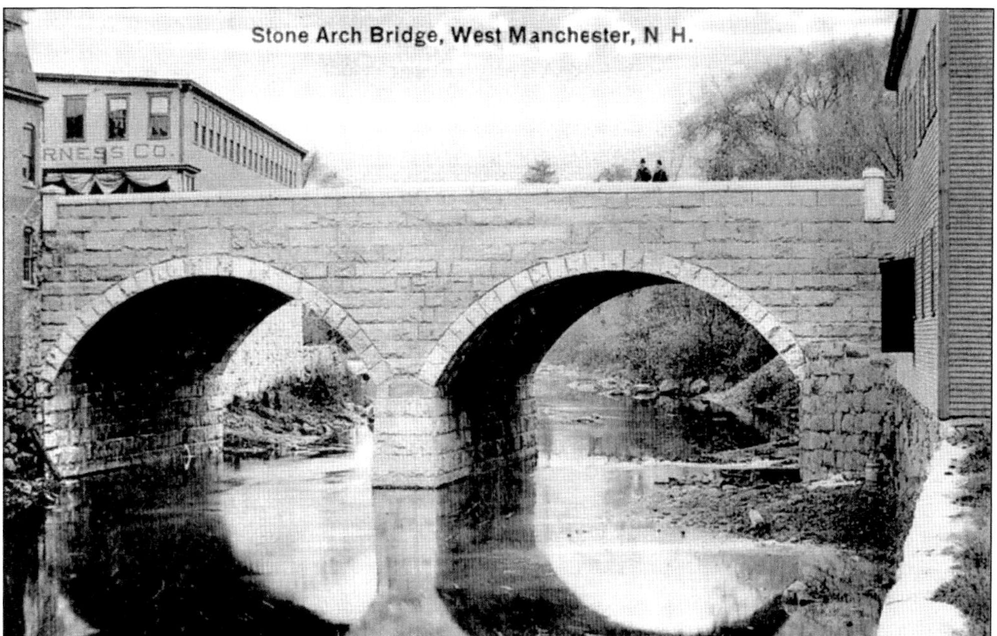

Officially unnamed but referred to generically by those aware of its architecturally significant substructure, the Stone Arch Bridge has spanned the Piscataquog since 1894. Unlike Manchester's other bridges, it has survived aging, floods, and urban renewal. It is the city's oldest existing bridge and the only one made of stone. Many of its daily users have never even seen its underside.

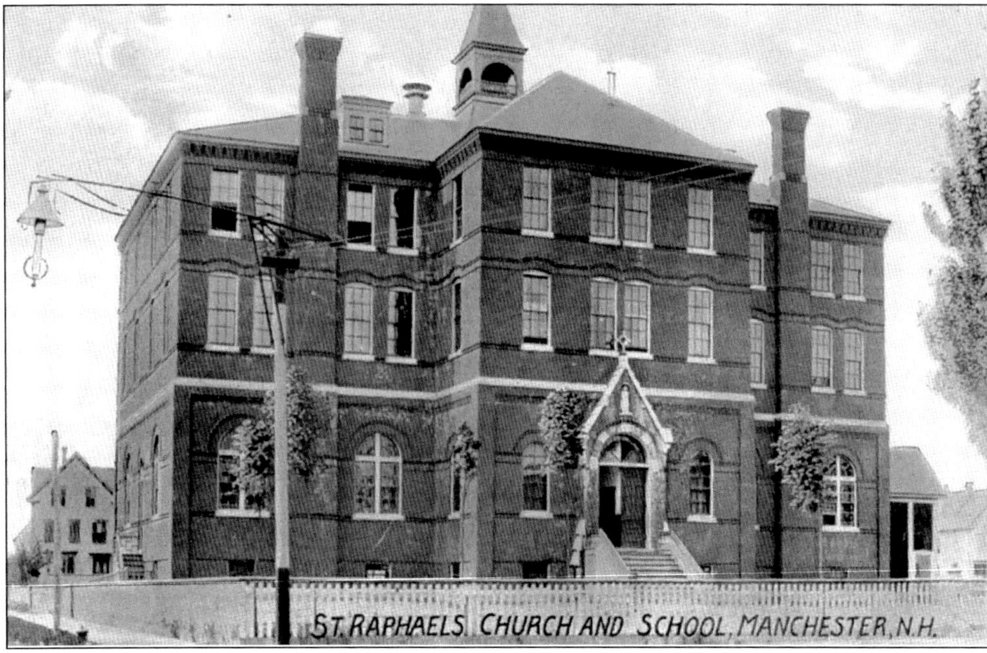

Benedictine monks founded St. Raphael Parish in 1888 to serve Piscataquog's German-speaking Roman Catholics. Completed in 1889, the building, located at the southwest corner of Ferry and Third Streets, served as a church and school until 1964–1965. The construction of new separate buildings involved the removal of the attic and two upper classroom floors and the transformation of the first floor from a church into a gymnasium. Today, it is Saint Benedict Academy's gym.

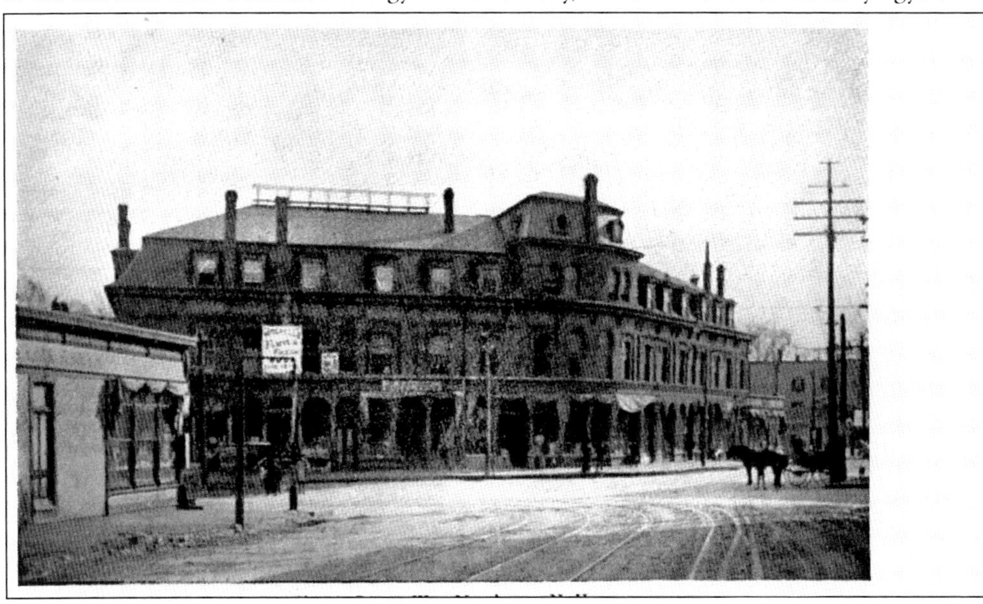

From 1871 to 1980, Squog's largest, most impressive business edifice, the Barr & Clapp Block, gracefully rounded the curve along Granite Street into South Main Street at Clapp's Corner, later Granite Square, seen here looking south about 1900. Built by longtime neighborhood grocers Ira Barr and Allen N. Clapp, the block housed stores, offices, and apartments. Because it gave Granite Square its character, the building's demolition left an enormous aesthetic and physical void.

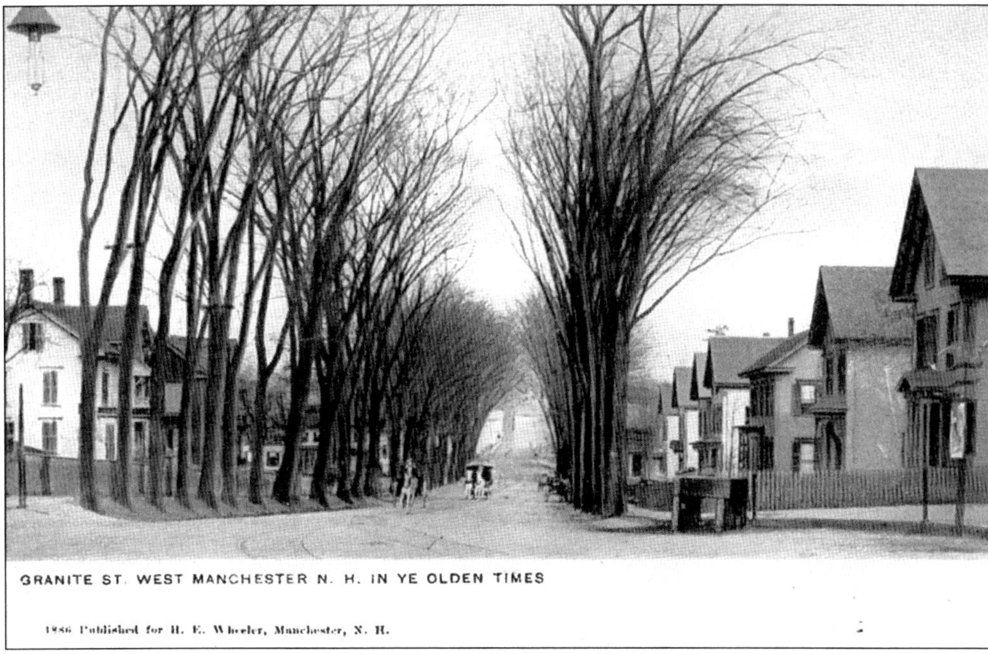

Harry E. Wheeler owned "H. E. Wheeler, ice cream, confectionery, and news dealer," an early-20th-century Granite Square landmark. He published this postcard showing a mid-1880s view looking east from Clapp's Corner. Wheeler's nostalgic choice of title, "Granite St. West Manchester N.H. in Ye Olden Times," suggests that even in his era, when life was slow by comparison with life today, Manchester's cityscape was already undergoing rapid change.

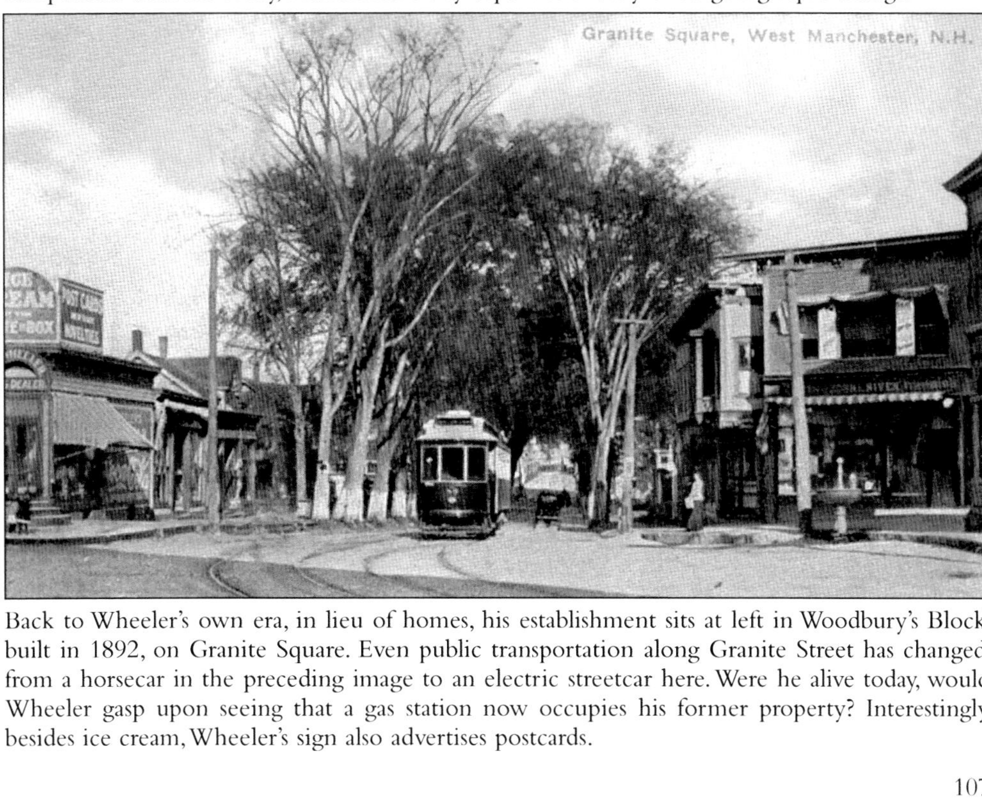

Back to Wheeler's own era, in lieu of homes, his establishment sits at left in Woodbury's Block, built in 1892, on Granite Square. Even public transportation along Granite Street has changed, from a horsecar in the preceding image to an electric streetcar here. Were he alive today, would Wheeler gasp upon seeing that a gas station now occupies his former property? Interestingly, besides ice cream, Wheeler's sign also advertises postcards.

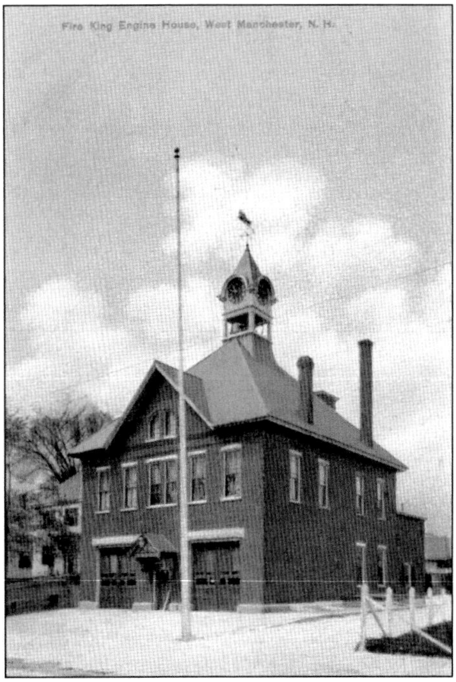

Opened in 1886, the Fire King Steam Fire Engine No. 2 house at 76 Main Street protected several West Side neighborhoods until its closing in 1977. Subsequently renovated, it was officially rededicated in 1979 as the West Manchester Senior Citizens' Community Center and the Manchester Public Library's West Branch. Before 1853, the boundary between Bedford and Goffstown ran east to west from the Merrimack River up through and beyond this precise location.

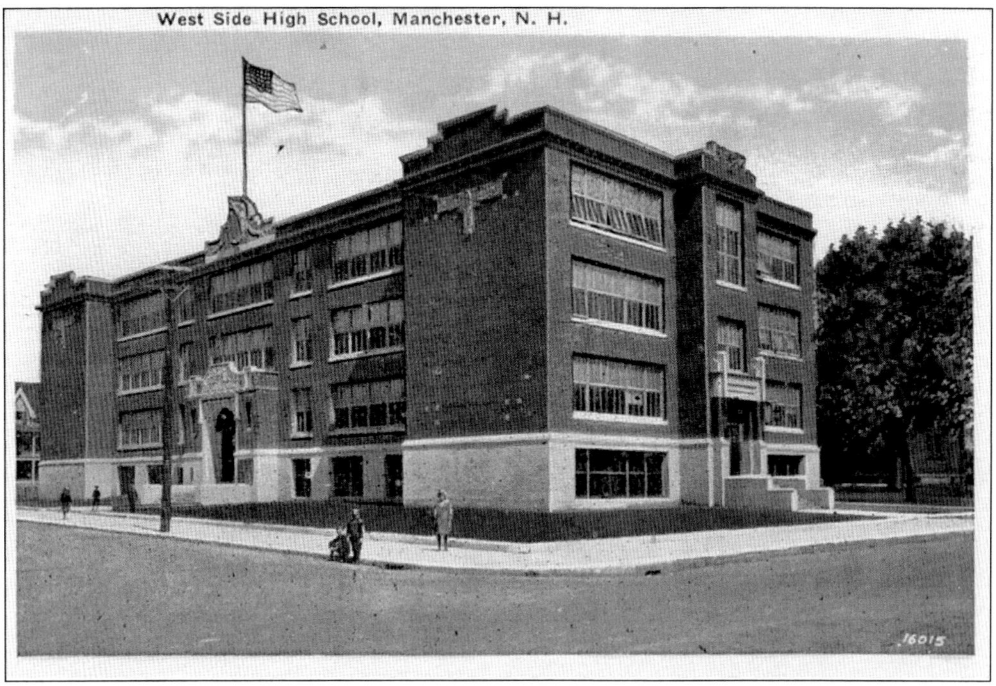

When West High opened in 1923, few imagined that the football team's substitute quarterback, called "Midge" due to his short stature, would reach greater heights. He was Martin Revson, who cofounded Revlon cosmetics with his brothers Charles and Joseph. Another student, whom the 1927 yearbook described as "quiet" but "sure to become a great man," revolutionized people's eating habits. He was Richard McDonald, who, with brother Maurice "Mac" McDonald, founded McDonald's hamburgers.

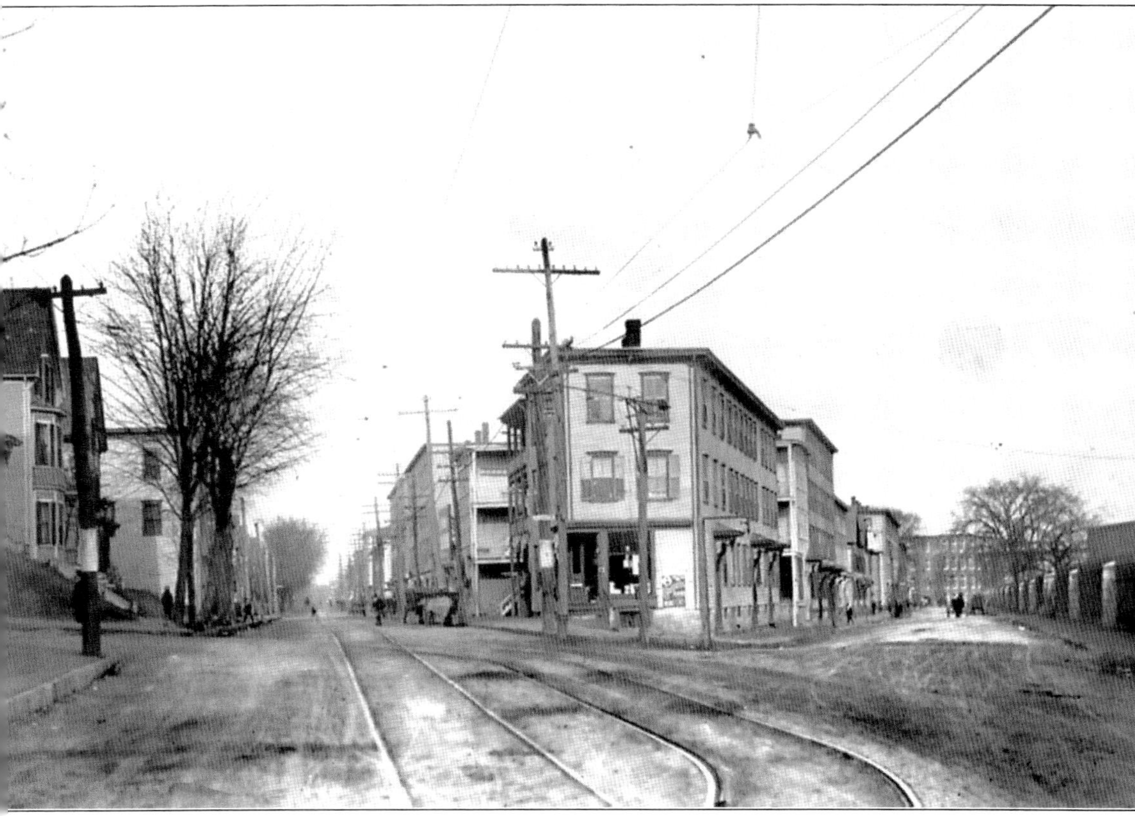

From a trickle in the 1830s to a deluge after the Civil War, Québécois immigrants to Manchester usually settled near St. Anne's and, later, St. Joseph's parishes. Eventually, they founded their own French-language parish, St. Augustin, nearby in 1871. When that church became overcrowded, Franco-Americans founded Sainte Marie Parish in 1880 and, with other groups to a lesser degree, began creating the neighborhood first known as McGregorville and subsequently as Notre-Dame. Here, about 1912, the Duclos Brothers recorded a scene looking north toward the Flat Iron district at the intersection of Main, McGregor, and Putnam Streets, with Amoskeag's new Coolidge Mill (1909) in the distance at right. This was McGregorville/Notre-Dame's veritable downtown business and residential area. Besides tenements, with their classic laundry-filled porches, the area had cafés; stores; offices; two theaters, the Modern and the short-lived Queen; the first credit union in the U.S., la Caisse Populaire Sainte-Marie; and even a small newspaper, *L'Écho de Notre-Dame*. With virtually every service available in French, some residents rarely ever felt compelled to visit downtown Manchester.

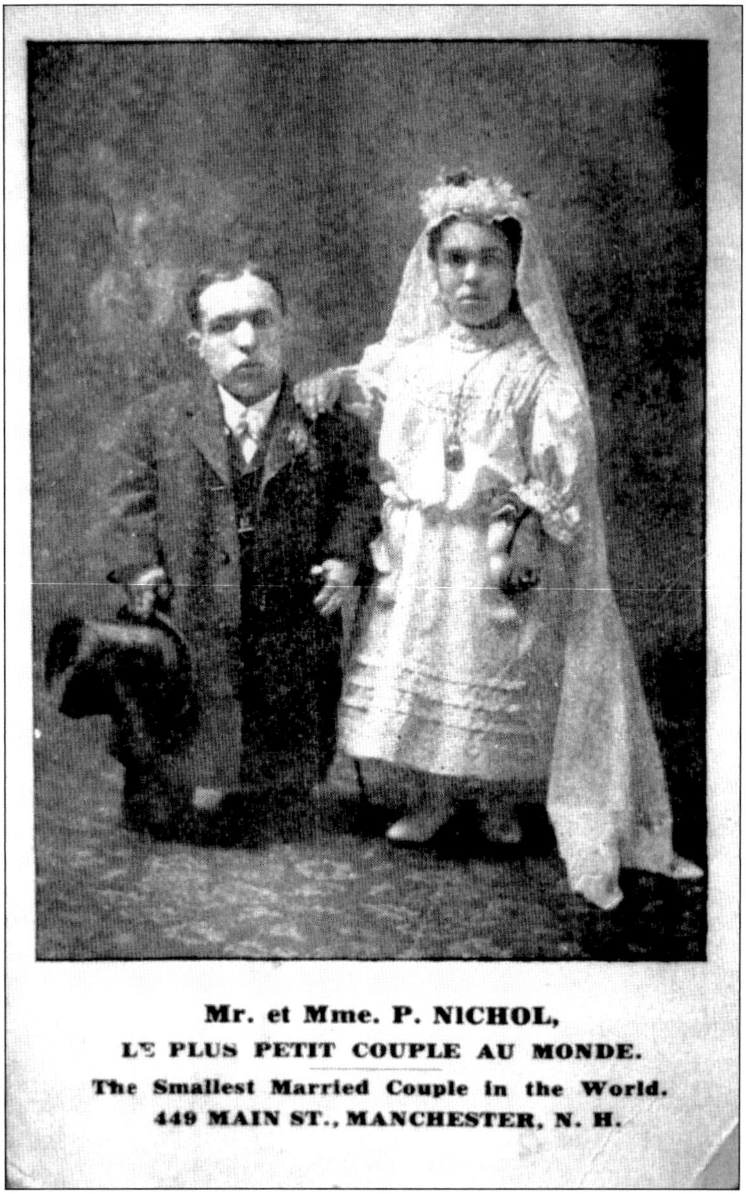

Born in 1881 in Saint-Henri-de-Lévis, Québec, to a father who stood 6 feet 3 inches tall and a mother who was 5 feet 9 inches tall, Philippe Nicol joined the circus by age three, when it became evident that he would never attain average adult height. In 1887, the family settled in Manchester, where Philippe went to school part time and continued his career. At 22, seeking a more tranquil lifestyle, he opened a variety store at 449 Main Street in McGregorville. Through the agent of Canadian strong man Louis Cyr, Philippe met Lowell-born little person and circus performer Rose Dufresne. A newspaper account of their wedding in 1906 states that Philippe and Rose stood 3 feet tall and 3 feet 4 inches tall, respectively. While they called Manchester home until 1910, they rejoined the circus and toured the United States and Europe as "Count and Countess Nicol, King and Queen of All Midgets." After a move to Lowell, they settled permanently in Montréal in 1912, where they built a home in which they designed everything to their scale. It later became a museum, le Palais des Nains, the Midgets' Palace.

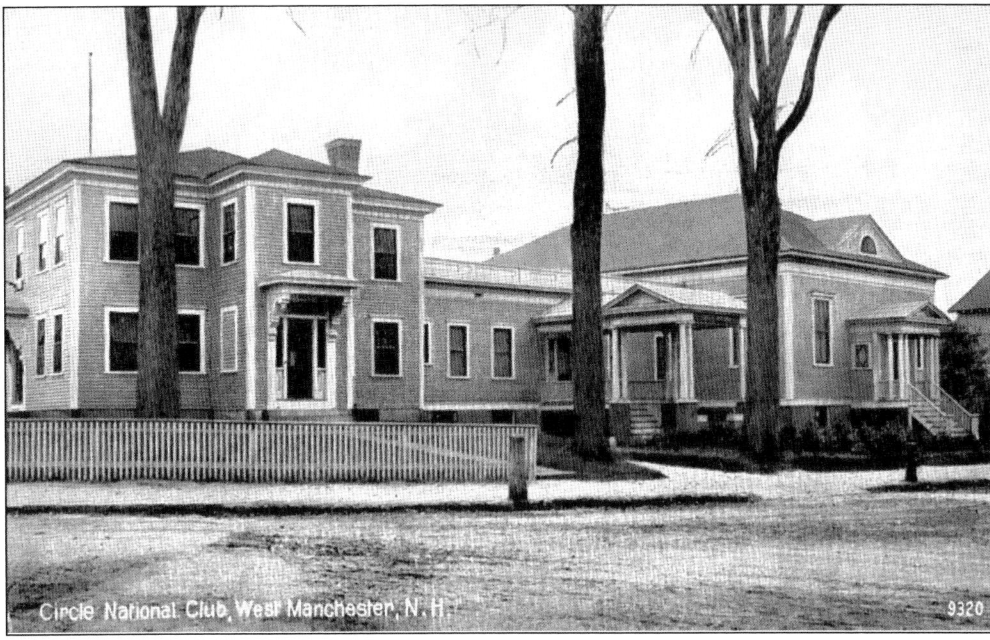

Founded in 1895 as a men's social club, le Cercle National occupied new headquarters at the northwest corner of McGregor and Amory Streets in 1906. Owned by the Amoskeag company, the building had been home to the late Horace Simpson, superintendent of the Jefferson Mill. The American Legion's Poste Jutras No. 43 moved in by 1920 and bought the building in 1927. It fell victim to urban renewal during the late 1960s.

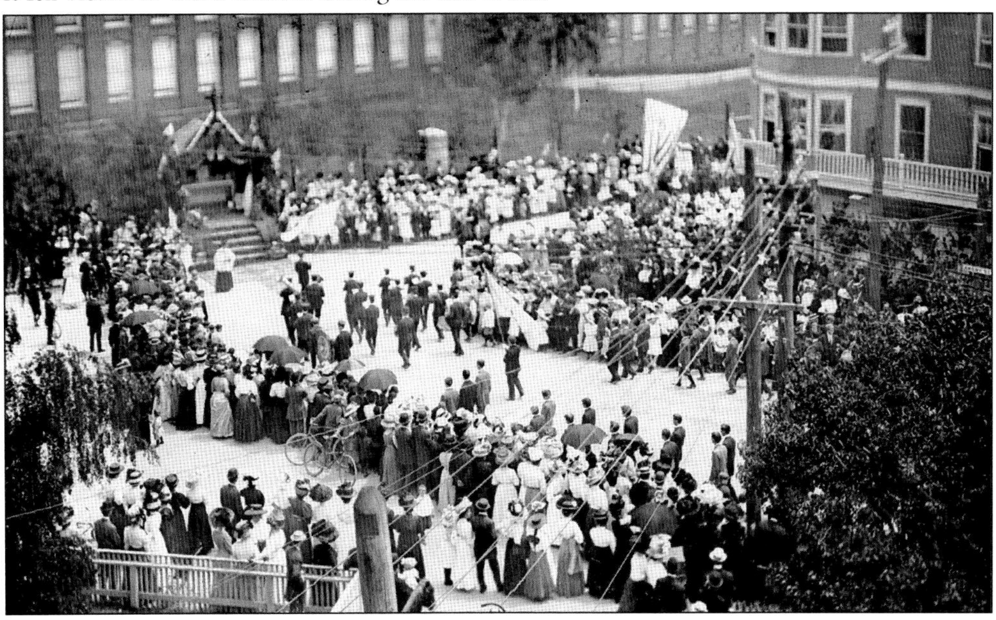

In this image, the feast of Corpus Christi, or la Fête-Dieu, is celebrated in Notre-Dame at the intersection of West Bridge, McGregor, and Amory Streets about 1910. The festivities feature a band marching toward the altar before Mass. With Amoskeag's No. 11 Mill in the background, the scene succinctly portrays the blend of two of the most important values around which people's lives revolved at that time: religion and work.

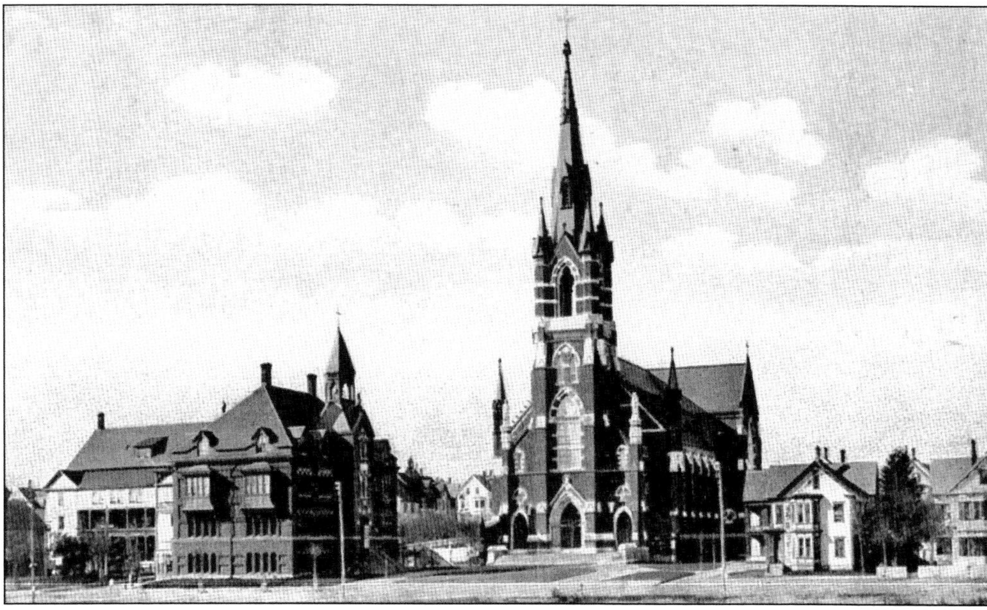

Built in 1880–1881 on Beauport Street, now Notre Dame Avenue, Sainte Marie's first building, a wooden chapel, burned in 1890 and was replaced by the present church, completed in 1898–1899. Pictured from left to right are the boys' school, l'École Sainte-Marie (1886–1910), which was replaced by l'École Hévey in 1911; the girls' school, l'École des Saints-Anges (1885); and the rectory (immediately to the right of the church), which was replaced by the present one in 1911.

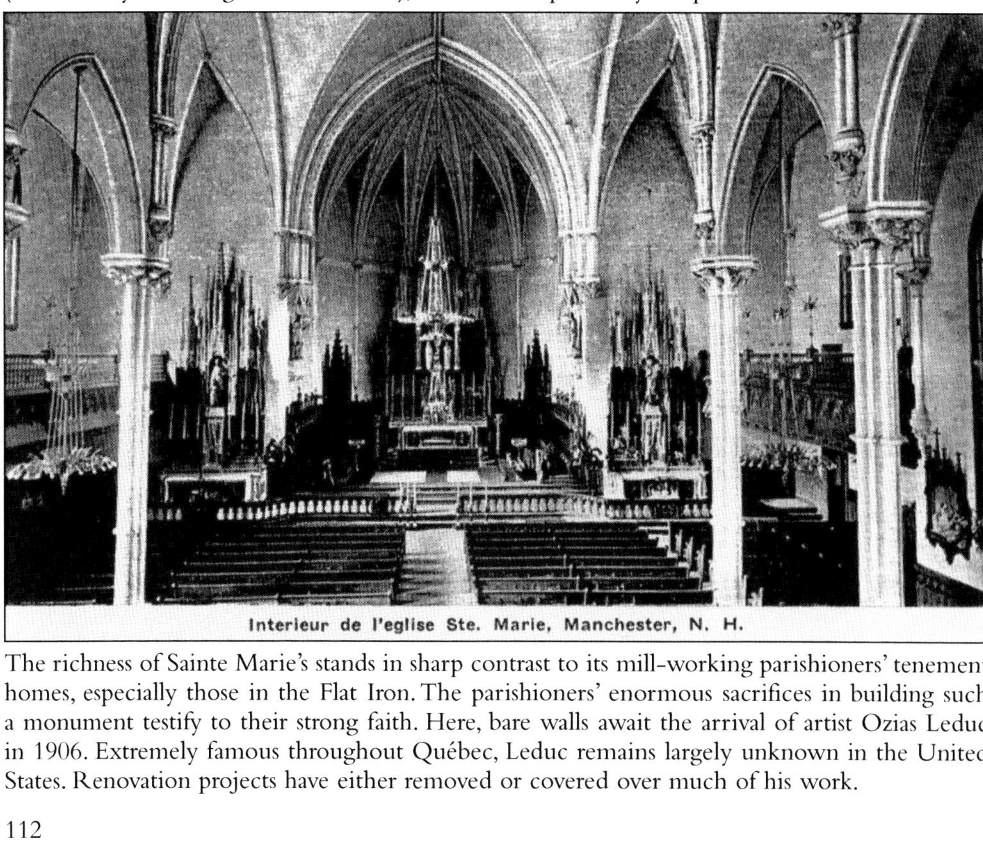

The richness of Sainte Marie's stands in sharp contrast to its mill-working parishioners' tenement homes, especially those in the Flat Iron. The parishioners' enormous sacrifices in building such a monument testify to their strong faith. Here, bare walls await the arrival of artist Ozias Leduc in 1906. Extremely famous throughout Québec, Leduc remains largely unknown in the United States. Renovation projects have either removed or covered over much of his work.

Although ranked as one of New England's most beautiful churches, Sainte Marie's has never been, as the caption reads, "St. Mary's Cathedral." Someone in a German print shop must have mistaken its neo-Gothic splendor for something deserving of cathedral status. As with any Roman Catholic diocese, that of Manchester has but one cathedral, the seat of the bishop, St. Joseph's.

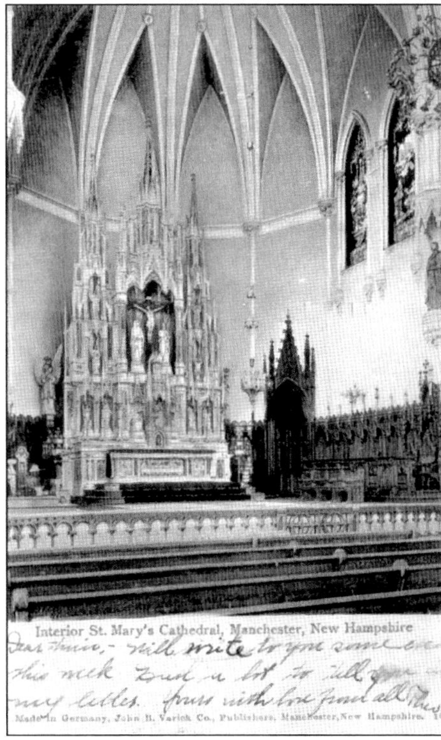

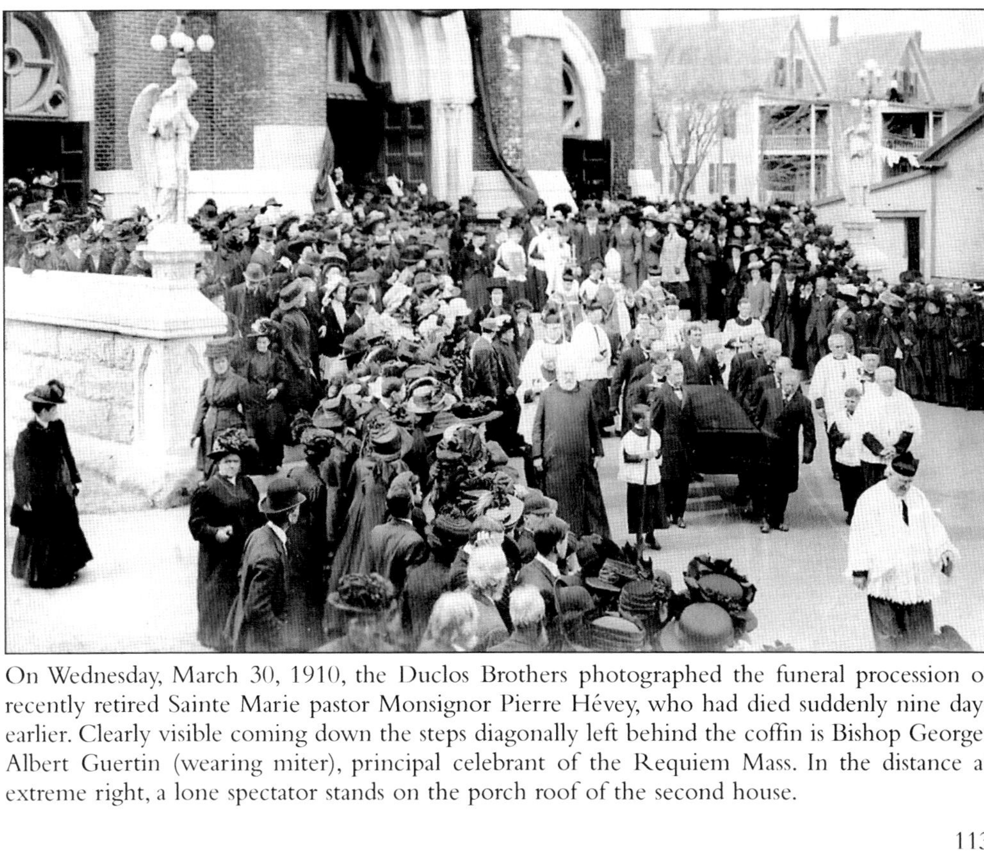

On Wednesday, March 30, 1910, the Duclos Brothers photographed the funeral procession of recently retired Sainte Marie pastor Monsignor Pierre Hévey, who had died suddenly nine days earlier. Clearly visible coming down the steps diagonally left behind the coffin is Bishop Georges Albert Guertin (wearing miter), principal celebrant of the Requiem Mass. In the distance at extreme right, a lone spectator stands on the porch roof of the second house.

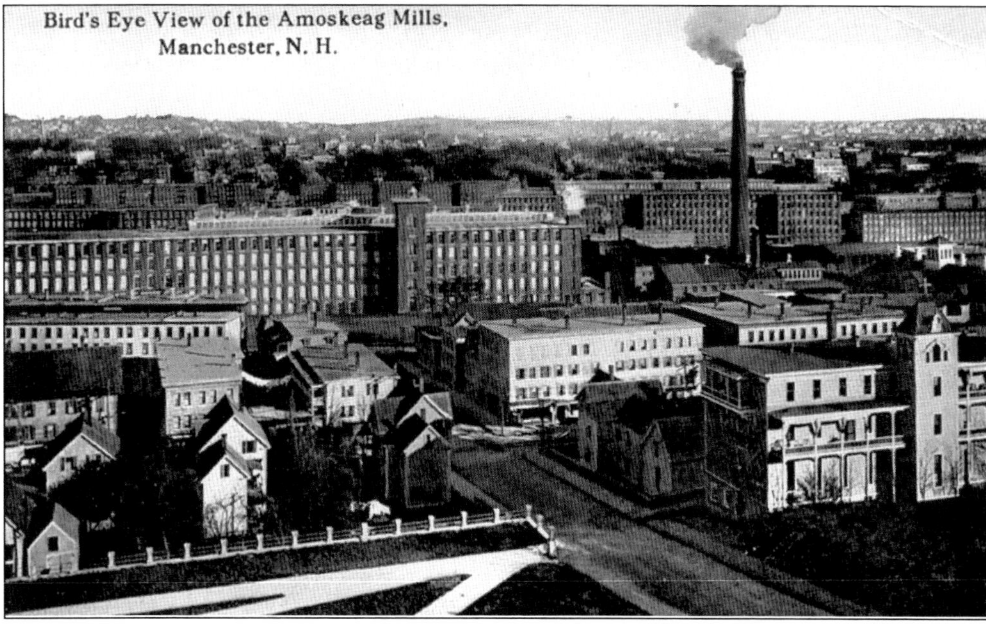

This *c.* 1915 view from Sainte Marie's shows Lafayette Park, l'Hôpital Notre-Dame, and, at the southeast corner of Wayne and Main Streets, the business and tenement building where Philippe and Rose Nicol had their variety store. Everything between the park and Amoskeag's No. 11 Mill was gradually razed between 1965 and 1970, wiping out an area overflowing with ethnic and working-class culture worthy of a best-selling novel.

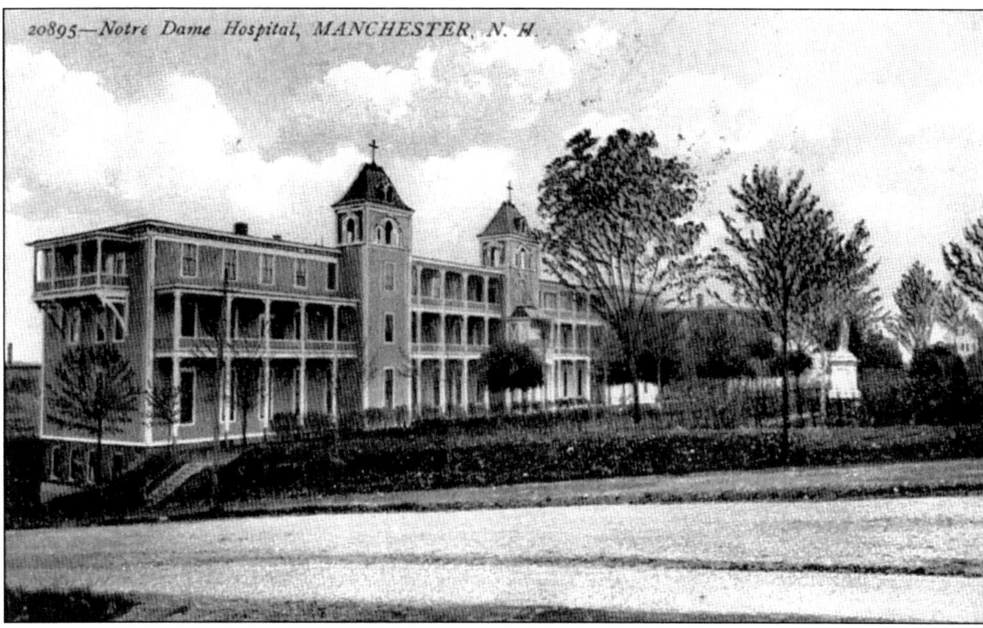

Opened in 1894 under the direction of les Soeurs de la Charité de Saint-Hyacinthe, known as the Grey Nuns, l'Hôpital Notre-Dame de Lourdes stood halfway up the hill from what was then Main Street between Wayne and Putnam Streets. An extension was built to its west in 1956. Having become Catholic Medical Center West in 1974, the original wooden structure was demolished in 1976 for the present CMC building.

Monsignor Pierre Hévey typified pioneer clergymen who migrated to this country to serve their compatriots. As Sainte Marie's second pastor, from 1882–1909, he served nearly until death, rebuilding the church and founding an infrastructure of parochial and neighborhood institutions: schools, orphanages, a hospital, a nursing home, a poorhouse, and a credit union. At his request, he rests here at the southeast corner of Wayne Street and Notre Dame Avenue, which was once a nucleus of parochial life.

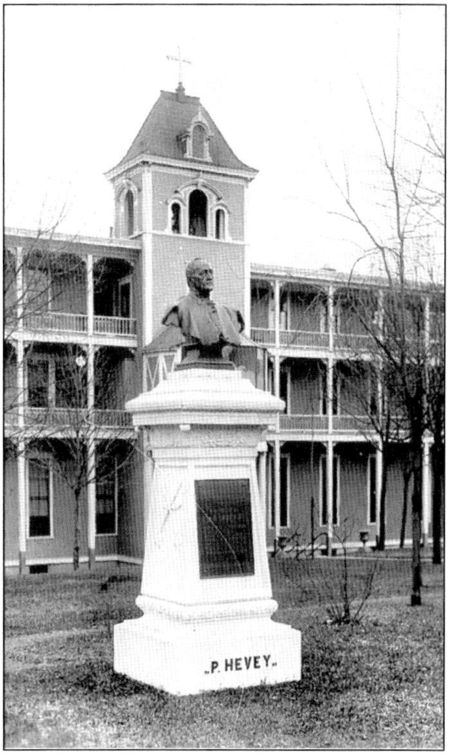

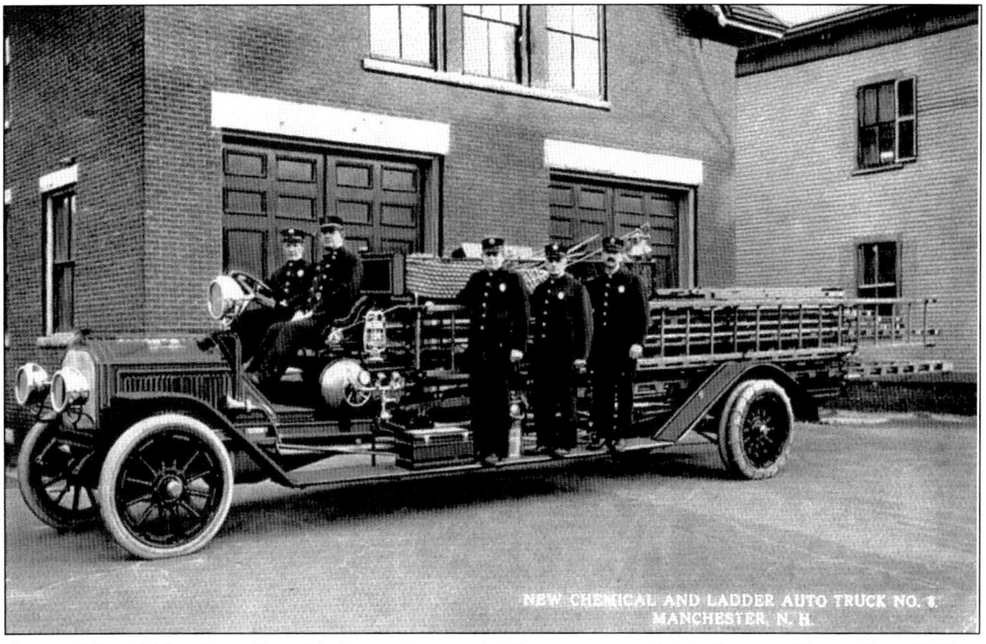

Opened in 1892 when Scottish-born Amory Mill overseer and McGregorville resident Walter M. Fulton was alderman for what then constituted Ward 8, the Walter M. Fulton No. 6 Engine House was located at the southeast corner of Rimmon and Amory Streets. Ironically, after having served the West Side for nearly a century, it burned on June 9, 1988, while firefighters were out on exercises. It was demolished in 1990.

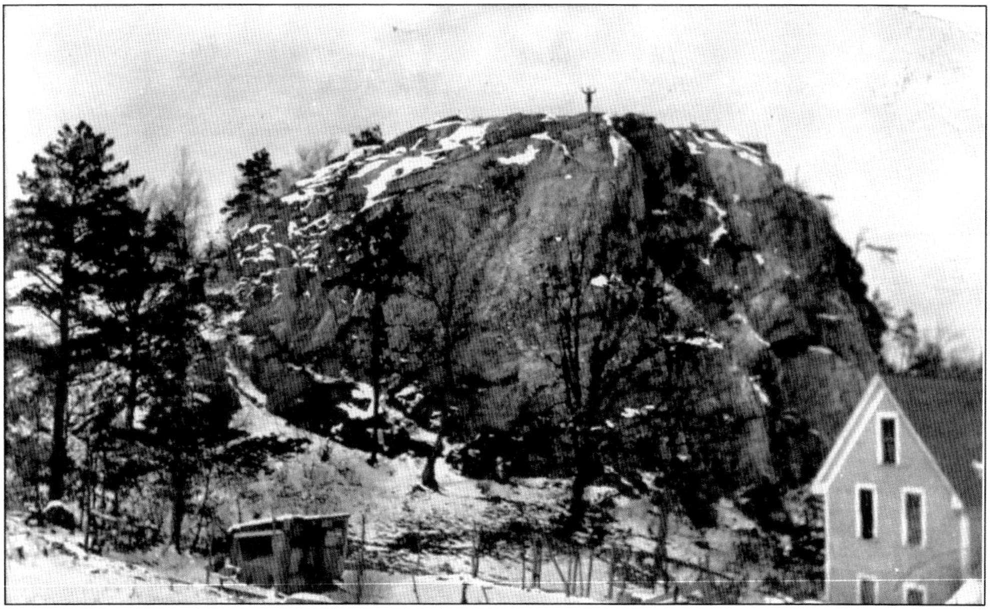

Towering majestically above the intersection of Boutwell and Mason Streets, Rock Rimmon offers numerous recreational opportunities. True adventure seekers climb the rock's nearly vertical face, while others take an easy path to the summit, which affords spectacular views. The scene of Sainte Marie's spire watching over the neighborhood recalls an old Québécois village. According to legend, a Native American maiden, disappointed in love, plunged to her death from Rock Rimmon.

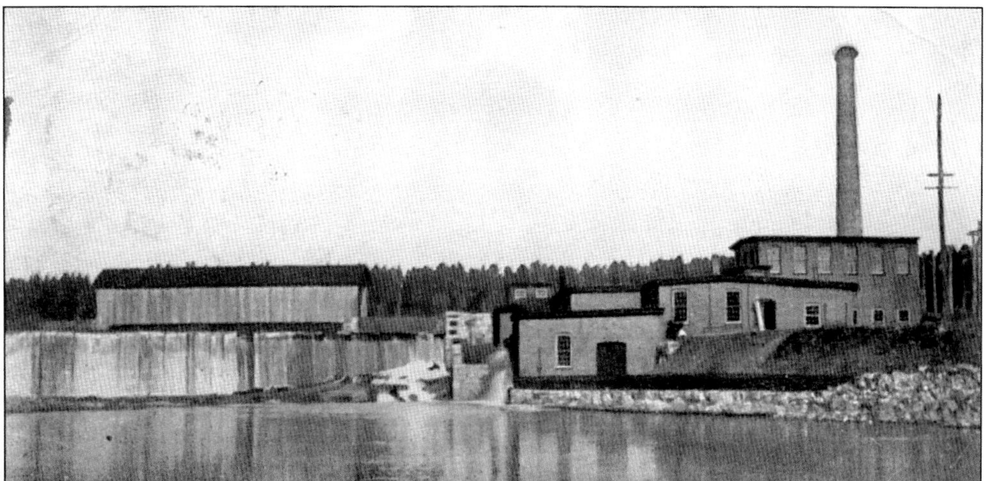

The scene at Kelley's Falls, seen here looking east across the Piscataquog River about 1905, has changed somewhat. The covered bridge along the B&M Railroad's North Weare line burned in 1941, leaving a trestle that has proven popular with swimmers. The Manchester Traction, Light & Power Company, forerunner of Public Service Company of New Hampshire, once maintained a hydroelectric power station here. It was demolished in the early 1970s.

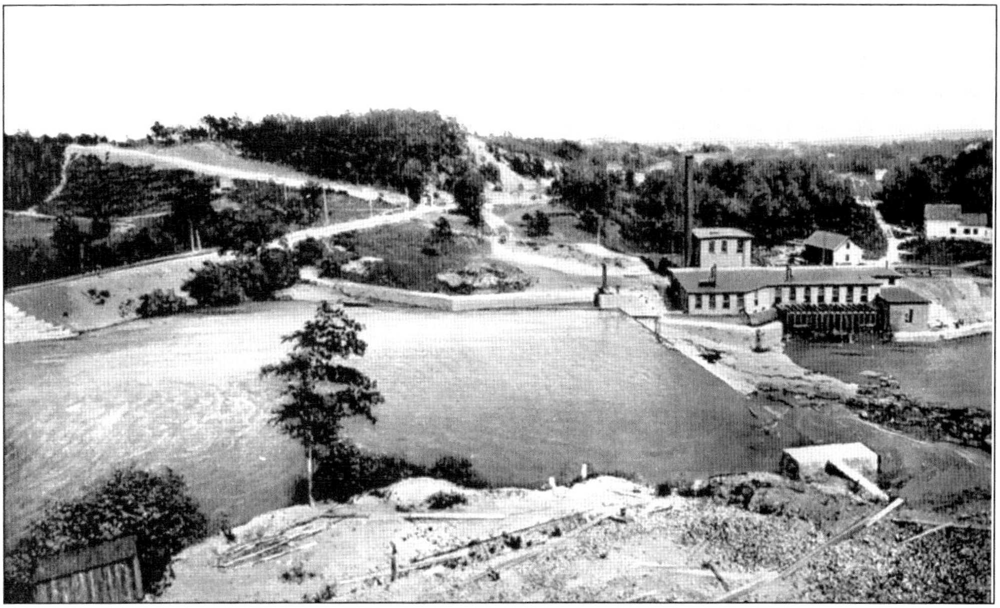

Prior to 1913, anyone wishing to get to the new, rapidly developing area known as Pinardville had to cross the Piscataquog River over the South Main Street Stone Arch Bridge and take Mast Street (renamed Varney Street) to Mast Road. When, as a solution to this problem, the city decided to build a bridge at Kelley's Falls, a dispute over land rights broke out, leading to rather interesting consequences.

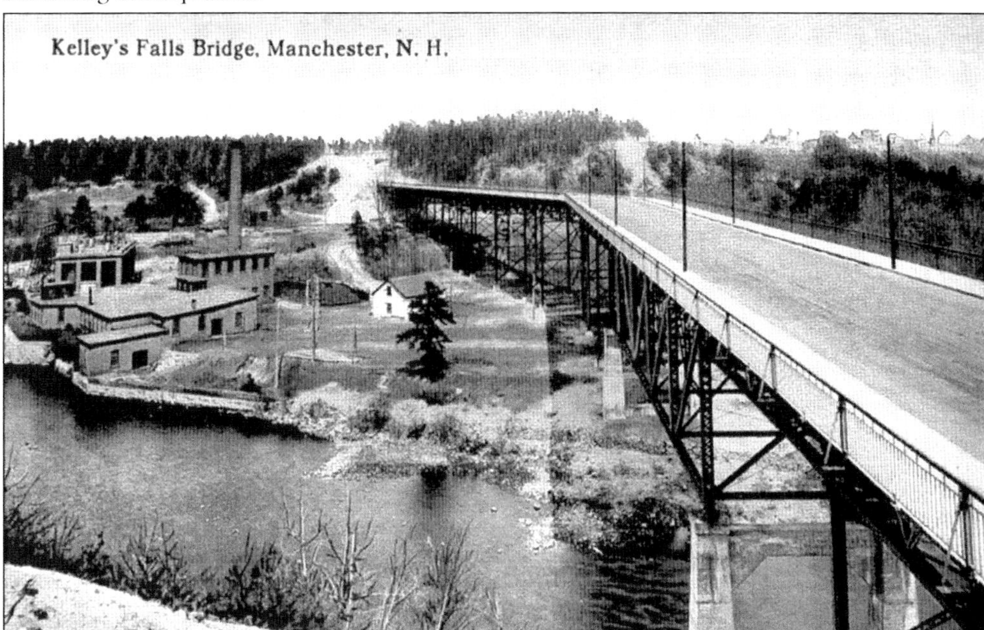

Named after the alderman who convinced the city to build it in 1913, the Nazaire E. Biron Bridge had a bend in it, somewhat like Elm Street. This unique characteristic won the bridge a mention in a Ripley's "Believe It or Not" cartoon. After many accidents, including fatalities, the city had the angle increased somewhat in 1949. A new, straight bridge replaced this one in 1974.

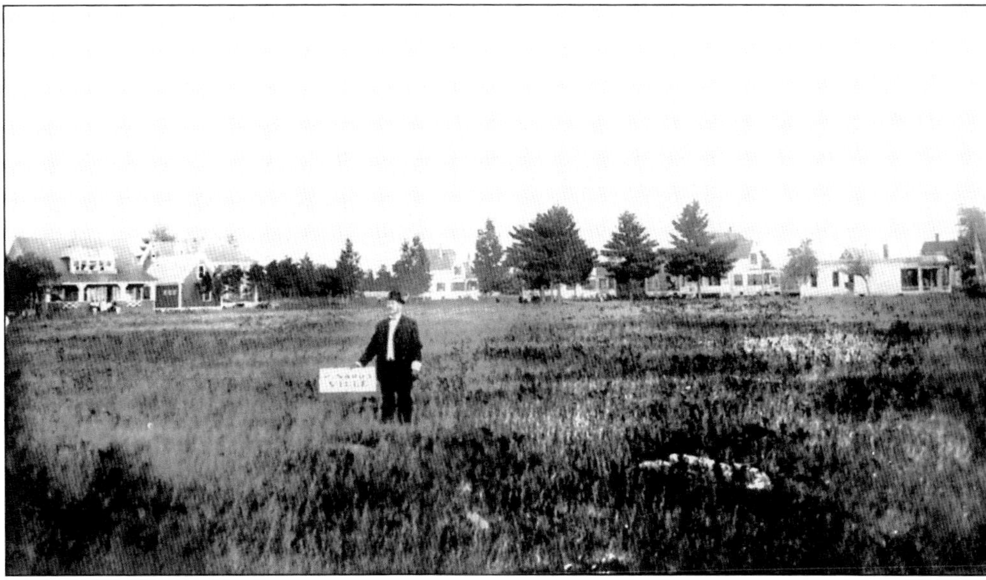

Edmond Pinard epitomizes the American Dream. Having come from Québec, he worked briefly at Amoskeag Manufacturing Company, then as a clerk in various shops, ending up with his own grocery store at 1157–1159 Elm Street. He is better known as the developer, beginning about 1907, of the area of the West Side that, according to his sign, was at first called "Pinard's Ville." Interestingly, he always lived on the East Side.

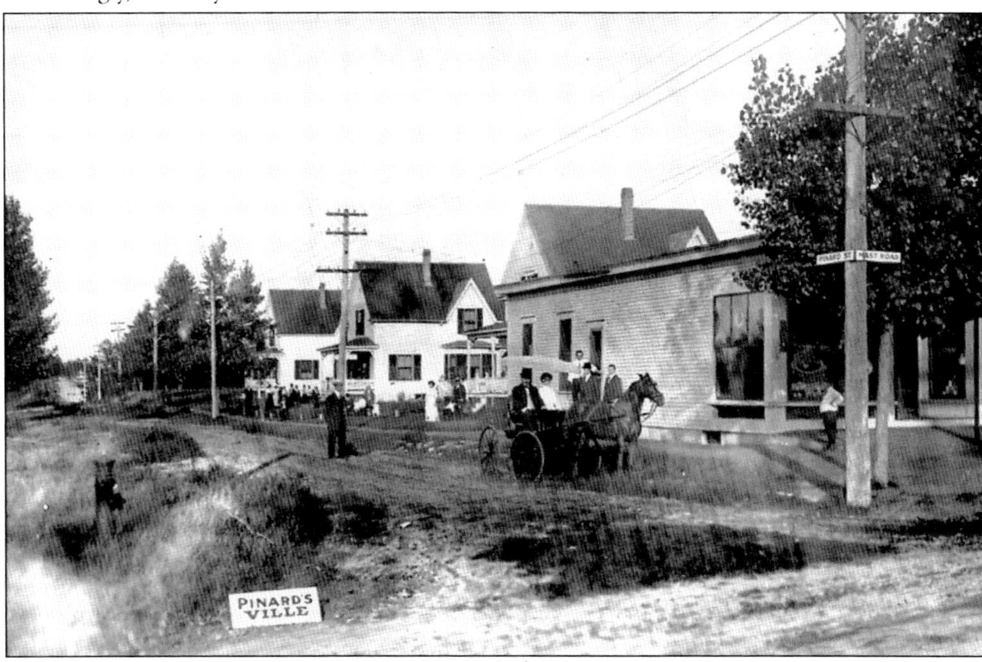

Here, Edmond Pinard and his wife, Henriette, pose in their buggy at the corner of Pinard Street and Mast Road, about 1910. Several streets in Pinardville bear family members' names. Besides Edmond, Pinard, and Henriette Streets—which meet by the former St. Edmond Parish, whose 12 lots of land Pinard donated—there are Théophile and Agnès Streets, named for Edmond's parents. An early map shows streets named Montréal and Sherbrooke.

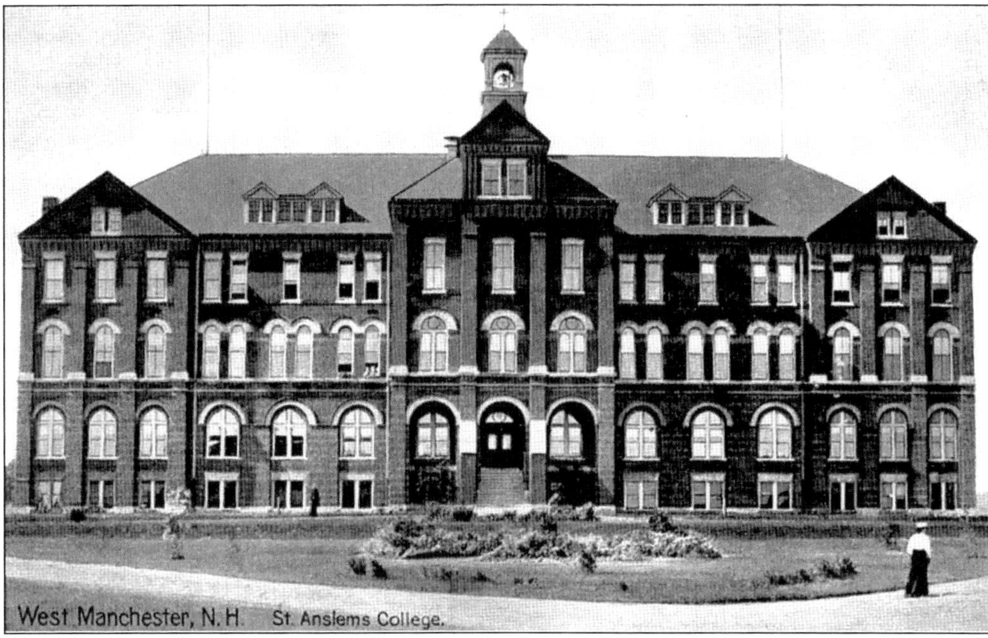

In 1889, having previously established St. Raphael's parish, Benedictine monks founded St. Anselm's (today St. Anselm) College. A fire destroyed the nearly completed original building in 1892. The Benedictines had it rebuilt by 1893. Renamed Alumni Hall, the building that today houses the college's administrative offices, several classrooms, some professors' offices, and other facilities, once incorporated the entire institution. For all practical purposes, this building *was* the college.

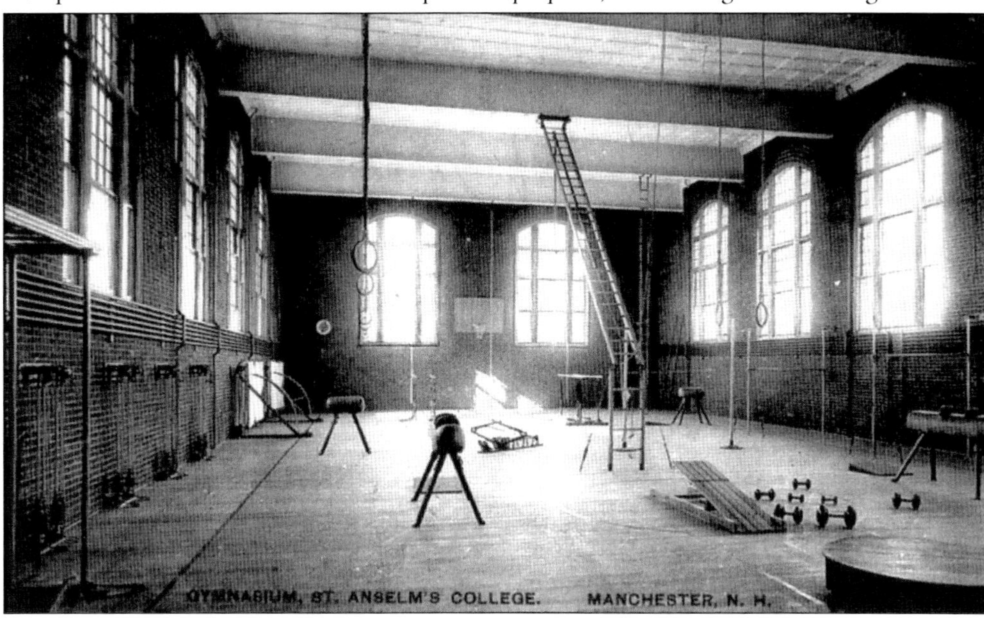

For many years, St. Anselm's gym occupied space in the north wing of what was then the college. After the opening of the Stoutenburgh Gymnasium in 1960, the old gym was partitioned into classrooms and, more recently, into offices. Alumni who knew this as their gym but who have never returned since their student days would be surprised by the transformation, as would younger alumni and current students upon seeing here how it previously looked.

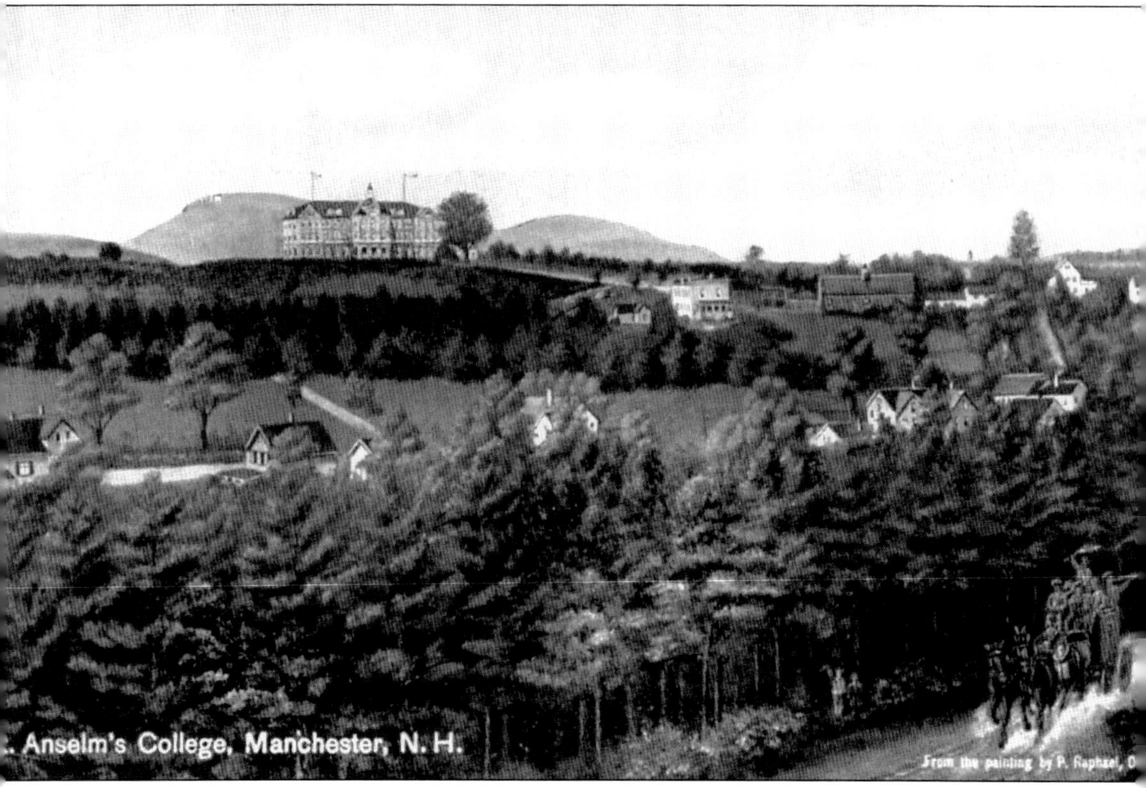

From a lone building in which monks taught philosophy and theology exclusively to men at both preparatory and undergraduate levels, St. Anselm College has evolved into one of the Northeast's best-known small Roman Catholic liberal arts colleges, with 50 buildings and an enrollment of nearly 2,000 women and men. Here is a reproduction of a painting by Rev. Raphael Pfisterer, O.S.B., who arrived at the college in 1900. This westerly view depicts the campus during its earliest era. Although Father Raphael's work enriches the decor of churches elsewhere in the country, his local reputation rests primarily upon his religious murals in the former student chapel, now the Alva deMars Megan Chapel Art Center. As both a monk at the college and the pastor of St. Raphael's, Father Raphael recruited students and parishioners to serve as models for much of his work, including his allegorical portrayal of the Queen City entitled *Progress of Manchester* (1917), now property of the Manchester Historic Association. Consequently, Manchester residents today can appreciate Father Raphael's art and perhaps even find in it familiar faces from their families' pasts.

Six

Notable Events and Lighter Moments

Manchester's history is filled with notable events and lighter moments, most of which never appeared on a postcard.

We have hosted many U.S. presidents. We have had our public halls, restaurants, and streets flooded with candidates, their staffs, celebrities, and the media every four years during the presidential elections. Who can forget the rousing speech that Sen. John F. Kennedy gave, quite fittingly, in Victory Park on the eve of his victory in November 1960? Or the agonizing moment on that snowy February day in 1972 when Sen. Edmund Muskie "cried" in front of the former Union Leader Building on Amherst Street? And we will always remember when Bill Clinton, no longer a candidate but a president, ate lunch at Chez Vachon on Kelley Street in 1993 and was reported to have scraped the cheese off of his poutine.

Other events brought large crowds together, such as when the Train de la Reconnaissance Française, more commonly called the "Merci Boxcar," was displayed in front of City Hall in 1949. The Freedom Train drew throngs for several days in 1975. Then came the huge U.S. bicentennial parade on Elm Street on July 4, 1976. And let us not forget September 6, 1989, when so many of us gathered to say good-bye to our beloved green arches and then watch, hear, and especially feel the Notre Dame Bridge go crashing down into the Merrimack River.

Here are a few scenes of notable events and lighter moments from our past.

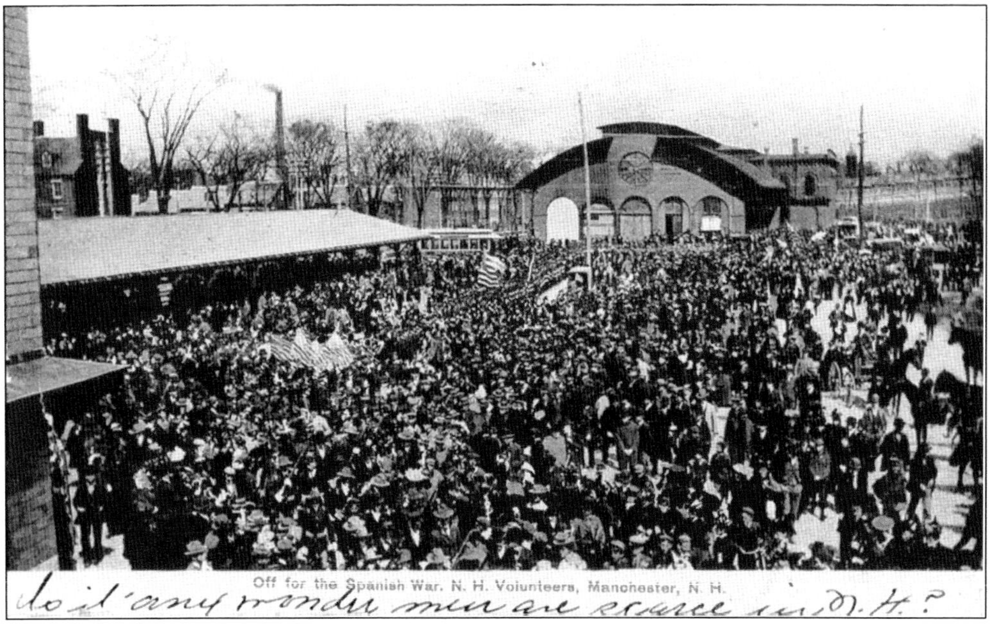

"Remember the *Maine*!" was the cry that led the United States to war against Spain in 1898 over the sinking of the American battleship in Havana harbor. Shortly after the opening of Union Station, barely visible here at extreme left with its predecessor at right, New Hampshire volunteers prepared to leave for war. In 1909, a Manchester woman wrote to another in Center Harbor, "Is it any wonder men are scarce in N.H.?"

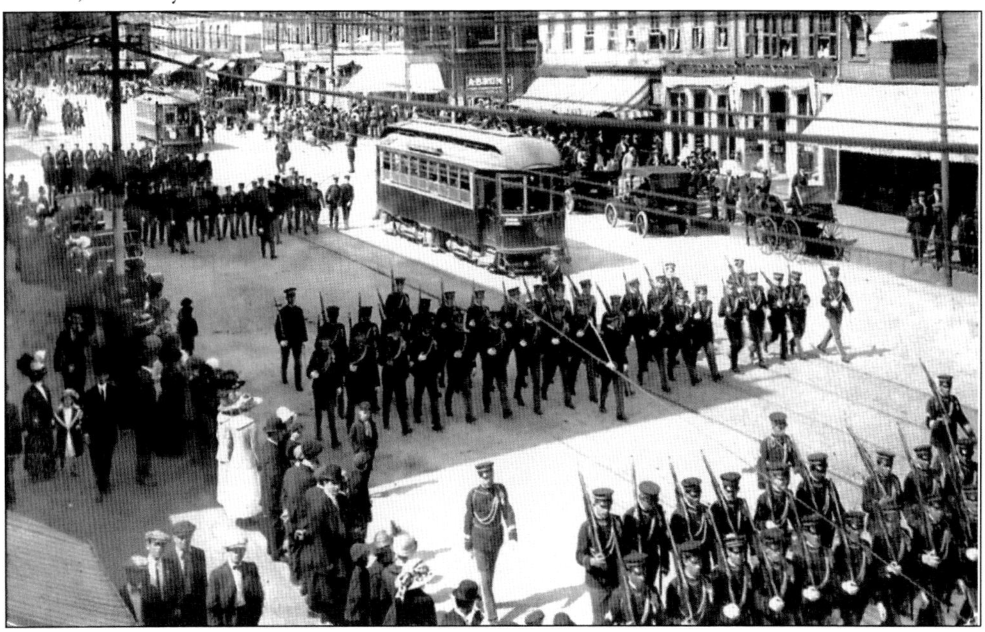

Elm Street has long witnessed parades of all types, such as the annual Memorial Day, Fire Prevention Week, and Christmas parades. With occasional exceptions, the processions usually go from north to south. Here, just south of the corner of Elm and Bridge Streets, soldiers from Battery A march in the Memorial Day parade in 1912. At right, the only business whose awning remains upright is Edmond Pinard's grocery store.

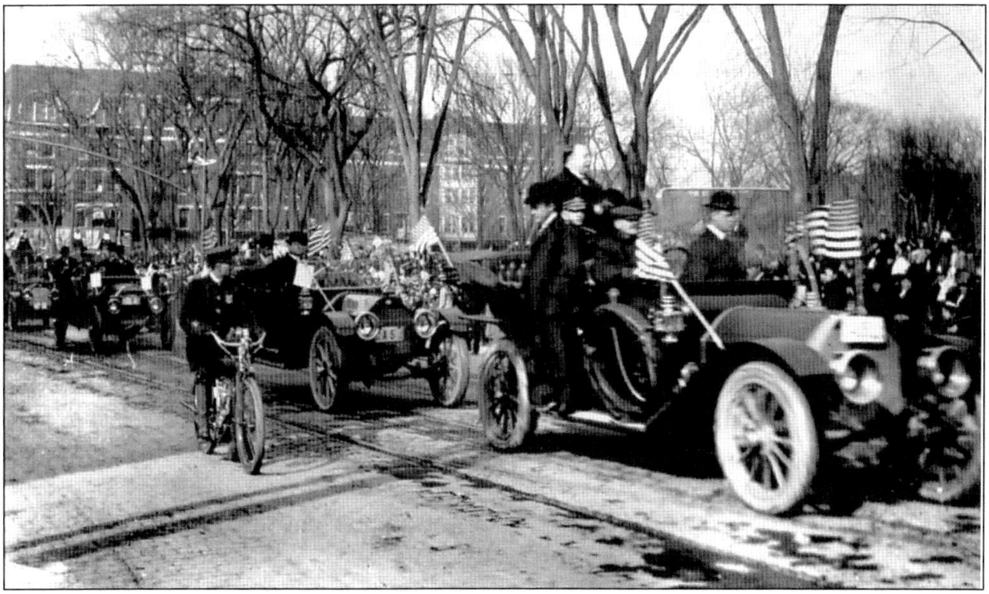

The campaign of 1912 brought Pres. William Howard Taft to Manchester on March 19. After several speeches and an official reception, President Taft rode along Elm Street, seen here near Merrimack Square, past throngs of adults and schoolchildren. However strong, the day's enthusiasm had waned by November, as Manchester and the nation elected Taft's opponent, Woodrow Wilson.

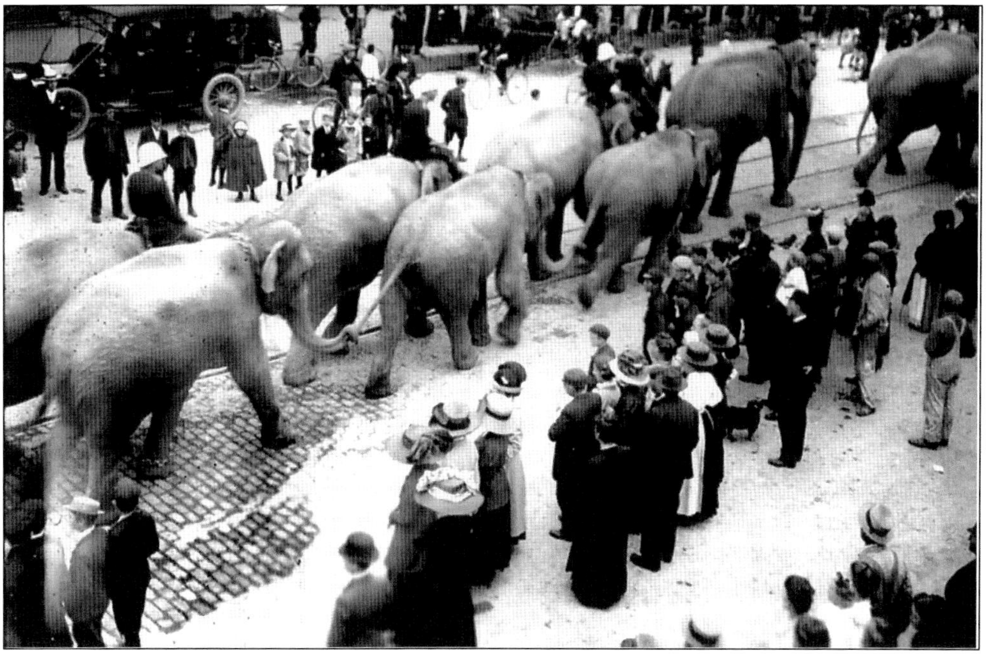

Upon arriving in Manchester, circuses have often held parades along Elm Street to attract attention, especially that of children, both young and less young. Such a parade is seen here about 1910. Today's children of all ages could have witnessed a similar scene as recently as autumn 2004, when the Ringling Bros. and Barnum & Bailey circus made a spectacular entry on Elm Street before proceeding to the Verizon Wireless Arena.

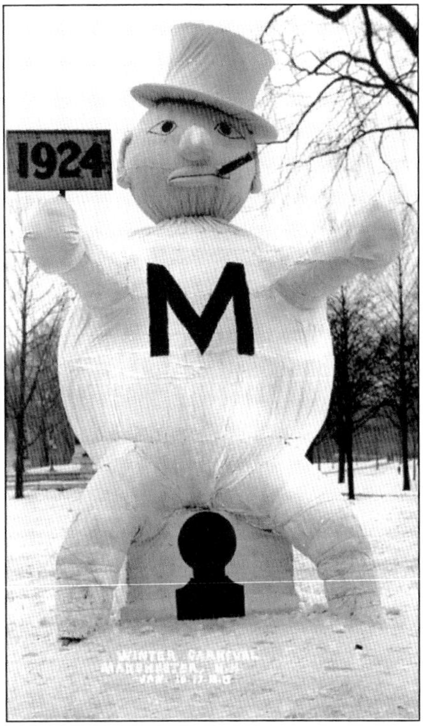

In the past, Manchester residents broke from the winter doldrums through winter carnivals filled with all types of sporting activities, competitions, and games. Here, during the Winter Carnival of January 16–19, 1924, Ulric Bourgeois caught this snowman sitting on the job in Merrimack Common. With the world's or the country's largest textile, shoe, and cigar factories located right here in Manchester, could this have been the largest snowman?

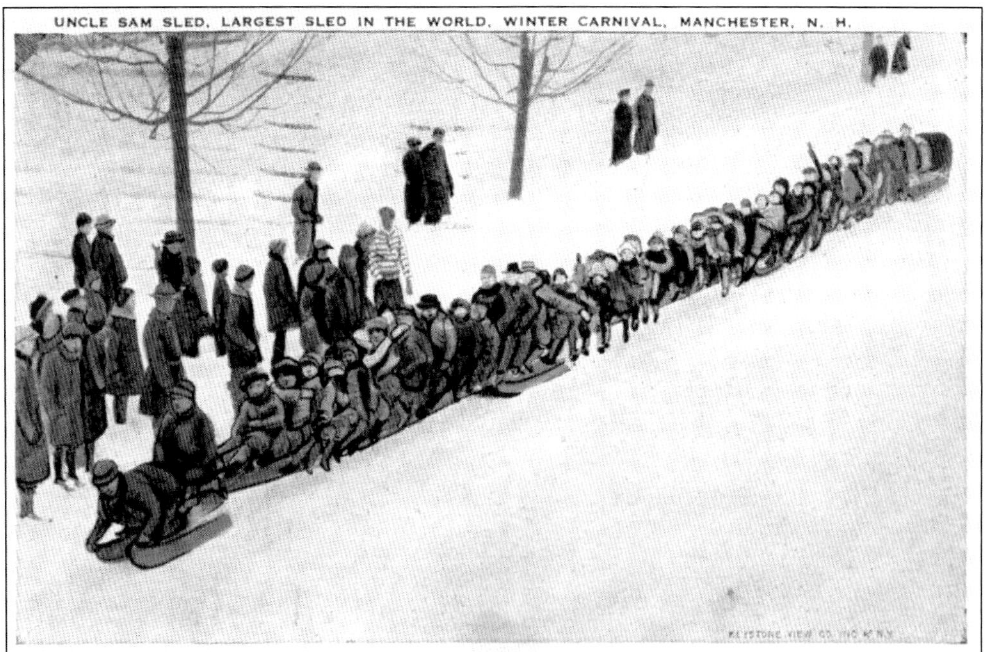

Speaking of large, this card, postmarked January 29, 1925, boasts what participants in the Manchester Winter Carnival believed to be the largest sled in the world, the "Uncle Sam Sled." With so many large structures and other apparent record breakers within its boundaries, the Queen City appears to have been well ahead of its time. The first edition of the *Guinness Book of World Records* didn't come out until 1955.

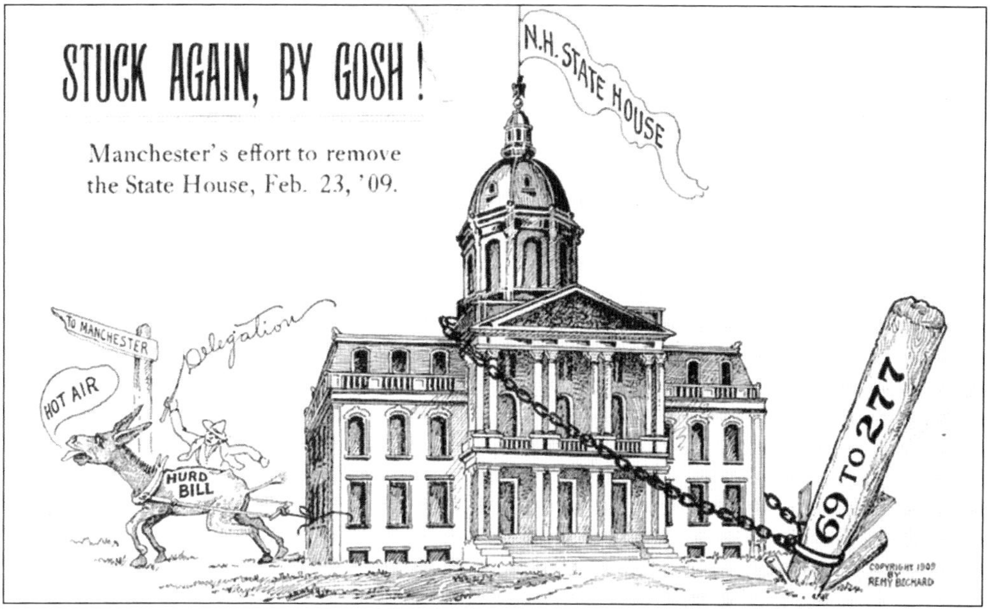

In 1909, state representative Henry N. Hurd, a Republican (despite the pictured donkey) from Manchester's Ward 2, characterized the State House in Concord as inadequate and outdated. His solution: Manchester would contribute up to $1 million, as well as a site, for a new state house—in Manchester! Queen City printer Rémy Béchard satirized Hurd's attempted coup, in which most of the few "yea" votes came, not surprisingly, from Manchester-area representatives.

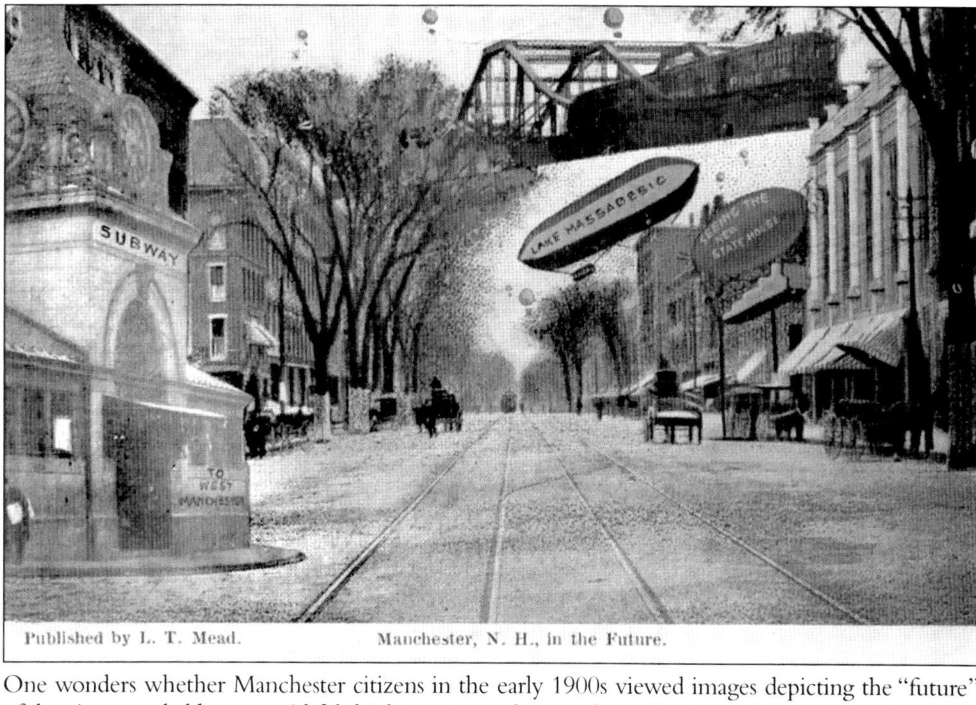

One wonders whether Manchester citizens in the early 1900s viewed images depicting the "future" of the city as probable or as wishful thinking, since subways, elevated trains, and blimps already existed elsewhere. Perhaps the most humorous image is the smaller blimp by City Hall, which reads "Seeing the New State House." The optimist who sent this card in 1909 wrote simply, "Not yet but soon."

Selected Bibliography

Blood, Grace Holbrook. *Manchester on the Merrimack.* Manchester: Lew A. Cummings Co., 1948.

Browne, George Waldo. *The Amoskeag Manufacturing Co. of Manchester, New Hampshire: A History.* Manchester: Amoskeag Manufacturing Co., 1915.

Clarke, John B. *Manchester: A Brief Record of Its Past and a Picture of Its Present.* Manchester: John B. Clarke, 1875.

Clayton, John. *In the City.* Portsmouth, NH: Peter E. Randall Publisher, 1993, and subsequent volumes.

Cummings, O. R., and Manchester Historic Association. *Manchester Streetcars.* Charleston, SC: Arcadia Publishing, 2000.

Dionne-Eaton, Aurore. *The Currier Gallery of Art: A History 1929–1989.* Manchester: Currier Gallery of Art, 1990.

Hareven, Tamara K., and Randolph Langenbach. *Amoskeag: Life and Work in an American Factory-City.* New York: Pantheon Books, 1978. Corrected paperback edition.

Hareven, Tamara K. *Family Time and Industrial Time: The Relationship Between the Family and Work in a New England Industrial Community.* Cambridge: Cambridge University Press, 1982.

Kenison, Arthur M. *Dumaine's Amoskeag: Let the Record Speak.* Manchester: St. Anselm College Press, 1997.

Metalious, Grace. *No Adam in Eden.* New York: Trident Press, 1963. A novel set in Manchester.

Page, Elwin L. *Abraham Lincoln in New Hampshire.* Boston: Houghton Mifflin, 1929.

Paradis, Wilfrid H. *Upon This Granite: Catholicism in New Hampshire 1647–1997.* Portsmouth, NH: Peter E. Randall Publisher, 1998.

Perreault, Robert B. *L'Héritage.* Durham, NH: NMDC for French, Department of Media Services, Dimond Library, University of New Hampshire, 1983. A novel in French set in Manchester.

Piotrowski, Thaddeus M. *A Bibliographical Index to Manchester's (N.H.) Ethnic Groups.* Manchester, 1977.

Potter, C. E. *The History of Manchester, Formerly Derryfield, in New-Hampshire.* Manchester: C. E. Potter, Publisher, 1856.

Samson, Gary. *A World Within a World: Manchester, the Mills, and the Immigrant Experience.* Dover, NH: Arcadia Publishing, 1995.

Schade, Gerhard R. *The Germans and Their Descendants in the Manchester, New Hampshire Area.* Concord, NH: Repro Graphics Publishing, n.d.

Tarrant, Isabel H., and Elizabeth W. Edwards. *Stark House: Boyhood Home of General John Stark.* Manchester: Molly Stark Chapter, Daughters of the American Revolution, 1969.

Thoreau, Henry David. *A Week on the Concord and Merrimack Rivers.* Orleans, MA: Parnassus Imprints Inc., 1987.

Thorp, L. Ashton. *Manchester of Yesterday: A Human Interest Story of Its Past.* Manchester: Granite State Press, 1939.

Verrette, Adrien. *Paroisse Sainte-Marie Manchester, New Hampshire: Cinquantenaire 1880–1930.* Manchester: Imprimerie Lafayette Inc., 1931.

Willey, George Franklin. *Willey's Semi-Centennial Book of Manchester 1846–1896.* Manchester: George F. Willey, Publisher, 1896.

INDEX